POLITICAL TRADITIONS IN FOREIGN POLICY SERIES

Kenneth W. Thompson, Editor

TOYNBEE'S PHILOSOPHY OF WORLD HISTORY AND POLITICS

TOYNBEE'S

Philosophy of World History and Politics

KENNETH W. THOMPSON

Louisiana State University Press
Baton Rouge and London

Copyright © 1985 by Louisiana State University Press
All rights reserved
Manufactured in the United States of America
Designer: Barbara Werden
Typeface: Linotron Trump
Typesetter: Moran Colorgraphic

Library of Congress Cataloging in Publication Data

Thompson, Kenneth W., 1921–
Toynbee's philosophy of world history and politics.

(Political traditions in foreign policy series)
Includes index.
1. History—Philosophy.   2. International relations—
Philosophy.   3. Toynbee, Arnold Joseph, 1889–1975.
I. Title. II. Series.
D16.8.T448   1985   901   85-11290
ISBN 0-8071-1252-6

To
Good and Faithful Friends
Who
Through
Loyalty, Devotion, and Trust
Make Possible
Research and Writing

CONTENTS

TOYNBEE'S PHILOSOPHY OF WORLD HISTORY AND POLITICS

INTRODUCTION

D ONALD KAGAN of Yale University writes in the lead article
in the *New York Times Book Review* (November 11,
1984): "Disagreements among the Western nations, increased attention to the non-Western world, the fear of nuclear war
and, no doubt, the hopes raised by detente have all helped to produce a renewed interest in a unified history of the world." Kagan
believes that the historian must provide illumination of certain
fundamental questions: "What are the enduring elements of human nature? How broad and deep is that complex of human traits
we call by that name? How great, on the other hand, is that part of
our lives freely open to our own will? To what extent was Herod-
otus right in saying 'Custom is king'? Or Thucydides, who sought
'an exact knowledge of the past as an aid to the interpretation of
the future, which in course of human things must resemble if it
does not reflect it'?"

Kagan considers these "the important questions world history
must address, for whatever the proportions may be, a vital part of
man's destiny is in his own hands, and he needs a broad and accurate picture of where he has been if he is to decide where he can
and should go." It is striking that Arnold J. Toynbee saw in these
same questions a similar challenge for his work and contributed
more than is commonly understood to their examination.

Present-day theories of international relations are often criticized for their narrow base in experience and historical examples.
It is said that scientists in their laboratories proceed with hun-

I

dreds and thousands of experiments. The student of international affairs, even looking back to the birth of the nation-state system and the Treaty of Westphalia in 1648, can at most draw on the history of a comparatively few political societies. Furthermore, the majority of these examples taken together represent no more than a handful of categories or patterns. Yet generalizations which relate to their structure and functioning are necessarily restricted to a subspecies of a larger whole. If international political theory is to achieve a more comprehensive definition, the theorist must spread his net more broadly, looking at examples of nation-states in different historical periods and other forms of political organization as well.

The main argument for a volume on universal history in this series, Political Traditions in Foreign Policy, is to expand the discussion of contemporary world politics to encompass world history and world affairs. If we are to trace in a more fundamental way the interconnection between purpose and interest, it is important to look to the interplay of the two as manifested in different systems of world order. When we consider where to uncover such systems, we must turn to world history because it can carry us beyond the limitations of time and place of separate national histories. We are transported from the political configurations we are presently discussing to large political groupings that, in the case of Arnold J. Toynbee, are called civilizations. The size and shape of those units within and among which politics occurs are expanded. At the same time, we are enabled to view international society as it existed under different social, geographical, and technological circumstances.

Toynbee's "pattern of the past" lends itself to such an inquiry in a distinctive way. Although Toynbee's predecessors such as Buckle, Gibbon, and Spengler were surely not unmindful of the times in which they wrote, they were not in their day full-time students of the present. Because of his position as Stevenson Professor at the Royal Institute of International Affairs in London, Toynbee was as renowned for his writings on contemporary diplomatic history as he was for his philosophy of history. He moved back and forth between past and present in the two realms of history. In the *Surveys* he edited, reviewing the year's events in international politics in the decades preceding and following World War II, Toynbee continually searched for lessons from the past. Because he could never set aside the past as he studied the present or the present as he thought about the past, he wove a many-colored tapestry of world affairs that no one before or since has matched.

If we are to look, then, to a universal historian whose chronicles on past civilizations are informed and inspired by the most urgent concerns of the present, the choice of Toynbee's history appears indisputable. All the great issues of our times are present in his work: nationalism, war, industrialism, international law and organization, and the related institutions of world order and peace. Yet Toynbee was too outstanding a historian to imagine that patterns of history simply repeat themselves. If Graeco-Roman civilization is a forerunner of Western civilization, the two cannot be seen as carbon copies. For the historian in search of patterns, the unique and the recurrent are intermingled. They manifest all the similarities and differences of individual persons who resemble one another because they are human but differ because they are individuals. If only differences prevailed, we would not study Plato and Aristotle to learn about man and politics. If only similarities existed, we would have no need for contemporary observers. We can speak about man in general because human nature is not fundamentally different in the twentieth century from what it was five thousand years ago. We must also recognize that the circumstances today in which men and nations work out their destinies bear almost no resemblance to those in the time of Alexander the Great.

What Toynbee provides, then, is a far broader canvas on which to trace the interaction of political philosophy and foreign policy interests. That is, the philosopher of history helps us to view the present crisis and its distinct characteristics against a background that safeguards us from parochialism. We dimly sense that Western civilization is no more immortal than were past civilizations. Having recognized that, we cannot be sure about our present point in history, nor can we know what threatens us because each period in history has its own uniqueness. Rather than settle for political prophecy, Toynbee provides concepts that merit further study by succeeding generations of students of international affairs. It is important that we ask which of those concepts have enduring value in our day and which satisfy our curiosity about the past but have little relevance in the present.

At this point, it is possible to discover congruence between some of Toynbee's "principles" of history and the "principles" which respected students of international politics advance. For example, present-day theorists of world politics have concentrated on concepts such as world order and the balance of power. Yet these same theorists acknowledge that some of these principles may be the products of postwar international affairs. They ask, and even more emphatically their critics ask, whether their ideas are merely reflections of the contemporary scene. Are they a manifestation of underlying social forces determined by human nature, or are they a phase of politics likely to be transformed in the future? If the answer were of mere scientific and academic importance, the subject would still be worthy of study. However, the future of the human race in the nuclear age depends on what can be said with some degree of certainty and credibility about the rise and fall of civilizations. It depends on the principles we can extract which will help us understand the forces at work in the world in our times.

What makes the study of Toynbee's philosophy of history valuable is not primarily his prescience in charting the future of civilizations including our own. Critiques abound in which the prophecies of Toynbee and others are revisited with the sole aim of judging their authors as prophets. As Toynbee acknowledged in numerous occasional writings, the mission of the prophet is fraught with grave perils and uncertainties. A more modest task, but one of no less consequence, is to evaluate the usefulness of the concepts with which he worked and test them for contemporary civilizations. If he should be able to help us understand the extent to which certain working principles are timeless, we might face the gravity of the present situation with greater confidence. He may have left us with some of the intellectual tools we require for grappling with our problems.

Political realists whose writings are grounded in history suggest that the nation-state persists in international politics. The same writers also point out that new political arrangements are possible and indeed show signs of evolving in the foreseeable future. The nation-state, though a stubborn fact of contemporary international politics, appears inadequate to meet the requirements of world order. It is no longer possible to assert that a sovereign nation-state can solve the problems of the nuclear age or cope with worldwide environmental or demographic problems. The time will come or may already have come when larger, more inclusive groupings are required. Underlying economic and strategic forces are driving mankind toward new solutions and new patterns of relationship.

In the face of this worldwide condition of political societies, two approaches are possible. One is to construct new international institutions to remedy the harsh problems that confront mankind in the twentieth century. The League of Nations and the United Nations are only the most recent forms of this approach. Toynbee over a period of five decades devoted himself to a detailed analysis of these emergent world institutions. His writings provide a barometer, not only of the hopes and fears of mankind seeking to give greater substance to the work of such institutions, but also of his own moments of optimism and pessimism as he observed their work. Toynbee, however, in contrast to many students of world politics, never totally relied on international institutions, for such organizations come and go, but the intractable problems of world politics persist.

The other approach is to reach down into the lessons of history to illuminate the present. If the nation-state is not immortal, neither are the structures and patterns which mankind has used to cope with past problems. Studying only the structures of world order, one risks isolating them from the profound forces that determine their success or failure. Especially in the United States, this approach has been imperiled by the fateful disease of parochialism. It has been a recurrent American illusion that institutions which have introduced a reasonable degree of domestic harmony and order can readily be transplanted to the international system. This tendency has been augmented by the central role that lawyers and institution builders have played in shaping the American world view. For one thing, an overwhelming proportion of secretaries of state have been lawyers, and a continuing debate has resulted between those who espouse a legalistic approach and those who call attention to the differences between national and international politics. Down to the present, the clash between the two schools of thought remains unresolved as successive administrations shift back and forth in their approaches to such issues as human rights and acts of aggression.

The best hope for resolving the debate may be to renew in our time the study of world history. Philosophers of history, and notably Toynbee, may help the world to clarify the important differences in the two perspectives. It is vital that we understand the relation between social forces and worldwide international institutions, and the study cannot be confined to the post–World War II period. History does repeat itself, and understanding is possible not through a tidy blueprint but through an examination of the complexities of the past. Principles of history offer ways to crystalize thinking about world politics, not panaceas for eliminating human conflict.

The framework which world history provides—a more promising approach than are certain oversimplified concepts of world order—gives pointers to direct our thought. It invites scrutiny of the role of religion as a recurrent force in world politics. It challenges the student to explore connections between internal and external developments that magnify or reduce political struggles. Whatever the more detailed studies of particular foreign policy developments may teach us in the volumes to follow in this series, world history is an essential route to understanding the relations among philosophy, politics, and national interests. Toynbee's subject may serve to encompass the separate subjects of authors of forthcoming volumes and may help us to view particular studies in a larger perspective.

PART ONE

Historical and Philosophical Foundations

CHAPTER I

Approaches to History and International Relations Reviewed

O NE CRITERION by which to evaluate a historian's work is the accuracy of his portrayal of past events. This applies as well to the philosopher of history, but for the latter, we must also consider his world view and how it helps us understand the present. In the case of Arnold J. Toynbee, then, attention should be given both to his chronicles of world events and to his theory of history. Although we could profitably examine Toynbee's interpretation of what history means or his assessment of its logic, this discussion will focus on his historical method. First, however, let us turn to some of the sources upon which he drew.

Central to Toynbee's methodology was a duality in which the scientific approach and a mythic or spiritual element were seen as mutually enhancing. In his use of the former he seemed a direct intellectual descendant of Buckle and Pareto, scholars who were convinced, albeit in differing degrees, of the primacy of science and its techniques for studying human behavior. Toynbee himself observed that he was trying "to apply the scientific notion of 'law,' 'regularity' and 'recurrence' to the history of human affairs and find out experimentally how far this way of looking at things will go in this field." He added, however, that the application of methods based on the natural sciences had certain limitations, but he was determined to see how far he could go, especially in relating the study of history to the physical environment and human interrelationships. Societies can legitimately be examined and compared, Toynbee believed, and in this he acknowledged the influence of E. A. Freeman's *Historical Essays.* Although geography was important for Toynbee—here we see the influence of Huntington—he did not see it as a primary determinative factor in history. In this context he argued that historians can properly use myths, since the objects of their study, after all, are "living creatures . . . [not] Inanimate Nature."[1]

If one speaks of the influence of Buckle, Pareto, Freeman, and Huntington on Toynbee's scientism, one must also cite those who contributed to his mysticism and idealism. Significant in this regard were Sir Frederick Maurice and Charles Kingsley, founders of the Christian Socialist movement; his uncle Arnold Toynbee and Canon Samuel Augustus Barnett, pioneers in social settlement work; and his father-in-law Gilbert Murray. It was, however, the writings of Henri Bergson which inspired the idea of creative evolution that permeated Toynbee's work. The Bergsonian emphasis on change, on purpose despite impermanent values, and on the relationship of mind and intuition to truth led Toynbee to a new stance, one which later became dominant in his historiography. His concern was still with a science of society, but he turned his thought to the cosmic drama in which the spirit of God in man struggles against the Adversary. This confrontation of mythic forces could, he believed, be studied in men's social relations. Such an element of myth did not necessarily overshadow or subvert Toynbee's use of scientific techniques. As Jacob Burckhardt, for example, argued, events have both historical and spiritual aspects, and it is history's task to reveal them.[2]

Toynbee's knowledge of classical literature, the Bible, and the works of Goethe and Blake was deep and profound. Nor should one overlook the influence of Oswald Spengler. His attempt to establish laws of history convinced Toynbee that his own plan to study civilizations was valid. Although Spengler viewed those laws as immutable, Toynbee was not convinced they were, recognizing with fellow historians the importance of proceeding empirically. On another point, however, they were in substantial agreement: man's spirit and inventiveness make an exclusively scientific methodology impracticable. As we have seen, it was such a con-

1. Arnold J. Toynbee to Kenneth W. Thompson, September 22, 1949, in possession of the recipient; Arnold J. Toynbee, *A Study of History* (12 vols.; London, 1934–61), I, 339, 292, 271; see also Kenneth W. Thompson, "Arnold J. Toynbee: World Civilizations and World Politics," *Masters of International Thought: Major Twentieth-Century Theorists and the World Crisis* (Baton Rouge, 1980), 225–49.

2. Tangye Leon, "A Study of Toynbee," *Horizon,* XV (January, 1947), 24; Jacob Burckhardt, *Force and Freedom* (New York, 1943), 83.

viction on Toynbee's part that led him to consider societies in human and spiritual terms. As important as Spengler's theory was for Toynbee, other influences were no less important. These included Winwood Reade's *Martyrdom of Man*, which speaks of man's struggle against nature as a spur to action. Here we see a possible prefiguration of Toynbee's theory of challenge and response. Another is Michael I. Rostovtzeff's *History of the Ancient World*, the final chapter of which implicitly treats the concept of an internal and external proletariat. In an interview, Toynbee confirmed the importance of these sources and added that Browning's poetry also led him to formulate his idea of challenge and response. Further, he noted his earlier attraction to Turgot's concepts as reflected in Teggart's writings.[3]

Identifying the intellectual contributors to Toynbee's historical method is easier than analyzing his approach, which developed in three distinct stages. As a young man, he believed in the primacy of the nation-state with a fervor inspired by Wilsonian nationalism. Intimations of a later "universalism," and the importance of some form of international authority, foreshadowed the link between idealism and nationalism.[4]

World War I and its carnage shattered his euphoric outlook. Toynbee's work for the government involved the reading and rewriting of reports of German atrocities. Not only did he conclude that certain conditions can provoke bestiality in any people, but he began to doubt that the nation-state was the measure of all good things. In the spring of 1918, when German victory seemed imminent, Toynbee had a growing sense that civilization itself was ephemeral.

The second stage in the evolution of Toynbee's methodology began in 1922, when he briefly outlined the plan of *A Study of History*. What distinguished his approach was a concentration not on nation-states but on civilizations. Further, these entities have life histories, that is, they can be described as "biological organisms" and hence can be subject to compilation, comparison, and generalization. This morphology of history generated another metaphor: one must study the plot and the three "Acts" of civiliza-

3. Oswald Spengler, *Man and Technics* (New York, 1932), 28–31; Winwood Reade, *The Martrydom of Man* (1872; rpr. London, 1925), 26; Michael I. Rostovtzeff, *A History of the Ancient World* (2 vols.; Oxford, 1927), II, 351ff.; private interview with Toynbee, December 2, 1950, Princeton.
4. See, for example, Arnold J. Toynbee, *Nationality and the War* (London, 1915), 476ff.

tions—development and growth; crisis, breakdown, and rally; and final dissolution. What intrigued Toynbee, moreover, were the encounters which gave rise to new civilizations. In some instances a universal religion is the point of contact, the "chrysalis" from which a new society emerges. This theme, of primary importance in Toynbee's later volumes, is merely adumbrated at this point.[5]

In 1939, however, the third stage in the development of his historical method became evident: his approach centered on "higher religions," which may be "representatives of another species of society . . . at least as distinct from the species 'Civilization' as the civilizations are distinct from the primitive societies." The change in concentration had to do with patterns of disintegration, which include internal and external proletariats as well as religion. Toynbee's surprising but perceptible shift from national states to civilizations to higher religions, then, changed his interpretation of history and his methodology for studying the past. The consequence was, as he observed, that "the greatest new event will then not be the monotonous rise of yet another secular civilization out of the bosom of the Christian Church in the course of these latter centuries; it will still be the Crucifixion and its spiritual consequences."[6]

This examination of Toynbee's historical method, which has considered three distinct periods in his thought, is a common way of looking at the methodology of any scholar. Another way may be worth notice, since it is the one which Toynbee as historian employed in talking about himself. In trying to answer the question, What are the chances for the survival of Western civilization? he discovered that three routes or historical methods could be followed. To some extent he pursued all three throughout his writing. The order in which he ranged them is therefore of significance.[7]

One method is the statistical approach, which some would call the scientific method. In general Toynbee had a high regard for the science of statistics, though he questioned its usefulness in at least two spheres. In a letter to this writer he referred to one reservation: "When I study Sorokin's attempt to bring this last field [that is, any

5. See Arnold J. Toynbee, *The Tragedy of Greece: A Lecture Delivered for the Professor of Greek to Candidates for Honours in Literae Humaniores at Oxford in May 1920* (London, 1921).

6. Toynbee, *A Study of History*, V, 23, 3; Arnold J. Toynbee, *Civilization on Trial* (New York, 1948), 237.

7. Arnold J. Toynbee, *The Prospects of Western Civilization* (New York, 1947), 3–60.

area where free will or intellect may be in command of man's be-
havior] under the rule of statistics, I find myself skeptical of the
applicability of this method here." And in his inquiry into the future of Western civilization, he rejected the statistical method for
another reason. Natural scientists have an almost unlimited number of specimens for their experiments; a historian looking at civilizations has twenty or thirty. Whether this sample is adequate or
not is something the historian, standing in history and perceiving
only the dim shadows of the future, has no way of knowing.[8]

Another method is one he designated "psychological," referring
to the appraisal and comparison of feelings of any kind. What are
the "impressions" and "judgments" of various leaders past and
present on the future of civilization? is the question asked. Some
of the keenest insights about historical problems come from the
visions of prophets and poets. Goethe, the Chinese philosophers,
and imagery from the Bible have earlier helped the historian un-
ravel the mystery of the origin of civilizations, but on the West's
future, if it has a future, the method draws a blank. There are so
many contradictions in the testimony of the prophets that the future must remain an open question.[9]

Finally, Toynbee introduced what he called the "comparative"
method. If a scholar should find certain experiences recurring in a
number of civilizations, he would have grounds for formulating a
working hypothesis. If militarism in Assyria, Rome, and other civilizations had certain inevitable consequences, then one would be
justified in looking for it and its consequent manifestations in
Western civilization as well. In some ways, this method is more a
rule of thumb than a science. In its most elementary form, it is
simply an attempt to look at a historical question from as many
sides as possible—as Toynbee did in dealing with contemporary
diplomatic problems: "By taking the bearings of his contemporary
object of study from various local observation-posts and then combining these several readings into a single formula, the student [of
foreign policy] is able to bring the object into focus and to calculate
its position and to measure its dimensions with some approach to
objectivity even though the time-vista is denied to him."[10] With
civilizations, he takes his bearings in both time and space. Having
made certain readings, he examines these for elements of recurrence and novelty between the genus civilization and the partic-

8. Toynbee to Thompson, September 22, 1949, in possession of the recipient.
9. Toynbee, *The Prospects of Western Civilization*, 7–9.
10. *Ibid.*, 15–22; *Survey of International Affairs*, 1931, pp. 13–14.

ular one he is observing. The fruits of these comparisons are of little value until they are pondered by the imaginative mind. Even
then, their purpose is to illuminate the understanding rather than
to provide ready-made previews of events. For the sanguine scientist of society, this may suggest craven incompetence. For
someone who will settle for the rewards of greater insight and
deeper understanding, the use of this method is not without value.

Philosophy of history characteristically has been identified as a
method for dealing with history, as a diagnosis of its meaning, or
as a review of its laws. Toynbee's work, as we have seen, can be
appraised from all three of these viewpoints; his method is evaluated at greater length in Chapter VII. Now it is essential to sketch
the broad outlines of the pattern of history Toynbee presumes to
discover, its meaning and its laws.

One thing appears to have been clear to him from the beginning.
If there is a meaning to history, one must search for it in part in
the structures or unities within which men live. Today this structure is the nation-state, but in earlier days there were world empires and city-states. Is there no intelligible field which the historian can trace through all of history? Toynbee found that societies
are such units and that more than twenty have undertaken the ex-
traordinary adventure of crossing from the torpor of primitivism
to the creative rhythm of civilization. They are units which "appear to have a genuine life of their own." Take a familiar, concrete
case and let Toynbee apply his criteria in detail:

> I mean, by civilization, the smallest unit of historical study at
> which one arrives when one tries to understand the history of
> one's own country: the United States, say, or the United King-
> dom. If you were to try to understand the history of the United
> States by itself, it would be unintelligible: you could not un-
> derstand the part played in American life by federal govern-
> ment, representative government, democracy, industrialism,
> monogamy, Christianity, unless you looked beyond the bounds
> of the United States—out beyond her frontiers to Western Eu-
> rope and to the other overseas countries founded by West Eu-
> ropeans, and back beyond her local origins to the history of
> Western Europe in centuries before Columbus or Cabot had
> crossed the Atlantic. But, to make American history and insti-
> tutions intelligible for practical purposes, you need not look be-
> yond Western Europe into Eastern Europe or the Islamic World,

nor behind the origins of our Western European civilization to the decline and fall of the Graeco-Roman civilization. These limits of time and space give us the intelligible unit of social life of which the United States or Great Britain or France or Holland is a part: call it Western Christendom, Western Civilization, Western society, the Western world. Similarly, if you start from Greece or Serbia or Russia, and try to understand their histories you arrive at an Orthodox Christendom or Byzantine world. If you start from Morocco or Afghanistan, and try to understand their histories, you arrive at an Islamic world. Start from Bengal or Mysore or Rajputana, and you find a Hindu world. Start from China or Japan and you find a Far Eastern world.[11]

In an even more elaborate illustration, he used the example of England to show that at every crucial stage in modern European history, most notably at the time of the Industrial Revolution, of sixteenth-century expansion, of the Reformation and the Renaissance, and of late feudal history, not even England, the European *alter orbis*, was self-sufficient. In each of these periods, only Western civilization had a life of its own. In all history, Toynbee found twenty-one full-fledged civilizations. Five others, which failed to achieve normal growth because their full energies were consumed in premature feats such as the Polynesians' crossing the Pacific to reach Easter Island, were the Spartan, Eskimo, Nomadic, Osmanli, and Polynesian. There were four "abortive" civilizations—the Celtic or Far Western, the Scandinavian, the Hyksos, and the Nestorian or Far Eastern Christian. Two early civilizations, the Andean and Egyptiac, were "unrelated" to any other subsequent societies.[12]

The Sumeric, Mayan, Sinic, and Minoan civilizations are "apparented" to later societies which are either still extant or are "apparented" to existing civilizations. The Sumeric civilization was the "parent" of the Indic, Hittite, and Babylonian. The contemporary Hindu civilization (India and Pakistan) is an offspring of the ancient Indic civilization. Mayan civilization sired the Yucatec and Mexic; the Aztec civilization sprang from the former. Sinic civilization is responsible for the Far Eastern civilization on the mainland and its offshoot in Japan and Korea. Both the Syriac and Hel-

11. Toynbee, *A Study of History*, V, 339; Toynbee, *Civilization on Trial*, 222–23.

12. For the discussion of civilizations, see Toynbee, *A Study of History*, I, 17–44.

lenic (Graeco-Roman) civilizations are affiliated with the ancient
Minoan, which has become known only through efforts by archaeologists such as Sir Arthur Evans. Syriac civilization is the
"parent" of the Iranic (Turkey and Persia) and Arabic (Arabia, Egypt,
and North Africa). Hellenic civilization is the source both of Western civilization and the two branches of the Orthodox Christian
(the Greek and the Russian). None of these civilizations is identical or even similar in all respects. They are, however, comparable in some ways, and since they occur in approximately the same
period for the timepiece of a universal historian (that is, within the
past six thousand years), they share an identity as "civilizations."

If this is the "pattern of the past" as regards form and structure,
its dynamic is nothing less than what Toynbee called a drama in
three "Acts." Act I opens with the eternal problem, how do civilizations originate? For the physical determinist, the answer is
simple. Buckle stated that civilization depends "entirely on soil and
climate: the soil regulating the returns . . . the climate regulating
the energy and constancy of the labour itself. . . . There is no instance in history of any country being civilised by its own efforts,
unless it has possessed one of these conditions in a very favourable
form." Toynbee proceeds on this same path for some distance
himself. His first road map is the Hellenic environmental theory
as preserved in the works of the Hippocratic School of Medicine:
"Inhabitants of mountains, rocky, well-watered country, where . . .
seasonal climatic variation is wide, will . . . [be] adapted for courage and endurance, and . . . ferocity and brutality. . . . Inhabitants
of rolling, wind-swept, well-watered country . . . [have] a vein of
cowardice and tameness in their characters. . . . Where seasonal
changes are most frequent . . . there you will find the greatest dif-
ferentiation in the human body, character and organism."[13]

There is but one way of verifying this theory and that is to test
it for each of more than twenty civilizations. This exposes the in-
adequacy of the theory. If we are concerned only with the influence of changes in environment, such as those brought about by
the retreat of the ice from Europe, then we can speak in reasonably
precise language. Climatic variations can be measured and so can
the changes they induce. But if the plan is to account for the nature
and existence of civilizations, then we discover that an important
dimension of the human drama has been left out. Why was it, for

---

13. Buckle, *Introduction to the History of Civilization in England*, I, 25; Toynbee, *A Study of History*, I, 251–52.

example, that the same forests of North America which subdued the Indians were a challenge to the white man? After his survey of twenty-one civilizations, Toynbee concluded: "Even the total geographico-social environment . . . cannot be regarded as the positive factor by which our twenty-one civilizations have been generated. . . . Civilizations can and do emerge in environments which are utterly diverse." "Fluvial" environments have given birth to the Egyptiac and Sumeric civilizations, "archipelago" types to the Minoan, Hellenic, and Japanese Far Eastern civilizations, and the "continental" to the Sinic, Indic, Russian Orthodox Christian, and Western civilizations.[14]

If the key to the riddle of civilization is not environmental, then perhaps it is human. In every period of history, some particularly successful or spiritually self-conscious group has identified itself as "chosen people"—"race is the term used to denote some distinctive innate quality in any genus or species." Especially in the early 1930s when Toynbee was writing his first three volumes, racial theories were much in vogue. But his empirical survey of civilizations persuaded him to reject the notion that some unique magical quality is the monopoly of a small fraction of mankind. Instead he discovered a "prevalent law . . . to the effect that the geneses of civilizations require creative contributions from more races than one." If some races have to this moment been less creative than others, this is due "to the inter-play between a Human Nature which is common to all Mankind and certain exceptionally unfavourable circumstances in the local environment." This is the reason for the gap in the participation of the "Mediterranean" race in ten civilizations, the "Alpine" in nine, the "Nordic" in four, and the "Black" in none. Obviously, some modern anthropologists might wish to qualify this rather sweeping assertion.[15]

Therefore, neither of these once widely held theories proves particularly helpful. At this point, civilization's emergence remains as much a mystery as it was before these surveys were undertaken. But an earlier assumption, taken from Bergson, offers a way out for Toynbee. What is the difference between primitive societies and civilizations? Clearly it is that the one is static, the other dynamic; one looks back to its old men, the other forward to what is new. After not more than a page or two of discussion, Toynbee accepted this proposition.[16]

14. Toynbee, *A Study of History*, I, 251–52.
15. *Ibid.*, 207–49.
16. *Ibid.*, 205–207.

Modern anthropologists would probably seek more evidence because even full-fledged civilizations in their last agonies are no less likely to revert to the past. Moreover, most primitive societies that Westerners have studied have become senescent, and their early history can sometimes only be interpolated. But this suggests a means for dealing with the problem. There is a factor X which must be accounted for. If neither environment nor race provides an explanation, but each throws some light on the problem, then logically a civilization comes about as a result of their interaction. It is as simple as that. Toynbee, with Spengler, turned at this point to a great metaphor. The journey of a man is a series of encounters with the totality of his environment. The first of these ordeals historically was between God and the devil:

> Goethe's "Prologue in Heaven" opens with the archangels hymning the perfection of God's creation. But, just because His works are perfect, the Creator has left Himself no scope for any further exercise of His creative powers, and there might have been no way out of this impasse if Mephistopheles—created for this very purpose—had not presented himself before the throne and challenged God to give him a free hand to spoil, if he can, one of the Creator's choicest works. God accepts the challenge and thereby wins an opportunity to carry His work of creation forward. An encounter between two personalities in the form of challenge and response: have we not here the flint and steel by whose mutual impact the creative spark is kindled?

This conflict is the reflection of a fundamental law. There is a rhythm in history and in men's minds which is manifested in alternate periods of tranquillity and turbulence, quiescence and action, Yin and Yang. Toynbee invokes this fragment of Chinese imagery again and again. In a summary passage this recurrence is described:

> The play opens with a perfect state. . . . In the Universe, Balder keeps all things bright and beautiful through keeping himself alive. In Heaven, "Die unbegreiflich hohen Werke / Sind herrlich, wie an ersten Tag." On Earth, Faust is perfect in knowledge; Job is perfect in goodness and prosperity; Adam and Eve, in the Garden of Eden, are perfect in innocence and ease; the virgins—Gretchen, Danae, Hippolytus—are perfect in purity and beauty. In the astronomers' universe, the Sun, a perfect orb of incandescent matter, is travelling on an unimpeded course

through Space. In the biologist's universe, the Species is in perfect adaptation to its environment.

When Yin is thus complete, it is ready to pass over into Yang. But what is to make it pass? A change in a state which, by definition, is perfect after its kind can only be started by an impulse or motive which comes from outside. If we think of the state as one of physical equilibrium, we must bring another star to raise a tide on the spherical surface of the Sun, or another gas to evoke an explosion from the inert air in the combustion-chamber of the motor-engine. If we think of the state as one of psychic beatitude or nirvana, we must bring another actor on to the stage: a critic to set the mind thinking again by suggesting doubts; an adversary to set the heart feeling again by instilling distress or discontent or fear or antipathy; in fact, an enemy to sow tares in the field; an access of desire to generate karma. This is the role of the Serpent in the Book of Genesis, of Satan in the Book of Job, of Mephistopheles in Goethe's *Faust*, of Loki in the Scandinavian mythology, of Aphrodite in Euripides' *Hippolytus* and Apollo in his *Ion*, of the passing star in Sir James Jeans' cosmogony, of the Environment in the Darwinian theory of Evolution.[17]

The point that becomes clear only as Toynbee proceeds is that this element of conflict and development is common not only to mythological and historical encounters but also to the integration of psychological forces within individual minds and to the engagements between man or his social group and his environment, whether geographical or human. The struggle that takes place in the mind of the individual depicts in "Microcosm" what ultimately occurs in the "Macrocosm." Man thus becomes both the "field of action" for a society's fate and the point in the universe upon which all supernatural energy is focused. This is the earliest hint that ultimately we are to deal not with civilization but with religion.[18]

Here the "myth" is used merely as the positive factor X which accounts for the origin of civilization. It is the first statement of the formula of challenge and response. All peoples have been faced with a challenge peculiar to their environment; their existence as a civilization has depended on their response. It is possible to iden-

17. Toynbee, *Civilization on Trial*, 11–12; Toynbee, *A Study of History*, I, 276–77.
18. Toynbee, *A Study of History*, I, 315–30.

tify the particular challenge in "unrelated" civilizations (those without antecedents). Droughts, floods, and swamps were the challenges facing the Egyptiac, Sumeric, and Sinic civilizations; the bleak climate and grudging soil of a plateau evoked the response of the Andean civilization; a tropical forest the Mayan; and the sea the Minoan. With "related" civilizations, however, there is another civilization in the background which has occupied the same geographical environment. Hence it is impossible to say a priori whether one can identify the physical source of the creative act. With "related" civilizations whose "homes" do not coincide with their antecedents, as the Orthodox Christian in Russia, it is possible again to reconstruct the physical challenge. With all other "related" civilizations, the challenge of the human environment is more prominent than is the physical environment, for one social group has succeeded another, and so the historian must look to internal groups rather than external forces.[19]

There is in society a more general complex of factors capable of stimulating the building of a civilization. One of these is a reasonable measure of deprivation. Man's creative nature comes into play only as a problem-solving device. Too "soft" an environment has often led to demoralization. The thin and stony soil of Attica provided the stimulus for Athens to become a great naval and commercial center. In contrast, Boeotia, rich in soil and resources, was known for a people lacking in imagination and spirit. Prussia is a modern illustration of response to adversity. Change in environment, a crushing defeat, pressure at a threatened frontier, or a particular infirmity or handicap may serve to inspire the supreme act of creation. Thus Western civilization found its creative force in the Carolingian Frankish regime, which was jeopardized by its position athwart the path of advancing barbarians. England and France not only came into existence in response to the maritime challenge from Scandinavia but found centers of gravity in London and Paris, which had borne the full force of the Scandinavian onslaught.[20] Challenge and response is the key which opens all doors in Toynbee's account of the genesis of societies.

The final scene in Act I is that of "growth." By an inner logic, one successful response calls forth a new challenge which requires in turn a new and creative response. Thus civilization moves forward as it responds to perpetually new challenges now primarily

19. *Ibid.*, 335–38.
20. Toynbee, *A Study of History*, II, 98–99.

from within rather than from without. A civilization becomes its own challenger, environment, and field of action, and there is a movement or rhythm of stasis or equilibrium, overbalance, motion, and stasis. The vitalism or psychic energy which makes this possible is the psychological quantity X missing in the racial and environmental approaches. Toynbee described the process thus: "The single, finite movement from a disturbance to a restoration of equilibrium is not enough, if genesis is to be followed by growth. And, to convert the movement into a repetitive, recurrent rhythm, there must be an *élan* which carries the challenged party through equilibrium into an overbalance which exposes him to a fresh challenge and thereby inspires him to make a fresh response in the form of a further equilibrium ending in a further overbalance—and so on in a progression which is potentially infinite."[21]

Growth in a civilization is characterized, then, by two principal developments: "self-determination" and "etherealization." The one universal measure of growth is the transference of a society's field of action from the natural world to the heart of the civilization itself. This is self-determination. Similarly, through "etherealization," there is increasing simplicity and efficiency in the way things are done in both the material and spiritual spheres. For instance, the wireless replaced the telegraph and writing took the place of hieroglyphics. The law of etherealization is defined: "In morphological terms, 'etherealization' appears as a progressive change in organization from complexity towards simplicity; in biological terms, it appears as a *saltus Naturae* from Inanimate Matter to Life; in philosophical terms, as reorientation of the mind's eye from the Macrocosm to the Microcosm; in religious terms, as a conversion of the soul from the World, the Flesh and the Devil to the Kingdom of Heaven." Through this process, energy is liberated and transferred from a lower level of action to a higher. Here men are able more fully to realize their potentialities.[22]

But Toynbee felt that one could be more specific on the whole process of growth. The agent is normally a leader of a creative minority, whose action is conditioned by a movement of withdrawal and return. Perpetually new challenges arise, and some creative minority devises a program to meet them. Approval for such a policy is gained not through democratic education but through mass imitation or *mimesis*. The gulf between leader and led is so great

21. Toynbee, *A Study of History*, III, 119–20.
22. *Ibid.*, 191–92.

that only through the "charm" of the former and the spontaneous admiration and trust of the latter is the society carried forward. But these devices have within them seeds of destruction. Success can be only momentary, for a minority tends either to rest on its oars or become the object of a demoralizing idolatry.

This image of creative leadership is at the same time one of the most imaginative and least scientific of Toynbee's concepts. An individual or a minority invents solutions to problems of group life and enlists a kind of mechanical adherence. Only the dominant minority, when civilization is in decline, employs coercive political power. This does not ring true to any observer of the contemporary scene, for modern man believes that no society can be held together without the use of political power. Mechanical mimesis is one kind of power, but only one. It deals with the acquired habits of men, but there are other less subtle forms of power by which men are led. Toynbee's purpose may be to use the notion of mimesis symbolically at this point, but there is nevertheless a problem with his use of the concept which can hardly be ignored.[23]

Act I closes on a note of mysticism. The creative minority gains its vision only by withdrawal from the flux of human events to contemplate transcendent realities. In modern psychological terms, withdrawal may be described as the movement of the ego from the objective world into the unconscious, and return would be the movement of the ego back to the world. The latter is for Toynbee the crucial experience, since it is the overt expression of a practical use of the fruits of this creative experience. Even with an inspired leadership and a responsive and docile following, no civilization has yet proved capable of endless growth. The tragedy of history is that somewhere in midpassage the chain of successful responses is broken and civilization reaches an apparently inevitable point of breakdown. Creativity falls prey to its nemesis, and society rejects a leadership which has failed it.

Act II is from the outset a parable of man's moral failures. It begins when a major challenge receives an unsuccessful response. In contrast to the new challenges presented in a civilization which is in growth, this same challenge is repeated and other unsuccessful responses are made. During growth a creative minority has drawn on inner sources of strength. In the moment of crisis and breakdown, the minority either fails to use or does not possess this inner strength. Breakdown comes earlier in Toynbee's pattern of history

23. *Ibid.*, 217–49.

than it does in that of some other historians. Gibbon, for example, dated the breakdown of the Roman Empire in the second century A.D., following the death of Marcus Aurelius. But to Toynbee this date and the preceding Age of the Antonines represent not the apogee of the Roman Empire but its Indian summer. Hellenic civilization and not Rome is the proper unit for study, and the failure of this larger unit came in 431 B.C. when it did not respond creatively to the challenge of the Peloponnesian War.[24]

Three lessons can be drawn from such breakdown. First, the challenge to which no response was given was the need for a larger political society than the Athenian city-state. The cause for this failure Toynbee attributed to the "idolization of an ephemeral institution." This tendency to cast useful institutions as absolutes is but one example of the devices by which a once creative, now only dominant minority can maintain power and conceal its failures from the masses. Again and again civilization is confronted by the same challenge and the old progressive rhythm of challenge and response is replaced by a contra-rhythm of challenge and failure to respond.[25]

Second, a deep schism appears within the society threatened by breakdown. The creative minority no longer exerts any influence over an "internal proletariat," which has lost the sense of belonging to an inclusive society, or over an "external proletariat," barbarians at the fringes of a civilization who by now have gone their own way. Each group creates a religion or institution by which it seeks to extend its power. The "internal proletariat" in some civilizations creates a higher religion; the "external proletariat" employs military force to exert constant pressure on the frontiers. Finally, after an extended period of internecine war, designated as a "Time of Troubles," the dominant minority crushes its opposition in a great "knock-out blow" and a universal state comes into being. This is the last bastion of the beleaguered dominant minority, and although such a state is incapable of growth, it may last a long time, as did the Egyptiac civilization, if its inner and outer enemies are not too strong. The end comes when those inner and outer groups combine to overthrow the civilization.[26]

The development which held Toynbee's attention in Act II was not, however, the breakdown but rather a long and apparently in-

---

24. Toynbee, A Study of History, IV, 245, 594, 263–74; Edward Gibbon, The Decline and Fall of the Roman Empire (6 vols.; New York, 1900).
25. Toynbee, A Study of History, IV, 303–423.
26. Toynbee, A Study of History, V, 35–337.

evitable period of disintegration. One of the characteristics of this is the division within society to which we have already called attention. Another is a "schism in the soul." In a civilization in growth, there is a sense of "wholeness" to life; in a society in disintegration, this is replaced by a kind of schizophrenia which manifests itself in art, religion, and politics. A civilization which has lost its sense of equilibrium and direction is driven, in its responses to challenges, to choose between extremes. For example, either it is encouraged to return to the past or its leaders try to inspire a utopian or "futurist" course of action. All this takes place with mechanical regularity. Having commenced its period of disintegration, a civilization moves with clocklike certainty toward the final doom.

This relentless movement, however, is punctuated by variants of "rout and rally." After the "Wars of Religion" in Western civilization, for example, the "rally" was the period of temperate warfare in the eighteenth and nineteenth centuries. Another "rout," the "Wars of Nationality," followed inevitably. The fourth "rout" in the sequence is fatal. Although these episodes extend the agony of eventual destruction, they are incapable of postponing it permanently.[27]

If there is any "determinism" in Toynbee, it comes in the second part of Act II. However valiantly he insisted on the freedom of will of a civilization to avert breakdown and destruction, he never denied that once disintegration sets in, no power short of God Incarnate can alter man's destiny. Nonetheless, this act ends with a question. If civilization is destroyed, does history itself come to an end? For Hegel, the Prussian state was the end point of history. For Spengler, each culture was unique, and therefore the issue never arose. For Toynbee, this question is by far the most significant. In writing about it, he endeavored to summarize his whole theory of history.

Act III is the chapter in the pattern of the past in which Toynbee posed a succession of far-reaching and fundamental questions. What is the nature of the contacts or encounters in time and space between civilizations? Is religion merely a vessel for carrying shipwrecked humanity from one civilization to the next, or does it possess a positive function that transcends this role? Where do we in the West stand in such a pattern, and what are the prospects that we shall join our predecessors and bow to the ruthless forces of

27. Toynbee, *A Study of History*, VI, 49–132, 278–326.

history? In the following analysis of Toynbee's theory of international relations, we shall refer again to these questions.

Despite Toynbee's questioning some of the tenets of modern social science, he can be considered a social theorist. One of his foremost objectives was to erect laws and principles which would demonstrate recurrence and regularity in history. A respected American scholar has argued on this point: "The absolutely unique, that which has no element in common with anything else, is indescribable, since all description and all analysis are in terms of predicates, class concepts, or repeatable relations." Such predicates and repeatable relations are keys to Toynbee's concept of history. He asserted unequivocally that he conceived the search for recurrence to be a necessary and a manageable task. In a letter to this writer he noted: "As to the issue between recurrence and uniqueness, I think both elements are present in History as in everything else, and the logical difficulty of reconciling them is neither greater nor smaller in History than in other fields of thought." There was, he felt, a compelling urgency to formulating principles of recurrence, and he asked: "May not it mean that we ought all of us to give far more time and far more serious and strenuous thought than many of us have ever given to this job of forming one's general ideas?"[28]

It is possible here to illustrate Toynbee's laws and principles only insofar as they have a bearing on international politics. One can indicate the trends in his thinking by enumerating some of the principles which he developed within five distinct areas. First, with respect to the broad area of history and social phenomena, he proceeded on the assumption that historical events display a sufficient similarity to warrant treating them as representative of a class of events. The crisis in American history, for example, at the time of the Civil War is in some respects an example of the same class of events as the Bismarckian wars of 1864–1871. What was involved was the prospect that an imperfect political union would dissolve altogether. History was to show that this issue was resolved in both cases by war. Furthermore, after each war a great increase in industrial activity took place. In a limited but important sense, therefore, the American Civil War and the wars for

<hr />

28. Morris Cohen, *The Meaning of Human History* (La Salle, Ill., 1947), 84; Arnold J. Toynbee to Kenneth W. Thompson, April 19, 1950, in possession of the recipient; Arnold J. Toynbee, Pieter Geyl, and Pitirim A. Sorokin, *The Pattern of the Past* (Boston, 1949), 90–91.

German unification were not separate and isolated events but examples of a particular species of event. Again, when a federal form of government emerged in Great Britain, America, and Germany, and later in Canada, Australia, South Africa, and Brazil, these were not isolated occurrences. Although each development was unique, there were features common to all.[29]

It is illuminating to contrast this view with other popular modern attitudes. For Charles Beard, Toynbee's conception of laws of history is unquestionably too ambitious. In his introduction to Brooks Adams' philosophy of history, Beard wrote: "It is not true that history repeats itself. . . . Mankind never returns to the events . . . of a previous age." In writing specifically of *A Study of History*, Beard charged that "no meaning can arise from such comparisons, even assuming that there are such . . . classes of societies—an assumption based on a physical analogy." At the opposite pole is a statement by Buckle: "Two doctrines . . . represent different stages of civilization. According to the first doctrine, every event is single and isolated. . . . This opinion, which is most natural to a perfectly ignorant people, would soon be weakened by that extension of experience which supplies a knowledge of those uniformities of succession and of co-existence that nature constantly presents." Buckle's application of this doctrine in important political and social spheres is quite extravagant. For him, uniformity in nature becomes a basis for predicting the character of all human relations: "The food of a people determines the increase of their numbers, and the increase of their numbers determines the rate of their wages. . . . When the wages are invariably low . . . the distribution of political power and social influence will also be very unequal . . . [and] depend upon . . . nature." This extreme illustration of a particular philosophy of history can be compared, as can Beard's viewpoint, with Toynbee's outlook to help us form our judgments about Toynbee's laws and principles. If we make a further comparison between Spengler and Toynbee on this point, it becomes apparent that Toynbee's view of law and recurrence in history is closer to that center on the spectrum than we at first imagined. It also gives some ground for believing that he is more a genuine historian than are some of his predecessors in the philosophy of history.[30]

There is a second type of law which Toynbee discussed. It is rep-

29. Toynbee, *Civilization on Trial*, 33–36.
30. Brooks Adams, *The Law of Civilization and Decay: An Essay on History*

resented by the balance of power in the sphere of political dynamics which, in his words, "comes into play whenever society articulates itself into a number of mutually independent local states." All political constellations in which multiple units carry on relations are characterized by the operation of this principle. In the history of political theory, the greatest of English-speaking philosophers has written, "the balance of power had been ever assumed as the common law of Europe at all times and by all powers."[31]

Since 1930, Toynbee was fascinated particularly by one aspect of this common "law." Throughout most of history, the balance of power appears inevitably to have shifted from the center of any political system to its periphery. Europe's declining position in world politics after World War I can best be comprehended in terms of this law:

> In the third century B.C., we see the city-states of Greece—an Athens, a Sparta, a Sicyon, a Megalopolis, a Rhodes—encircled and dwarfed by a ring of outer Powers which owed their own vitality to the elixir of Hellenism—a Macedon, a Syria, an Egypt, a Carthage, a Rome. . . . [In] the Far Eastern extremity of the Old World, we shall similarly perceive the little states in the centre— a Song, a Chou, a Lu—which had been the seedbeds of Chinese culture, on the point of succumbing to the contending Great Powers on the Periphery: a Ts'i, a Ch'u, Ts'in.
>
> From these analogies, it would appear that the plight in which . . . Europe found . . . [itself] was not after all an unprecedented departure from the ordinary course of history.[32]

With comparable illustrations from ancient and contemporary history, Toynbee endeavored to prove that states which occupy the homeland of any civilization sooner or later are dominated by emerging "Great Powers" which inevitably spring up on the fringe of the old order. This is not the only principle of the balance of power worth observing, but it is the one on which Toynbee placed greatest emphasis. There are other examples of the function and

---

(New York, 1910), 51; see also Lynn White, Jr., "The Changing Past," Harpers Magazine, CCIX (November, 1954), 29–34; Charles A. Beard, "Review of a Study of History," American Historical Review, XL (January, 1935), 308; Buckle, Introduction to the History of Civilization in England, I, 4–5, 39.

31. Toynbee, A Study of History, III, 301; Edmund Burke, "Third Letter on the Proposals for Peace with the Regicide Directory of France," Works and Correspondence (8 vols.; London, 1852), V, 381.

32. Survey of International Affairs, 1930, p. 133.

purpose of the balance of power to which he gave some attention, and these will be mentioned later.

Toynbee considered but briefly a third type of laws, those concerning the interrelationship of forces in a civilization. These are essentially little more than general working hypotheses for dealing with complex problems. Tests to determine their accuracy and consistency are restricted to fewer civilizations than are the laws previously enumerated. Two striking illustrations are the laws of the relation between democracy and education and between religion and politics. From his examination of the historical experiences of Greece and Rome and of Western civilization, Toynbee put forward the theory that the diffusion or democratization of learning invariably lowers its quality. In Hellenic history the spread of elementary education within the Roman Empire was the harbinger of the disappearance of a vital intellectual life which was over one thousand years old. In our own time, the tyranny over men's minds exerted by some private and public leaders through the mass media illustrates the same proposition.[33]

Another hypothesis is Toynbee's law that religions bring ruin on themselves by going into politics. This law is a two-edged sword in effect, for not only have all religions, with the exception of Islam, broken down as a consequence of excursions into politics, but political systems have suffered equally thereby. In this same category of laws concerning the interrelation of forces is a law which Toynbee formulated thus: "The possibility of borrowing this or that element of an alien culture at choice, without eventually making an unconditional surrender to the inclusive alien force, is a fundamental law of the contact of cultures."[34]

Toynbee's ability to conceptualize intriguing principles of history and international affairs with insight and cogency is nowhere more clearly indicated than in his laws of war, revolution, and international peace and order. Curiously enough, however, these learned comments must be placed in a fourth class of laws of descending order of universality, because their application presents certain problems. Plainly, one of the underlying revolutions of our time has been the technological revolution, and those who formulate theories and laws applicable to the contemporary scene are obliged to think within new frames of reference. For a people who have lived a major portion of their lives in the flux of social change,

33. Toynbee, *A Study of History*, IV, 194.
34. Toynbee, *A Study of History*, V, 359n2, VI, 229. (See also the last series of four volumes.)

what Toynbee had to say about laws of revolution is indeed appropriate: "If old institutions obstruct the action of new social forces without ultimate success, the degree of violence of the eventual revolution is proportionate to the time-span of its retardation."[35] In this sense the American Revolutionary War could be considered among those "temperate and undecisive contests" of the eighteenth century. The outbreak of nationalist wars in Latin America, Italy, and Germany in the nineteenth century took heavier tolls than did their predecessors. And the uprisings in Eastern Europe, Southwest Asia, and the Middle East have shattered two empires and threatened civilization as a whole.

A student can have but one major objection to these propositions. This law, surely one fraught with meaning, ought probably to be reformulated in light of the immense and novel power of the organized state with its monopoly over the instruments of power and violence. It ought also to be tested more widely than Toynbee was ever able to do. Nevertheless, it provokes us to think more broadly about a recurrent problem.

Few insights on political and military strategy are more immediately relevant for citizens of a new empire than is Toynbee's law of strategic interests and power: "On a stationary military frontier between a civilization and a barbarism, time always works in the barbarians' favour; and, besides this, the barbarians' advantage increases (to borrow Malthus's famous mathematical metaphor) in geometrical progression at each arithmetical addition to the length of the line which the defenders of the civilization have to hold." If one accepts the proposition that bolshevism is the second great barbarian reaction or threat to Western civilization, the implication of this law is sobering.[36]

No less pertinent is the law by which Toynbee accounted for the pattern in the recovery of great nations following major wars. The situation of Germany following World War I could have been forecast with at least a rough-and-ready reckoning based on France following the Napoleonic Wars: "The post-war recuperation of France after the General War of 1792–1815 declared itself when the Bourbon Restoration was supplanted by the Orleanist regime of Louis Philippe through the Revolution of July 1830, in the fifteenth year after the decisive military defeat of Napoleon at Waterloo. The post-war recuperation of Germany after the General War of 1914–18

35. Toynbee, *A Study of History*, IV, 189.
36. Toynbee, *A Study of History*, II, 283.

declared itself in the fifteenth year after the capitulation of the
Prussian General staff."[37] The recovery of Germany and Japan after World War II, though accelerated by the beneficence of Western assistance, displayed a roughly similar pattern.

A final illustration of such a law may be found in Toynbee's thesis that in a conflict between more and less civilized antagonists,
the latter enjoys decisive advantages in any protracted struggle. The
reasoning supporting this law has primary interest for us. The civilized power has greater ability to mobilize moral and material energy in peace and war. In peace, this accounts for remarkable social
and economic progress; in war, this forces the expending of blood
and treasure to the point of self-destruction. After World War I,
Germany lay prostrate for over a decade but Russia and Turkey re-
covered in a few years. A backward country is less likely to con-
sume its full strength in war and thus retains a margin of power for
bold adventures and new programs.[38] One might wonder how this
applied to the United States or even Great Britain after World War
II. It may offer a warning against excessive defense expenditures
and massive deficits in the 1980s.

The fifth and final type of law represents those principles of history and politics which are founded on Toynbee's conception of the
nature of man. We must note, however, the deviation of some of
Toynbee's principles from the findings of modern social psychologists. For example, he assumed that social and political leaders in
a society's creative minority were each able to come forward with
a solution for only one problem or crisis and with a means of gaining support for it. He based this notion upon a law of human nature set down by ibn-Khaldun that the individual with the capacity for a particular art seldom masters another art well: "If he did
achieve this, that would mean that he did not yet possess, to perfection, the former capacity; it would mean that the dye of that capacity in him had not yet taken fact."[39] As a commonsense dictum, this law has a certain meaning; as a principle of practical
politics for leaders of an ever-expanding government, it is surely
more difficult to fathom and apply. The general criticism leveled
against Toynbee's laws of history and politics arises from questions about their application to current problems.

That leads to international studies. International relations, and particularly international politics, is a young discipline among ac-

37. *Survey of International Affairs*, 1933, p. 112.
38. Toynbee, *A Study of History*, IV, 393–94.
39. Quoted in Toynbee, *A Study of History*, V, 354–55n6.

ademic fields of study. It has drawn on older disciplines when problems have arisen on which they could speak with greater authority. Some scholars have suggested that one such related discipline which should be consulted was universal or world history. It is fortunate that, as we have seen, the scholar whose philosophy of history we have been examining acquired stature in both the fields of international relations, as editor of the *Survey of International Affairs*, and of universal history. His theories, therefore, provide a bridge between the two disciplines whose relationship forms the principal basis for the inquiry which follows.

From the beginning, there has been no unanimity among scholars in the field as to a proper definition of international relations. For his part, Toynbee moved uneasily through three separate definitions at three different stages in his thinking. In the 1920s he conceived of the field as limited narrowly "to the relations between sovereign independent states." He showed faint awareness of the kind of problem which would be presented by the Spanish civil war. In a preface to the first *Survey* he offered one prophetic addition to his theory: "Not states but relations between states have been chosen as the units, except in a few cases . . . in which the status or internal condition of a country was itself an international affair." In the 1930s, however, Toynbee abandoned the sharp distinction between internal and foreign affairs. A respected American scholar emphasized that "there is no clear dichotomy between internal and foreign affairs." Toynbee pointed out that such a distinction was really little more than a convention which in most cases merely confused the individual who was seeking a proper understanding of international affairs.[40]

More specifically, in the 1930s he was impressed that two outstanding events, the American depression and the German political revolution brought about by the rise of Hitler, could not have been properly defined under his first classification of international relations. Whenever the internal affairs of any one of the sixty or seventy countries affected the potential world distribution of power, then and only then would they become a bona fide topic within the field. At this time, he was arguing that the interpenetration of domestic and international affairs had become the rule rather than the exception. The episode which confirmed this belief was the Spanish civil war, which, he wrote, presented "the his-

---

40. *Survey of International Affairs*, 1929, p. 202; preface to *Survey of International Affairs*, 1920–23; Edward M. Earle, "National Security," *Yale Review*, n.s., XXIX (Spring, 1940), 452.

torian with another case of the . . . breakdown of the conventional
distinction between 'international' and 'internal' affairs." From the
moment hostilities began, the burning question was whether the
war was in fact a civil war or an international war fought on a
Spanish stage. Far from an academic exercise, this was a political
issue fraught with grave danger—the five Great Powers might move
in the direction of a general conflict.[41]

A third concept which occupied Toynbee's attention was Janus-
headed in character. One type of international relations is among
communities within a civilization; another is among civilizations
themselves. These two influence one another, and it is therefore
incumbent upon scholars to explore the latter as carefully and as
thoroughly as they do the former.

Beyond definitions, Toynbee spoke about methods of study in
international relations which appeared the most fruitful to him.
One combination was based upon the cooperation of historians,
political scientists, and psychologists. For him, as we shall see,
foreign policy inevitably has an important psychological compo-
nent. The attitudes of Central and Eastern European states in the
1920s and 1930s toward domination by Germany or the alternative of active participation within an effective collective security
system was an example. It would require a historian to point out
how the lack of experience of newly sovereign states influenced
their policies and a psychologist to show the "subconscious res-
ignation to the inevitability of a coming German hegemony."[42]

On other problems the cooperating disciplines might be history
and military science, for Toynbee recognized the close connection
between war and international politics. He dealt at length with the
history and art of war, using the writings of military experts to as-
sist him in this enterprise. Indeed, there are times when Toynbee
seems to include all disciplines, from agriculture to zoology, as
handmaidens of his own historian's discipline. This practice, which
is comprehensive in scope, can of course be destructive to the unity
of any discipline, an issue we shall explore later.

Since World II, one of the foremost practical concerns in international relations has been the analysis of power politics. On numerous occasions, Toynbee made plain that in contemporary international society the precepts of Machiavelli are more appropriate

41. *Survey of International Affairs,* 1935, II, vii; *Survey of International Affairs,*
1937, II, v.
42. *Survey of International Affairs,* 1934, p. 345.

for action than are those of Grotius. As he remarked: "I certainly believe that anarchic power politics are simply the reflection of the power drives of a number of individuals." In the Far East, for example, the prestige of the Confucian scholars enabled them to dominate and sometimes even ruthlessly exploit the peasants. In other civilizations, the peculiar positions of priests, philosophers, or warriors permitted them to dominate. This underlying force shaping human conduct, which is often concealed or disguised within a nation, was for him self-evident, fundamental, and universal on the contemporary international scene. Therefore, if Machiavelli's exposition of the nature of politics "seemed shocking to Western minds for several centuries after the date of the publication of *The Prince*, it offended through being innocent of both obtuseness and hypocrisy, and not through being guilty of any misrepresentation of the principles on which the philosopher's contemporaries and successors were acting in real life."[43]

There are ample illustrations of the workings of power politics in Hellenic history. These include the curious shift in alliances among Greek city-states culminating in the policy of the Aetolian League aligning itself with Rome against Macedon which ultimately involved Greece in the Hannibalic War.[44] But power politics as such attains its present character only with the passing of the *Respublica Christiana*. Significantly, in Toynbee's discussion of the handling of the Crusades and relations with the House of Hohenstaufen, the papacy is criticized not for engaging in power politics but for making such poor guesses about which political causes and leaders should be encouraged. Some of the strongest passages in Toynbee's writings concern the radical discrepancy between the pretenses and ideological rationalizations of statecraft and the political principles on which action is really based.

One event which he recounted concerns the meeting of a British and a Persian statesman following the Versailles Peace Conference of 1919. The latter repeatedly mentioned his great disappointment at the cynical sacrifice of his nation upon the altar of the Anglo-Russian entente. British policy, he acknowledged, had been honorable and fair before 1907, but to sacrifice Persia now in this way was an act of absolute moral degeneracy. The Englishman sought to explain by discussing Britain's strategic interests and the threat of a Russo-German alliance. The British, he said, saw a

43. Toynbee to Thompson, April 19, 1950, in possession of the recipient; Toynbee, *A Study of History*, IV, 420; *Survey of International Affairs*, 1933, pp. 116–17.
44. Toynbee, *A Study of History*, III, 341n3.

choice between the probable sacrifice of Persia to Russia and the possible destruction of the whole of Western civilization. At this, the Persian lost his temper. To speak with complacency of the sacrifice of Persia, "the priceless jewel of civilization," on the off chance of saving a worthless Western society was sheer impudence. He concluded: "What should I have cared and what do I care now, if Europe perishes so long as Persia lives!" For Toynbee, such views reflected the present standards of international society and the primacy of loyalty to the state in power politics.[45]

In explaining the setting for this way of thinking, Toynbee offered a broader framework. Two philosophies of international relations have coexisted in Western society for at least a century and a half. The one, idealistic and moralistic in character and crusading in spirit, views rivalry or conflict among nations as a mere temporary distortion of the normal pattern of international life. The other, which interprets politics as an unending struggle for power, focuses on practical choices in diplomacy, on permanent aspects of foreign policies, and on techniques of accommodation and adjustment. The question it deals with is, what techniques are necessary for international peace and order when there is no world state in existence or any binding system of world law? In a striking and revealing fashion, Toynbee combined these two philosophies in his own theory and emphasized first one and then the other in the unfolding of his thought.

In the 1920s and well into the 1930s, Toynbee was a prominent spokesman of the idealist school. In the early 1920s, he appeared to agree with Lord Curzon that a new alliance between England and France would be inconsistent with the League of Nations. He noted with displeasure that the Franco-Polish military alliance "introduced an unfortunate element of *raison d'état*" into French policy respecting the sanctity of the European peace treaties. In appraising the work of the Temporary Mixed Commission on Armaments of the League of Nations, he emphasized the overweening influence of the munitions makers. At times he verged on accepting the "devil" theory of politics, namely, that a handful of evil men were responsible for war and conflict.[46]

His faith in the League of Nations was sometimes extravagant. He criticized Austria for turning to Italy at the time of the Ethio-

45. Toynbee, *A Study of History*, I, 162–63.
46. *Survey of International Affairs*, 1924, p. 13; *Survey of International Affairs*, 1932, pp. 308, 296–97.

pian crisis. It seemed inconceivable that nations would depend upon traditional alliances when a collective security system was available. He spoke of the "sinister play of 'power politics'" within the League, which "represented an attempt to reconcile peace with growth. . . . A relapse [from the League] . . . would signify . . . the problems of post-war Europe would not or could not, after all, be settled by the new method of reason, debate and conciliation." The underlying cause of these lapses was human weakness and wickedness. He spoke of British and French foreign policy as "negative, weak-willed, cowardly egotism [and] . . . the reigning politicians . . . in deference to what they believed to be the will of their constituents . . . stop short of an effective fulfillment of their own covenants." The foreign policy of the United States was "captious and perverse . . . in the sight of a neutral observer." All during this period, British interests, international law, and universal morality were equated. This is the Toynbee with whom students of power politics, such as E. H. Carr, had little patience.[47]

There is a second Toynbee, however, who sets forth a philosophy of international politics which goes back to what some have called political realism. This is the Toynbee who emphasizes underlying political issues and the problem of conflicting foreign policies. In the mid-1930s he began to wonder whether a settlement between Germany and France was not more important than the perfecting of the new machinery of international organization. In one illustration, Toynbee wrote: "A definitive territorial settlement between Germany and France would assuredly do more than any other single international transaction . . . to assure . . . the peace of Europe. It could not, perhaps, absolutely ensure that France and Germany should live, henceforth, in perpetual peace with one another; for the territorial question was not, unfortunately, the sole question. . . . [But] if once the territorial conflict between the two principal Powers of Continental Europe were removed from the arena the whole international situation in Europe was likely to improve almost beyond the range of imagination." The second illustration represents Toynbee's outlook on the United Nations, which can well be contrasted with his earlier view of the League: "The present constitution of the U. N. represents the closest degree of cooperation that the United States and the Soviet Union can reach at present."[48]

47. *Survey of International Affairs*, 1937, II, 132; *Survey of International Affairs*, 1930, p. 10; *Survey of International Affairs*, 1935, pp. 2, 96.
48. *Survey of International Affairs*, 1934, p. 627; Toynbee, *Civilization on Trial*, 135.

The final step in Toynbee's disenchantment with the idealist philosophy of international relations was reached as the world moved into a period of deepening Soviet-American crisis. In 1947 he declared, "Anything that would enable us to buy time seems worth thinking about; and therefore I suggest a provisional partition of the world into a Russian and an American sphere by agreement between the two."[49] In the 1930s, Toynbee was critical of what he called cynical views designed merely to gain time. The unqualified character of his later statements, however, places him among students of diplomacy who have recognized the need for practical techniques more appropriate to the unregulated character of international politics.

Finally, there is an interesting correlation between Toynbee's general historical method at a given period and his philosophy of international affairs. In the 1920s, for example, his emphasis on nations bears a rough correspondence to his strongly idealist philosophy of international relations. As his focus shifts from nation to civilization to higher religion, there is a perceptible change from idealism to realism in international politics. Cautious at first, this change becomes ever clearer as his thinking mirrors the mounting crisis between East and West. It is worth noting that this same combination of theological absolutism and political relativism can be found in Niebuhrian Protestantism and the proclamations of the Vatican on the cold war. Those whose religious views approximate some measure of certainty can perhaps afford to be more tentative about politics.

There remains the question of science. Throughout, it is clear that even when he spoke of "science," Toynbee recognized its limitations. The historian Huizinga once observed that if the scientific character of history were emphasized, the greatest historians of former times would have to be excluded.[50] Despite Toynbee's dedication to the empirical method, he too would probably be placed in this group. There are four limitations inherent in the nature of history which restrict any science of politics and thus Toynbee's attempt to construct a more rational theory.

The first is the limitation of materials, which he appeared to have surmounted. The screen upon which A Study of History is reflected is large enough to permit the illumination of from twenty

49. Toynbee, The Prospects of Western Civilization, 46.
50. Raymond Kilbansky et al., Philosophy and History (London, 1936), 3–4.

to thirty civilizations over a time span of six thousand years. But this amplitude of material is more apparent than real, for on numerous occasions it becomes clear that Toynbee proceeded from mere shreds of evidence. Minoan civilization is the key to several of his principles, but he admitted he was "hampered by having no access to written records."[51]

Another handicap which confronts any historian is the limitation of his own energy and knowledge. Herbert Butterfield spoke of this when he resisted publication of his *Origins of History* delivered in the form of the Gifford Lectures. In Toynbee's *Study*, the architectural design is often much better than a good deal of the building material. The fund of available knowledge for the study of man today is so massive that no one can presume to speak authoritatively on all phases and periods of history. An isolated scholar, no matter how enormous his learning, must draw heavily upon secondary sources. One must distinguish with reliability between good and inferior examples, and the strong and weak points of those sources. In his dependence upon Bergson and Huntington, for example, Toynbee fell victim to this limitation. Perhaps only through cooperative efforts by teams of scholars can we expect amelioration of such a problem.

The third limitation is the paradox that historians must be both researchers and artists. History can be comprehended only through its narration. The form of great history on occasion approaches that of the novel. The observer stands not outside but curiously within the network of events he describes. The collection and ordering of data may be scientific up to a point; its recording and analysis require gifts of creativity, imagination, and artistry of another order.

The fourth limitation for the historian is the epitome of the others. The formulation of method in the social sciences has been largely defective because it has been predetermined by achievements in the natural sciences rather than being evoked from its subject matter. In this way facts are amassed beyond any conceivable use, observation is restricted to data that may be isolated, measured, and verified, and events are torn from the context which produced them and which continues to give them meaning. The ready-made formula of the "scientific method" has brought prestige to history and politics, but has often obscured the need for modes of observation and analysis more appropriate to the study of man.

51. Toynbee, *A Study of History*, I, 93.

Certain limitations are, in addition, the outcome of Toynbee's own personal philosophy and outlook. At the launching of his grand project, his method was to formulate explanations and then test or illustrate them by certain passages of history. This is the eternal dilemma of anyone who strives toward general principles and theory. The very selection predetermines to some extent the laws and principles which will emerge. The testing is even more precarious since events which confirm the theory must be detached from the life of the society from which they take their real meaning. All students of comparative history expose themselves to this snare, but the boldness of Toynbee's endeavor places him squarely in this dilemma.

One further problem involves Toynbee's religious faith. Certain spiritual histories have succeeded to some degree in separating the spiritual and material; Toynbee makes no such effort. Instead, the two spheres become virtually interchangeable. Buddha and Machiavelli are illustrations of "withdrawal and return," and spiritual progress is identified both with the City of God and the City of Man.[52] These vertical analogies, in which illustrations are drawn from separate dimensions of life, are probably the least scientific of all the techniques employed.

What can be said, therefore, is that Toynbee clearly falls short of the scientist's picture of the proper study of society. His failure is a dual one and provides a commentary on the predicament of any student of human behavior. Both the observer and the object of study are subjective in character. Man, "a subject," deals with objects, but these objects are men and forces. Therefore a scientist who aims at objectivity at any cost excludes that aspect of historical occurrence from which his "object" takes its own meaning. Toynbee has not done this. A scholar who bans these overtones or undercurrents of human conduct because their action can seldom be verified may build an impressive scientific edifice but he will probably not disclose the mysteries of human behavior. If he tries, however, to deal with them through legend and poetry or by examples from particular events taken arbitrarily from history, then he must expect to be classed as a mystic and spiritualist.

The other failure in Toynbee's *Study* becomes especially plain in the second and third sets of his volumes. Not only do they offer a spiritual interpretation, but it becomes increasingly clear that

52. Toynbee, *A Study of History*, III, 270–309; Toynbee, *Civilization on Trial*, 234–52.

there is a central vision. Christianity becomes not only a higher religion which bridges the chasm between two civilizations but also the sole basis for ultimate salvation of the only remaining progressive civilization. For those "scientific" theorists who assert the importance of inquiries that are value free, this commitment to Christianity is unforgivable. For Christians like Toynbee, it is the only path to survival.

PART TWO

Political Foundations

CHAPTER II

International Relations and the Problem of War

F EW WOULD dispute that the most urgent and threatening problem today is that of war. Contemporary scholars identify at least three distinct theories about the nature of war which have been articulated in Western civilization—the romanticist, the idealist, and the realist. All three find a place in Toynbee's writings but only the last two are in any sense representative of his philosophy. In *A Study of History* he quoted from von Moltke's famous letter of December 11, 1880, to Bluntschli: "Perpetual Peace is a dream—and not even a beautiful dream—and War is an integral part (ein Glied) of God's ordering of the universe. . . . In War, Man's noblest virtues come into play." Bernhardi, Nietzsche, and Spengler shared this view. Spengler conceived of man as a beast of prey who "lives by attacking and killing and destroying." A British military man wrote: "If honour be worth safeguarding, war sooner or later becomes inevitable, for in this world, there are always to be found dishonourable men, and if war does not bring a nation against these, then must vice live triumphant."[1]

However, the German Romanticists were even more brazen in their emphasis upon the intrinsic value of war as such. The most outspoken among them, Heinrich von Treitschke, asserted that "all movement and all growth would disappear with war, and . . . only the exhausted, spiritless, degenerate periods of history have toyed

1. Arnold J. Toynbee, *A Study of History* (12 vols.; London, 1934–1961), IV, 643; Oswald Spengler, *Man and Technics* (New York, 1932), 28; J. F. C. Fuller, *The Reformation of War* (New York, 1923), 282.

with the idea." He had the last word for this group of theorists: "War . . . will endure to the end of history, as long as there . . . [are] States." The laws of society and the fundamental nature of man make it inevitable that war will continue with no foreseeable prospect of its eradication.[2]

To a degree, the communist theory of war is romanticist in character. It maintains that war is inevitable under the capitalist system and encourages revolutionary wars and wars of national liberation. What is missing, however, is the idealization of war that characterized German romanticism. Instead, communism holds that war results in a negative selective process in which the fit are more often destroyed than are the unfit. The paradox of war within and among nations is that it inverts the laws of survival. In Toynbee's view, however, "some people say that war is inseparable from Human Nature. . . . I think the historical parallels show that this view is mistaken."[3]

A second theory of war, particularly dominant in contemporary Western society, proclaims that war is not inevitable, but can be eliminated through the achievement of a new and better form of international relations. This claim is at the heart of the idealist or rationalist theory of war. Its origin goes back to the Enlightenment. Reason and science are the foundation upon which this utopian edifice is built, and morality and democracy are its façade. War is conceived of as an anachronism which international organization, social conditioning, or increased contacts among peoples will eliminate. Power politics and aristocratic government are singled out as the primary causes of war. Those who persist in disrupting international harmony, a handful of leaders or a nation or two, are all that stands in the way of a peaceful and warless world.

There are at least four examples in as many separate areas of this philosophy as it manifested itself in Toynbee's earlier thinking. The first is the idealist view which seeks to eliminate war by substituting organization for politics. The spokesman whose words brought inspiration and dignity to this view was undoubtedly President Woodrow Wilson. He declared that in the new age, "national purposes have fallen more and more into the background and the common purpose of enlightened mankind has taken their

2. Heinrich von Treitschke, *Politics*, trans. Blanche Dugdale and Torben De Bille (2 vols.; London, 1916), I, 68, 65.

3. D. Feodotoff White, "The Soviet Philosophy of War," *Political Science Quarterly*, LI (September, 1936), 323–39; Arnold J. Toynbee, "Parallels to Current International Problems," *International Affairs*, X (July, 1931), 479.

place." Only democratic nations were capable of holding to these high purposes. A better world required that the balance of power be supplanted by the new international organization. Wilson's vision of peace reflected principles drawn from Kant's *Perpetual Peace* (1796).[4]

More recently this view has been persuasively argued by other scholars and publicists, particularly in the Anglo-American world. Typical is a statement by Leonard Woolf: "It was not the Kaiser who made the war of 1914, but the system of power politics." By contrast, Toynbee was not permanently misled into accepting the glittering generalities of utopianism in international politics. Still, in the early 1930s he was prompted to say: "Indeed, the proposition that if there were no 'Great Powers' in the world there would be no danger to the peace of the world was a thesis which could hardly have been contested, in 1932, by any impartial student of public affairs." Earlier he had written that nationalism "is the one thing . . . that can and does produce the calamity of war." When the Nye Committee in the United States and the League's Temporary Mixed Commission on Armaments were making their inquiries into the activities of the munitions industry, Toynbee observed that "the information which was made public casts a sinister light upon the policy and proceedings of armament firms and their agents." On the face of it, he seemed attracted by the theory that the nefarious deeds of munitions makers were a cause of war.[5]

However, the evil aspects of power politics which were aggravated by the immorality of certain personal "devils" in politics— whether munitions makers or Great Power diplomats—showed signs of being mitigated, if not eliminated, by the new international organization. Less than five years before the outbreak of a world war, Toynbee optimistically affirmed that the new machinery for dealing promptly with international emergencies had diminished the prospect of minor crises spreading into general conflagrations: "It becomes evident that, in the short span of twenty years, a great and encouraging advance had been made towards safeguarding Mankind against the *old* danger of being plunged into war." Thus in a period when the idealist philosophy

4. Woodrow Wilson, "Fourth Liberty Loan," *War and Peace: Presidential Messages, Addresses, and Public Papers (1917–1924)*, ed. Ray Stannard Baker and William E. Dodd (2 vols.; New York, 1927), I, 255–59.

5. Leonard Woolf, *The War for Peace* (London, 1940), 53; *Survey of International Affairs*, 1932, p. 184; Arnold J. Toynbee, *Nationality and the War* (London, 1915), 10; *Survey of International Affairs*, 1935, I, 47–48n2.

of war voiced by such thinkers as Sir Alfred Zimmern prevailed, even Toynbee, a student of power politics, trimmed his sails in conformity with the overriding majority opinion.[6]

Second, the idealist theory of war is a manifestation of a particular type of rationalist viewpoint which has served as the intellectual assumption of some modern thinkers. Buckle was convinced that "it must happen, that as the intellectual acquisitions of a people increase, their love of war will diminish." He saw a natural ratio between peace and reason which preordained that wherever intellectual classes are weak, the military influence will be strong. It was for this reason that Russia in the mid-nineteenth century embarked on military adventures such as the Crimean War. Buckle could say: "Russia is a war-like country, not because the inhabitants are immoral, but because they are unintellectual." Writing in the nineteenth century at a time when Europe was enjoying a period of general peace, Buckle understandably confused the political condition of peace with the intellectual assumptions of the age. It is more surprising, though, that Toynbee, writing in 1915, should for similar reasons have been no less optimistic: "War as a constructive national activity is for us essentially a thing of the past: between our warlike ancestors and ourselves there is a great gulf fixed, the Industrial Revolution, which has put us into a new environment."[7]

A corollary to the rationalist philosophy is the conviction that there exists a natural harmony of interests among all nations and peoples. Yet what is true in Mandeville's *Fable of the Bees* and Adam Smith's economic cosmos is not true of the idealist view of international affairs. That natural harmony has been temporarily obscured by the specific actions of some arch-troublemaker or by the atavism of power politics in general. Toynbee found that a "supreme British interest was also the supreme interest of the whole World, inasmuch as international law and order were in the true interest of the whole of Mankind and all the parochial states among which the living generation was partitioned."[8]

A third illustration of the idealist philosophy of international relations is the still popular belief that war can be banished through contacts between nations and by programs of cultural understanding. A shrinking globe, which facilitates trade and travel, will

6. *Survey of International Affairs*, 1934, p. 353 (emphasis added).
7. Henry T. Buckle, *Introduction to the History of Civilization in England* (2 vols.; New York, 1925), I, 111, 113; Toynbee, *Nationality and the War*, 27.
8. *Survey of International Affairs*, 1935, II, 45–46.

gradually eliminate ignorance and misunderstanding from which wars grow. Buckle attempted to show that English conceptions of French morals and French notions of the Englishman's scorn of letters were undermined by their closer contacts: "The progress of improvement, by bringing the two countries into close and intimate contact, has dissipated those foolish prejudices, and taught each people to admire, and, what is still more important, to respect each other. And the greater the contact, the greater the respect." So shrewd a military analyst as Liddell Hart falls prey to this formula. He concluded: "To abolish war we must remove its cause. . . . The way to 'peace on earth' is by the progressive and general growth of 'good will.'" Modern anthropologists and psychologists offer similar generalities.[9]

There is little evidence of this expression of idealism in Toynbee's writings. It is true that in 1915 he believed that peace could be achieved not through "mechanical means" but only by converting public opinion throughout Europe from "National Competition" to "National Cooperation."[10] Otherwise, Toynbee was not sympathetic to this idealist view. Perhaps the tragic character of international relations and war in the Balkans, which he observed firsthand by crossing boundaries from one national observation post to another, dampened his faith in such a vision. Whatever the cause, he came to have ever fewer illusions about cross-cultural relations as the way to end warfare.

Easily the most popular of idealist conceptions of war stems from the theory that there are no inherent human instincts making for war. Modern psychology, anthropology, and biology have sought to demonstrate that war either was inevitable because of certain inherent characteristics in man or, more frequently, was not inevitable because of the absence of such basic instincts. A minority conclusion by social scientists is that "it would serve no useful purpose to endeavor to define principles to eliminate causes of war, for war is inherent in human nature." The majority view, however, is reflected in the answers given to a questionnaire sent to 528 members of the American Psychological Association. The question was, "Do you as a psychologist hold that there are present in human nature ineradicable, instinctive factors that make war

9. Buckle, *Introduction to the History of Civilization in England*, I, 125; Basil H. Liddell Hart, *Thoughts on War* (London, 1944), 35; Gabriel Almond, "Anthropology, Political Behavior, and International Relations," *World Politics*, II (January, 1950), 277–84.

10. Toynbee, *Nationality and the War*, 10.

inevitable?" There were 346 negative answers; 10 positive; 150 did not reply; and 22 were ambiguous in their answers. Most psychologists would probably agree with Julian Huxley's thesis that there are no specific human instincts which one can designate as "war instincts."[11]

Only three kinds of animals practice war at all, in the sense of organized conflict between groups of the same species. These are man and two sorts of social insects—certain bees and some ants. The motive forces in these two cases are quite different. Among the insects, wars have a mechanical and instinctive foundation— the tactics on both sides are identical in essentially every respect. War among humans, however, lacks this automatic character, and numbers are not invariably the final arbiter. Rather, the real basis of wars is the impulse of "pugnacity" which, when evoked by external conditions, merges with other sentiments such as patriotism. It should be possible to create situations so that this instinct could express itself in other more peaceful ways. Without examining the political means for approaching or attaining such goals, this school of modern psychology hopes that new conditions for peaceful relations will derive from world government and a world system of law.[12]

Another form of idealism is embodied in certain anthropological research. Malinowski, for example, could find no evidence of any biological impulse toward war. Instead, "aggression is a derived impulse. It arises from the thwarting of one or the other of the basic psychological drives." New cultural conditions are capable of ameliorating aggression and eliminating war; social engineering can redirect conflicting interests. William James discovered a "moral equivalent of war" in the conscription of young men into a glorified Civilian Conservation Corps where their aggressions would be spent struggling against nature rather than against rival nations. More recent schemes for channeling aggressions and frustrations into benign pursuits are equally removed from those factors which cause rivalry among nations.[13]

11. Arthur B. Keith, *The Causes of the War* (London, 1940), ix; John M. Fletcher, "The Verdict of Psychologists on War Instincts," *Scientific Monthly*, XXXV (August, 1932), 142–45; Julian Huxley, "Is War Instinctive and Inevitable?" *New York Times Magazine*, February 10, 1946, p. 7.

12. Huxley, "Is War Instinctive and Inevitable?," 7.

13. Bronislaw Malinowski, "War—Past, Present, and Future," in J. D. Clarkson and T. C. Cochran, *War as a Social Institution* (New York, 1941), 23; William James, "The Moral Equivalent of War," *International Conciliation* (New York, 1926), No. 224, p. 496.

Evidence abounds that Toynbee was influenced by anthropological and social-psychological thinking in the 1920s. He made it his business to criticize the popular confusion of "the species of War with the genus violence. . . . Sociological research . . . indicated that War was a specific and peculiar exercise of violence, in which that indefinite impulse was organized in a corporate form. . . . This institutional form of violence . . . had not existed in the primitive condition of society in which Mankind had spent all but the last 6000 years of its inconceivably long duration." Yet Toynbee recognized the popular objection that among those primitive societies which had survived, war was still very much in evidence. He showed that no primitive society remained which was immune to the cultural influences of advanced civilizations. Those societies in their final stages had been infected by the civilized world with a virus they had not always known. At least in the 1920s, then, Toynbee found the anthropological approach soundly based and reliable and made use of it in building his own idealist outlook.[14]

A fifth form of idealism can be mentioned which Toynbee recognized but which he consistently opposed and rejected. He cited a passage from *The Age of the Chartists* by J. L. Hammond and Barbara Hammond which is a striking illustration of the theory of Herbert Spencer. An anonymous letter from a citizen of Manchester is quoted: "The rise and progress of the industrial arts, and the extension of beneficent commerce indicate . . . a new epoch which shall substitute the plowshare for the sword and the loom for the battery. The cause of industry is the cause of humanity."[15] Toynbee did not comment directly on this passage, but on several occasions he discussed political relations in an economic context. In 1936 he suggested that the economic harmony then existent between Germany and the Soviet Union was a portent of peaceful relations. Yet history proved in this and other instances that economic factors were not the primary determinant of warlike or peaceful relations among nations. After World War II, the economic self-sufficiency of the USSR and the United States, which some viewed as advancing prospects for peace, was overriden by political rivalries and conflicts.

A final version of idealism is more difficult to identify and describe. It combines elements of the earlier schools within a more

14. *Survey of International Affairs*, 1928, pp. 1–2.
15. Quoted in *Survey of International Affairs*, 1930, pp. 9–10n1.

general philosophy. It interprets international affairs in exclusively moral terms and passes judgment on political behavior
measured against standards of individual morality. For example,
Toynbee described the invasion of Abyssinia as "Signor Mussolini's deliberate personal sin."[16] It was one man's sinfulness that led
to a nation's aggression.

It is unfair to suggest that Toynbee's ideas between the two
world wars squared completely with the idealist theory. What is
significant is that the prudent historian should so frequently have
evaluated political actions in terms of personal and national virtue
and wickedness. Yet signs of change were present especially as the
world crisis deepened.

The third theory of war differs fundamentally from the romanticist and the idealist philosophies. To answer the question, Is war
inevitable? the realist approach starts with the assumption that
international politics must be understood as an unceasing struggle
for power. The normal condition of modern international society,
as of all human relations, is one of rivalry, conflict, and strife which
will exist until the end of history alongside good will, comity, and
cooperation. This is of far-reaching importance in determining the
techniques of international relations. If cooperation is the norm in
the relations between nations, states can pursue policies based on
humanitarian and moral principles. When strife is the norm, however, states must base policy on the national interest and must seek
those temporary adjustments which will prevent any antagonist
from dominating all the rest. Under the realist theory of war, goals
and policies must be more tentative, immediate, and practical in
character.

After World War II, Toynbee clearly tended toward this theory
of war. There is a particularly revealing contrast between his indignant rejection in 1936 of a suggestion that a few years' post-
ponement of war might mean that the conflict would never come
and his statement in 1947: "I do not think that in our present circumstances playing for time is a wrong or unreasonable thing for
us to try to do. . . . Russia and the United States . . . [need] time to
get used to each other. . . . Anything that would enable us to buy
time seems worth thinking about." It would not be unfair to say
that Toynbee's position became increasingly that of the realist. He
proposed a negotiated settlement between East and West based on

16. *Survey of International Affairs*, 1935, II, 3.

spheres of influence, the traditional realist technique of postponing a general conflict. Shifts in the European balance of power had been as important in causing open hostilities, he saw, as had the moral factors which he previously emphasized. He examined the United Nations within the framework of power politics and characterized it as the boldest and most realizable step toward world government. He saw European union not as the creation of a "Third Force" but as a significant experiment in regional organization, yet of minor importance for the world balance of power.[17] Each of these perceptions reflected a growing sense of the realities of world politics.

International politics, if it can be reduced to a single formula, must be analyzed from the standpoint of the security-power dilemma. Nations seek security, strive for it through gaining power, threaten another's security through the dynamic working of power, and avert conflict through some rough-and-ready demarcation of the respective spheres in which they have dominant interests. In Africa and in the Near East, wars have been prevented for many years through spheres of influence, and the student of power politics who deals realistically with the present crisis can find nothing which can wholly take the place of such arrangements. Philosophically, such a view differs sharply from either idealism or romanticism.

In yet another arena, Toynbee demonstrated his realist point of view. He looked toward the future establishment of a world government. In contrast, however, to the pure consensus and cooperation theories, Toynbee believed that "without the metal support inside the reinforced concrete you cannot hold the concrete together. So I think, whatever form of world government we may arrive at . . . there will be in it an element of the ascendancy of one great power."[18] In his approach to the problem of war, Toynbee moved closer to emphasizing the imperatives of national security and aligned himself with modern international relations scholars in the United States who espouse the realist conception of war.

Compared with such scholars, he displayed a continuing interest in the concrete details of warfare. However widely he ranged across the social sciences, Toynbee was principally a historian, if essen-

---

17. Arnold J. Toynbee, *The Prospects of Western Civilization* (New York, 1947), 45–46; *Survey of International Affairs*, 1930, pp. 10–11; Arnold J. Toynbee, *Civilization on Trial* (New York, 1948), 140–49.
18. Toynbee, *The Prospects of Western Civilization*, 48.

tially a philosopher of history. It is not surprising, then, that along
with his theory of war he sought to trace the history of war. Although what he systematically worked out was primarily a history
of the development of the art of war, Toynbee dealt more broadly
with the continuities and novelties in the history of war. From the
time of the transition from primitive societies to modern civilizations, war has been with us. Little evidence exists of a decline in
the incidence or magnitude of war. In nineteen out of twenty civilizations, its role has been the same. War has heralded the breakdown and disintegration of particular civilizations and incidentally, therefore, the birth and emergence of successor civilizations
and religions.

War generally has been localized, even at the time of the Roman
Empire. In Greek history, it was limited in a second way, by the
professional character of those who fought. Not general conscripted forces but troops of mercenaries fought with Alexander the
Great and most of his successors. Curiously enough, these struggles, limited in time and space and conducted by mercenaries,
worked indirect burdens upon the populace at large, which historians sometimes overlook. Soldiers who served in expeditionary
forces under Alexander in Southwest Asia were paid in the bullion
which was the basis of currencies there. The resulting expansion
in the volume of currency in circulation meant that peasants and
artisans in Greek cities who had been spared military sacrifices
found themselves helplessly ground into pauperism. Somewhat
later in Rome the impact of war was felt directly by the groups who
at first had been immune. The peasants originally were affected
only by bold thrusts such as Hannibal's march from the north. As
Rome's interests and far-flung commitments continued to expand, as campaigns were conducted first in Greece and then the
Middle East, the demand for larger quotas of fighting men increased. Peasants were conscripted to meet expanded commitments, were taken from the land and separated from the only means
of livelihood they knew. Their descendants, in the century of rev
olutions and civil war from 133 B.C. to 31 B.C., were the troops with
which rival warlords contended for mastery within the new Roman Empire. In this way, the impact of war, which Toynbee considered civilization's "deadly disease," was also for earlier civilizations the ultimate cause of internal disintegration. There were
delaying actions both in Rome and in China, and peace seemed to
have been temporarily restored. These rallies, although lasting for

several hundred years, were in retrospect merely signs of the final dissolution.[19]

If war is the "deadly disease" of civilization, it is logical that historians who love humanity should seek conditions and precedents for getting along without it. Toynbee speculated repeatedly that war may have been absent from primitive societies. There is a romantic turn of mind in the suggestion that only upon infection by existing civilizations do primitive societies display this disease. It is a view to which Elbert Smith gave factual support. Even in the era of modern civilizations, this general notion recurs in historical writings. Here, the ruling groups first challenge the barbarians to combat. The techniques of war and the first offensive are the work not of the external proletariat but almost always of the dominant minority which represents the declining society.[20]

However, there are groups and individuals who can be cited as having not known war. For one, there were the Slavs who lived in the Pripet Marshes until several centuries after the dissolution of the Roman Empire. Only when the Teutonic invaders came to the end of an expansionist phase were these primitive barbarians carried off by the Avar nomads to colonize other conquered territory. The Slavs were described by Simocatta, the last Hellenic historian in the sixth century, in his *Universal History*: "Their only baggage consisted of harps . . . they were not trained to bear arms. Their country was ignorant of iron, and this accounted for their peaceful and harmonious life. . . . They were people among whom war was unheard of." In another case, we see the outright renunciation of war. The monk-emperor Asoka, one of the most successful imperialists in the ancient Indic civilization, conducted one great war and then refused to countenance others. He spent the remainder of his life preaching and organizing peace. In the ancient Chinese civilization, following the destructive civil wars of "the contending states," Ts'in Shih Huang Ti was the last in a line of great warriors before the emergence of a long pacifist tradition.[21]

We can also look to the Mayan civilization, the whole history of which, as Toynbee pointed out, "in so far as it is known to us at all, is markedly pacific. It is only on the northwestern fringes of

19. Toynbee, *A Study of History*, V, 62–63; Toynbee, *The Prospects of Western Civilization*, 28.

20. Toynbee, *A Study of History*, V, 337.

21. Simocatta quoted in Toynbee, *A Study of History*, II, 318; *Survey of International Affairs*, 1928, p. 3.

the Mayan World that there is any archaeological evidence for the
practice of the art of war; and here it seems merely to have been a
border warfare against outer barbarians. There is no evidence either of fratricidal warfare between the Mayan city-states themselves or of military collisions with any alien society of the Mayan
Society's own calibre."[22]

Some scholars might use these illustrations in support of a philosophy of pacifism. Toynbee, however, used them with far greater
caution; in his early writings especially, he formulated no general
principles. It is perhaps significant that a philosopher of history
with whom Toynbee seldom agreed was engaged in a similar pursuit. Gibbon saw as the model illustration of a warless people the
Laplanders, who probably originated in western China and were in
their language affiliated with the Hungarians. Gibbon wrote that
"the Arctic tribes, alone among the sons of men, are ignorant of
war, and unconscious of human blood." The Eskimos are also
comparatively warless. Both historians give the impression of
making notes for posterity concerning these peaceful groups, but
neither of them projects any elaborate theories.[23]

The breakdown of medieval Christianity released loyalties and
forces that were to transform the nature and function of conflict.
In the sixteenth century the emotions and convictions which men
had formerly directed toward religion were channeled into war and
politics. This change led to the Wars of Religion. Scholars who have
studied wars statistically, recording the number of participants,
casualties, and duration of battles, point out that with the Wars of
Religion begins a period of increasingly ruthless conflicts. Moreover, the invention of gunpowder and the voyages of discovery
provided new material resources for waging war. The gold and
treasures of overseas colonies, especially of Spanish America, made
possible the retention of well-trained and well-paid troops. What
was most important, however, was that soldiers and leaders fought
with political and military antagonists who were also religious
miscreants. These factors helped to shape the outlooks of Gusta-
vus Adolphus and the Duke of Alva, which contrasted sharply with
those of Saint Louis and Frederick II.

The eighteenth century is described by military historians as the
exception to the general trend toward the increasing scale and

22. Toynbee, *A Study of History*, IV, 108.
23. Edward Gibbon, *The Decline and Fall of the Roman Empire* (6 vols.; New
York, 1900), V, 520–21.

temper of conflict. In the context of a much wider discussion of war and society, Gibbon, writing near the end of the eighteenth century, observed that "the European forces are exercised by temperate and undecisive contests." For part of the century, war was a kind of sport in which kings engaged one another for limited objectives. The Enlightenment had been responsible for the separation of war and religion.[24]

Also significant was a sociopsychological factor arising from the relation between rulers and ruled. When wars are justified in terms of morals and religions, men participate with a deadly earnest commitment, regardless of the odds against them. When wars are interpreted as strategic moves by rival princes, the response is considerably more restrained. Since the leaders were aware of this, they kept their ambitions within limits. Wars were fought by rules of the game, and the goal toward which leaders aspired was final victory with a minimum of losses and engagements. Complicated and cunning principles were designed to facilitate overcoming an enemy without destroying him. Some writers assigned moral virtue to these techniques. Thus Ferrero wrote that the eighteenth century was "one of those peaks of human evolution which man painfully attains . . . [only] to slide back once more." Although these observations are undoubtedly true, statistical studies such as Sorokin's indicate that the toll in life and resources, not taking into account the relative size of armies, was in fact no less than in the two previous centuries and was indeed greater than in the nineteenth century. There is an inner contradiction in Toynbee's view, for at one point he recognized the uninterrupted intensification of war beginning in the sixteenth century, but here he contradicted this general observation.[25] One nevertheless gains a profound insight into the period through his description of the nature of war in the eighteenth century. It is not difficult to recognize the meaning of certain lessons for the present.

War as the sport of kings, however, was destined to be changed by the French Revolution and the Industrial Revolution. Mirabeau, for example, spoke to the French National Assembly about representative governments' proclivities for war. His warnings,

24. Gibbon, The Decline and Fall of the Roman Empire, III, 529–610. Contemporary writers on international relations including Hans J. Morgenthau have discussed in detail war as the sport of kings.

25. Guglielmo Ferrero, Peace and War, trans. Bertha Pritchard (London, 1933), 54; Pitirim A. Sorokin, Social and Cultural Dynamics (4 vols.; New York, 1937), III, 346–47; Toynbee, A Study of History, V, 43.

fully realized in the twentieth century, were obscured in the general peacefulness of the nineteenth. Industrialism provided new and more terrible equipment for war; democracy put the "lethal 'drive' into War." But the humane spirit of the eighteenth century died hard, and even Napoleon felt obliged to justify as reprisal his internment of British nationals. An American study of war provides these somewhat conflicting views: "Of the later centuries, the nineteenth appears to have been, comparatively, very peaceful, especially in its last quarter. The burden of war that it imposed upon the population by the relative size of the army, as well as of the casualties, was comparatively very low, much lower than in the seventeenth and the eighteenth centuries, and rather similar to the burden of the sixteenth century."[26]

Is there any way of reconciling Sorokin's statement with Toynbee's careful observation? It appears that there is. In the latter's appraisal of the nineteenth century, he was talking principally about the beginning of certain profound underlying changes. Before hostilities broke out, leaders would have to rouse the hatred and moral fervor of a whole people. But effective employment of the balance of power in nineteenth-century Europe prevented excessive hostilities and checked these forces before they could be called into play. In our century, however, the problem which Toynbee anticipated has become critical.

War in the twentieth century has seen both quantitative and qualitative changes. According to Toynbee, after wars or sets of wars of ten to twenty years' duration, there were extended periods of relative peace.[27] From the Battle of Waterloo to the Battle of the Marne, the casualties in civil wars were heavier than in international wars. Only in this century have we seen, instead of long peaceful intervals, two world wars which had the most devastating consequences. In Toynbee's view, precedents could be found not in modern history but in the Punic Wars and the Peloponnesian War. He was to return to this comparison again and again.

Further, war in the twentieth century ignores traditional distinctions between civilians and combatants. Universal military conscription is the basis on which most armies are formed. For the first time in history, total destruction is a possibility. Toynbee concluded: "Evils which hitherto have been merely disgraceful and

26. Toynbee, *A Study of History*, IV, 143; Sorokin, *Social and Cultural Dynamics*, III, 347.
27. Toynbee, *The Prospects of Western Civilization*, 33.

grievous have now become intolerable and lethal."[28] Tragically, the transformation of war has taken place within a matter of decades, not centuries.

It is a sign of the many-sided character of Toynbee's *Study* that he dealt at length with military institutions and practices in the civilizations which were his subject. Even those who are critical of his system of history concede that he throws a strong illuminating light on the problem of war. Despite a preoccupation with showing that militarism is our gravest social ill, he treated war's laws and history with the detachment of a scientist in his laboratory. He was impressed by the plurality of forms and systems through which military forces have been organized for battle. An army is not only the military arm of a state; its nature and role in a society have far-reaching significance for the culture. An army in fact sometimes molds the ethos of a civilization even as it reflects the structure of society.

Two kinds of problems exemplify Toynbee's interest in the institutions of warfare. They concern the size and the composition of any military group. In the first place, an army may be small, select, and specialized, or it may be conscripted from the whole of the citizenry. As a nation expands, the need may increase for larger standing armies. In Rome, for example, a growing fraction of the peasant population was uprooted from the soil by perpetual calls to military service. As ever more distant campaigns were planned, the need for manpower increased. Conversely, the social pressures produced by restless elements, those not engaged in military pursuits, encouraged new ventures in conquest and imperialism as a safeguard against internal revolution. Assyrian civilization formed a standing army in a parallel attempt to deal through military organization with both external aggression and internal tensions.[29]

In contemporary history, the size of armies is a reasonable index of the magnitude and intensity of military engagements. Over four centuries, Toynbee examined a variety of examples of both total and limited armies. In the seventeenth and eighteenth centuries, small numbers of technically superior troops were employed. Until the introduction of the *levée en masse*, compulsory military service was used only in exceptional cases, such as in Prussia. After 1870, all Continental nations adopted conscription, although

28. Toynbee, *Civilization on Trial*, 25.
29. Toynbee, *A Study of History*, IV, 481–82.

the system at first was not strictly applied and enforced. Most European countries followed France in calling to duty less than one-fifth of their potential conscripts, and those who could afford it were permitted to contract out. Others were called up and remained in military service for seven years, and thus a semiprofessional force, which compared with the professional armies of earlier centuries, was created. In Prussia, however, exemptions were granted to artisans and the technicians who produced the machines of war.[30]

The qualitative dimension of armies as representative groups of individuals is also a study in contrasts. The men who serve may be lords or peasants, freemen or slaves, citizens or aliens. No one has discovered any constant principles which prove that one social group is universally more effective than another. In the last century B.C., one of the Parthian armies which checked the ambitions of Mark Antony was reportedly composed of fifty thousand effectives, of whom only four hundred were freemen. The Parthian army which earlier annihilated the Roman army under Crassus had ten thousand slaves in its ranks. On the other hand, Sparta and the Ottoman Empire required large standing reserves in manpower, and young men were trained from childhood for permanent military service. Such men had no other loyalty than that commitment. When exceptions were made within the Ottoman system and free Muslims were enlisted side by side with the alien slave population, it was not long before the system broke down. Pride of family, community, race, and religion made intolerable the strictures of the totalitarian system. In both the Ottoman and Spartan systems, however, there were unemployed troops. Indeed, in Sparta the problem became unmanageable; the Ottoman system required that every child trained as a soldier must also learn a trade. Of these two supremely powerful military systems which sought to come to terms with social problems, only the Ottoman resolved them in an effective way.[31]

If the forms of organization of armies are diverse, their techniques of fighting are also infinitely varied. The military strategies of successful states are, according to Toynbee, based on certain operative principles. One is what he called successful "adaptation." Many armies have been impaired by conservatism, a tendency peculiarly characteristic of military organizations. In some societies, the leaven has come from nonprofessional groups. Within limits,

30. Ibid., 151–52.
31. Toynbee, A Study of History, III, 59–60.

amateurs have been the "salt" of an effective army. They have also been the source of innovations, as in the American Civil War and more recently in guerrilla warfare.[32]

Another principle requires leaders to plan and act in accordance with their available sources of strength. It was the Greek military genius to sense its own limitations and create specialized troops within each of its divisions. The Roman army, whose members were competent in several military techniques but whose overall organization was homogeneous, illustrates the wise use of the forces available. From the Assyrian use of armed cavalrymen, or cataphracts, to the Russian use of numbers and terrain, planning based on available resources has been crucial for warfare.

A final principle is "innovation." The Assyrians, when challenged by nomads from the Steppes, combined their own heavily armed infantrymen with the nomads' tactic of archers on horseback. However, one challenge follows another, each calling for innovations in tactics or strategy. One mystery in the history of the art of warfare is how Assyria, after two centuries of "innovation" in techniques of warfare, should suddenly suffer a mortal defeat in the seventh century B.C. On the eve of its destruction, the Assyrian army was scientifically prepared for any task and was differentiated into specialized units: archers on horseback, armed archers on foot, infantrymen (hoplites) similarly armed but who carried spear and shield instead of bow and quiver, and partially armored skirmishers (peltasts). In addition a corps of engineers was available. Yet Assyria was destroyed by overextending its commitments and by internal dissension.

Tactics is the management of troops in combat, and strategy is their deployment up to that point. Toynbee identified certain landmarks in the history of tactics and strategy in the classical period of warfare. The Spartan phalanx, a key to victory in the Peloponnesian War (431–404 B.C.), was based on heavy infantry in close-order formation and relied upon shock techniques. But the Athenians, recovering from their defeat slightly more than three decades after the Peloponnesian War, employed swarms of light infantry and were successful against Sparta. Later the Thebans improved the phalanx by distributing its power in depth and introduced an element of surprise. They interchanged special units in battle: infantry with spears exchanged places with infantry with

32. On the principles of military strategy, see Toynbee, *A Study of History,* IV, 472–75.

swords, and from successive depths or levels, specially trained and armed fighters were called up as tactically required.[33]

A second landmark Toynbee noted was the Macedonian strategy, which revamped the Spartan phalanx, used Greek mercenaries, and emphasized a war of movement. The source of its success was the integration into one organic unit of heavy and light infantry, cavalry equipped for deep thrusts into the flanks of the enemy, and specialized troops who made possible defense in depth. But Macedon lost the initiative when heavy defense units were substituted for mobile forces and fighting was no longer against the enemy in open country but came to mean the destruction of villages and towns. This latter change was analogous to that which took place in the nineteenth and twentieth centuries.[34]

Macedon's innovation was succeeded by the military strategy of Rome, which at first employed the old-fashioned phalanx, though it was less mobile than the Macedonian. After the slaughter of Roman infantry by Hannibal's heavy cavalry at Cannae, a mobile Roman legion was created. The second great Roman innovation was the tactic employed in the First Punic War. The Romans invented, as Toynbee described it, "a gangway, slung from a mast and fitted with a grappling-iron, by means of which they literally came to grips with the Carthaginian warships. By this shockingly unprofessional innovation in technique they seized the tactical initiative, inhibited their astonished and indignant opponents from employing their traditional tactics of manoeuvring and ramming, and forcibly substituted the tactics of grappling and boarding, with decisive effects upon the fortunes of the war." The Roman legion carried the principle of a mobile phalanx one step further: men with javelins in the front ranks engaged the enemy initially and then were replaced by the reserve of heavy infantry with spears and swords. This change in principal weapons—from spears to javelins and swords is in a sense comparable to the replacing of the pike by musket and bayonet in the sixteenth and seventeenth centuries. Each legionary was versatile enough to serve as skirmisher or heavy armed infantryman, and the Roman army, hardened in civil and border wars, attained an efficiency which was not eclipsed until the invention of firearms. However, the Battle of Adrianople against heavy armed cavalrymen from the East was the challenge which Roman leaders had foreseen but for which they

33. *Ibid.*, 432–34.
34. *Ibid.*, 464–65.

were unprepared. Rome failed to "adapt" to this threat, and it was the undoing of the Roman army.[35]

These examples of techniques and strategy could be multiplied. Although Toynbee was primarily concerned with classical warfare, he did direct attention to modern examples as well. The culmination of historical warfare in all its demonic fury is surely World War II. What in the late 1930s was expected to be another brutal and costly war of attrition became one of total destruction. Even this form of warfare, however, was to be replaced by techniques and strategy so ruthless and terrible as to bring the art of war to its final, self-destructive climax. The principles of innovation and adaptation, which Toynbee used as pointers to explain the military supremacy of states in classical times, also have relevance in modern history. Thus the Germans were defeated in World War I because they used the strategy of 1870 against their opponent's strategy of trench warfare and economic blockade. The Maginot line, a strategy designed by the French for a war of attrition, failed to stop German tanks and airplanes. Art in warfare must be construed as the peculiar skill of discovering successful techniques and strategy but abandoning them when new military problems arise.

Historically there has been an inevitable decay in even the most effective mode of warfare which moves an army seemingly by an inner logic to its ultimate and fated destruction. Toynbee described this tendency as the "suicidal" character of militarism. The model example for him is that of Assyria in the seventh century B.C. The principal reason for its deterioration is that Assyria under Tiglath-pileser III (who ruled from 746 to 727 B.C.) pursued a foreign policy which brought Assyria into collision with Babylonia, Elam, and Egypt. When Assyria extended its empire up to the frontiers of Egypt, such action was bound to evoke substantial opposition. The bold occupation of the outpost of Philistia in 734 B.C., which first appeared as a master stroke in Assyrian strategy, led to the conflict between Sargon and the Egyptians in 720 B.C. and Assyria's spectacular conquest of Egypt itself. However, Assyria was unable to sustain the occupation, and after five Egyptian campaigns, the Assyrian garrison in Egypt was withdrawn. The concession came too late, for Assyria was repeatedly unable to prevent uprisings within that inflated sphere of influence.[36]

A second cause of military decay is the idolatry of present tac-

35. *Ibid.*, 439–40.
36. *Ibid.*, 475–78.

tics and techniques as such. Macedon was unable to cope with Rome after five generations of unchallenged military supremacy primarily because of the almost pathological exaggeration of the precise length of the *sarisa*, the weapon used in the Macedonian phalanx, and thus the need for light infantry and cavalry was ignored. Macedon provides an example also of the third cause of military failure, the uncertainty and unpredictability of warfare itself. The most efficient tactic may prove worthless in an engagement which was never anticipated and for which it is singularly ill-designed. Strategy and tactics have had consequences precisely the opposite of those intended, and when psychological factors come into play, this is especially the case. In contemporary warfare, stories and pictures of enemy atrocities have filled men's hearts with hatred and violence. In his Asiatic campaigns, Philip of Macedon sought to rouse his men for mortal combat by holding public burials within his encampment. They were designed to fortify morale but served rather to leave men terror-stricken at the thought of close combat with the Romans. With demoralized troops under his command, Philip called back the garrison from a strategic pass, thus leaving all of Macedon exposed to attack by Pleuratus and the Dardanian troops.[37]

Broader issues arise for Toynbee concerning the relationship between war and society. Some historians seek an absolute distinction between war and politics—the two are considered qualitatively different in every respect. Others conceive of war as public policy pursued through other means. Spengler held to this view: "Politics is only a temporary substitute for war that uses more intellectual weapons. . . . The technics of government, war and diplomacy have all this same root and have in all ages a profound inward relationship with each other." Toynbee's view must be placed somewhere between these extremes. His interest in war throughout history reflects his belief that war forms an integral part in the life of a society. Moreover, as civilization's "deadly disease," war has profound effects upon the economy. In history one discovers a correlation between war and the distribution of wealth: "One of the commonest social effects of War upon the internal economy of a belligerent country is to produce a maldistribution of wealth or to aggravate a maldistribution that already exists. Classic examples are the effect of the Hannibalic War and its aftermath upon the

37. Toynbee, *A Study of History*, II, 163.

agrarian economy of Roman Italy, and the effect of the life-and-death struggle with the Danes upon the agrarian economy of the English Kingdom of Wessex. The corresponding effect of war in an industrial society is exemplified in the social consequences of the General War of 1914–18."[38]

Broader still is the connection between war and religion for students of war. Contemporary history has been characterized in two of its three major periods by the union of war and religion. The era of the Wars of Religion began with the breakup in the sixteenth century of the unity of Western Christendom and extended from the Reformation to the Treaty of Westphalia (1648), which terminated the Thirty Years' War. In England it lasted until the Restoration in 1660. The second period, sometimes called the age of the Wars of Nationality, had its origin in the successful attempt of the bourgeoisie to identify with the state and in the universal appeal of doctrines of popular government to extend the French Revolution throughout the world. This appeal was marked by the fervor embodied in the conviction that "the Revolution is a universal religion which it is France's mission to impose upon humanity."[39] In the present day, world communism and universal democracy are also examples of political religions. The interval between these two periods, roughly the last half of the seventeenth and most of the eighteenth century, is the one time during which the close tie between war and religion was temporarily severed. It corresponds to the "Age of Enlightenment," or the period of "Toleration."

During this era, we have one of the few examples of war being conducted as a kind of private game. The stakes, which were well defined in advance, were a piece of territory, an inheritance, or succession to a throne. Further, the players and the publicists agreed that the ideas of right and justice should never be mixed with strategies of war. When men's actions are inflamed with such passions, they can and do go on fighting until they are exhausted. Ferrero explained the attitudes of eighteenth-century participants in this way: "One must go to war admitting that the cause of one's adversary is as just as one's own; one must take care to do nothing, even for the sake of victory, that may exasperate him, or close his mind to the voice of reason or his heart to the desire for peace; one must abstain from treacherous and cruel acts, for there is nothing

---

38. Spengler, *Man and Technics*, 67; Toynbee, *A Study of History*, IV, 396.
39. Toynbee, *A Study of History*, IV, 142–43; Albert Sorel, *L'Europe et la ré-volution française* (8 vols.; Paris, 1889), II, 109.

that rouses an adversary to greater fury."[40] War was not a religious crusade but a "temperate and undecisive" contest.

But this respite soon passed, and the union between religion and war was reaffirmed. The Wars of Nationality were fought with a ferocity which is characteristic alone of fratricidal conflicts. Armies lived off the country, and the duration of each war increased progressively. In the Wars of Religion, the formula *cujus regio ejus religio* ("the religion of the ruler is the religion of the people") brought a short-lived truce in 1555. This principle was based upon a precept laid down at the Diet of Speier (1526), which stated that a prince should so conduct himself that he could be accountable to God and the emperor. The play of political and military forces upon religious competition intensified these struggles, as was the case in Germany, France, England, and the Low Countries. Quincy Wright has observed that these wars "were ostensibly fought for religion." The examples of such conflicts included the French Huguenot wars (1562–1598), the Dutch Wars of Independence (1568–1648), the Thirty Years' War (1618–1648), Elizabeth's wars against Ireland, Scotland, and Spain, and Charles V's wars in Mexico, Turkey, Peru, and France. Probably the clearest statement concerning the character of this kind of wafare is Burckhardt's:

> Of all struggles, the most appalling are the "wars of religions," more especially those between religions in which the thought of a future life predominates, or in which morality is in other ways completely bound up with the existing form of religion, or in which a religion has taken on a strong national coloring and a people is defending itself in its religion. Among civilized peoples they are most terrible of all. The means of offence and defence are unlimited, ordinary morality is suspended in the name of the "higher purpose," negotiation and mediation are abhorrent—people want all or nothing.[41]

In the sixteenth and seventeenth centuries, the use of gunpowder and increased material resources, when combined with the force of religious fanaticism, meant wars which "came very near to wrecking our Western Civilization." In the latter part of the seventeenth century, fortunately, the devil of "sectarian Religious Fanaticism was successfully cast out; and . . . the immediate effect

40. Ferrero, *Peace and War*, 8.
41. Toynbee, *A Study of History*, IV, 143–46, 221; Quincy Wright, *A Study of War* (2 vols.; Chicago, 1942), I, 198; Jacob Burckhardt, *Force and Freedom* (New York, 1943), 134–35.

was to reduce the evil of War in the eighteenth century to a minimum which has never been approached in any other chapter of our Western history, either before or after, up to date."[42]

The century which followed was marked not by deeper and more humane religious insights but rather by a negative cynicism, for fanaticism was weakened at the cost of extinguishing religious faith. The principle of toleration gave Western society a breathing spell after its "Time of Troubles." This era, however, which was in a sense a spiritual vacuum, led inevitably to the Wars of Nationality. Logically, this was so because man can never be restrained from choosing faith over cynicism; historically, because any civilization in its "Time of Troubles" moves from "rout to rally to rout."

The period of moderate warfare in the eighteenth century has not disappeared without leaving behind traces of its influence. As late as 1904, Napoleon's having imprisoned British citizens in 1803, which he called a reprisal for the seizure of two French merchantmen before war had begun, was condemned for an "unheard-of-action," one of which public opinion could hardly be expected to approve. Only ten years later, enemy aliens were interned as a matter of course by all belligerents.[43]

The transformation of war in the nineteenth and twentieth centuries thus had two aspects. In relations with other nations, the nation-state assumed a new posture. The popular will replaced the will of aristocratic elites. Princes and aristocratic governments may fight one another without excessive animosity; nations under arms must hate each other with a consuming passion, must know that their cause is righteous and that the threat they face is the most infamous and unparalleled aggression. The new weapons of propaganda become as essential as guns and bayonets. Strife must be rationalized in terms of ideologies rather than territorial ambitions.

The second aspect of the change in warfare is the transformation and transglorification of the state itself. For Augustine, the state was a necessary evil; for liberalism, it is a "Night-Watchman." In the twentieth century, the state has become the embodiment of the nation and the instrumentality through which political religion is mediated. This change has been more far-reaching than the profound differences brought about by industry and tech-

42. Toynbee, *A Study of History*, IV, 143.
43. Toynbee, *A Study of History*, V, 161–62.

nology: "Our modern Western nationalism has an ecclesiastical tinge; for, while in one aspect it is a reversion to the idolatrous self-worship of the tribe which was the only religion known to Man before the first of the 'higher religions' was discovered by an oppressed internal proletariat . . . [it] is a tribalism with a difference. The primitive religion has been deformed into an enormity through being power-driven with a misapplied Christian driving-force." So the second bout of religious wars is more dangerous than the first since religion and state form an identity. Fascist Italy, Nazi Germany, and Communist Russia were merely exaggerations "of something that constitutes three-quarters of the religion of the Western world today."[44]

A critic of Toynbee's theory of Wars of Nationality finds it difficult not to say that other explanations can be offered for the fanatical character of modern political religions. Toynbee's is exclusively a "spiritualist" interpretation. But one can also speak in "materialist" or psychological terms: frustrated individuals in modern society, having failed in the realization of their personal aspirations, transfer their aims to the nation and find rewards in its attainments. Toynbee significantly failed to mention the material sources of political religions.

The origin of the crisis in warfare is the result of a second underlying characteristic of international society. One of the few sources of common ground between students of world politics and crusaders for world government is agreement that collective security is infinitely more difficult in the absence of any supranational organization with effective powers of government. Thus it is not surprising that Toynbee settled on these same peculiar anarchic conditions of international politics as a fundamental cause of the intensification of modern warfare. Indeed, in his theory of history, the absence of government in the relations among sovereign political units is one of the unmistakable signs that civilization has entered its "Time of Troubles." In the mid-twentieth century, moreover, the object lesson from past civilizations that the absence of political unity is a portent of decay has been reinforced by the immediate peril of atomic destruction.

The parallel which Toynbee found most illuminating was the position of the Greek city-states. These political units were the

44. *Ibid.*, 160–61; Toynbee, *The Prospects of Western Civilization*, 89.

most spectacular innovations of their time. But with the emergence of new powers on the fringe of Greek civilization, they became inadequate to provide for the defense of their own people. They also failed to match the extent of unity achieved in the economic realm with some degree of political unity. When the separate states were unwilling or unable to unite successfully, the impending unification was accomplished through a "knock-out blow" by Alexander the Great.[45]

As Greece failed to mitigate the anarchic character of relations between city-states, so, Toynbee feared, we in Western civilization may flounder and fail. But particularly after World War II, he believed that we must change that condition of our international relations. One of his statements foreshadowed the conclusion reached in the final volumes of *A Study of History*:

> I believe that with such weapons as we have now let loose in the world the world cannot go on very long in the condition in which politics have been in the West since the fall of the Roman Empire, a condition in which a great many local sovereign states are each going their own way and occasionally colliding with each other and fighting each other. It seems to me most unlikely that that condition of things, which we have come to take for granted, as if it were in the order of nature, can go on. There have been times in the history of other civilizations when the old local sovereign states have been swept away by the establishment of a universal peace over the whole area of whatever the civilization might be, and it seems to me that we are on the eve of that political revolution in our world today.[46]

We shall discuss in another connection Toynbee's attitude toward a world state. Here we have seen his conception of the problems which arise under conditions of international anarchy. War becomes an effective instrument of national policy, a situation which could be viewed without despair, until the explosion of the atomic bomb. Now the question takes on tragic dimensions. War has become a problem calling for a solution one way or the other. As a historian, Toynbee recognized three solutions: the sudden achievement of cooperative world government by general consent; the gradual progress toward this goal through political means;

45. Toynbee, *Civilization on Trial*, 134.
46. Toynbee, *The Prospects of Western Civilization*, 29.

or world conquest. Later we shall see which of these he considered to be real possibilities and which he considered merely theoretical prospects.

Another dimension which Toynbee discussed was war's relation with industrialism. Changes in warfare resulted, as we have seen, from bitter competition between contending religious groups for political recognition and from the continued fragmentation of an already enfeebled political unity and the disappearance of older forms of control upon these new sovereign states and principalities. More profound, however, were the technological and political revolutions which took place in the nineteenth and twentieth centuries. The first of these, the Industrial Revolution, transformed social and political life and economic activities. It has permitted the unification of large groups of hitherto independent people and territories, as in Germany and Italy. In the beginning it seemed that the new economic forces might accommodate themselves to states the size of Great Britain and France, but that standard has been revised upward—to the United States and the Soviet Union. Anything smaller may not be practical in terms of the scale of warfare or the scope of domestic economic activity. Whether the standard is that of the nineteenth or the twentieth century, the fact remains that war potential is commonly measured in terms of ships and trains, submarines, tanks, and bombers, and rifles and other weapons. They are the products of industrial activity, and thus it becomes plain that a revolution in technology has promoted a parallel revolution in warfare.

The first clear evidence that so fundamental a change had occurred came during the American Civil War, when Generals Grant and Sherman implemented their strategy by the use of railways. With the German campaign in Denmark, France, and Austria, General von Moltke introduced the same strategy on the Continent. For the first time it became possible to convert the entire material wealth of a country into war matériel and to mobilize men and machines to achieve this purpose. If there was a will to use them, resources were now available for warfare infinitely more destructive than was any past struggle. Yet industrialism in itself was passive—indeed ecumenical. If it had moved forward under its own inner logic, industrialism would have embraced the world. The ultimate minimum effective unit for the industrial system is nothing less than the globe. Instead it has been restricted to the dimensions of the nation-state, and an 1870 model at that. Industrialism has supplied the explosive material of modern "total" warfare but a second new force has been needed to touch off the fuse: "In our own modern case . . . where the material force of Industrialism and the spiritual force of Democracy have both been engaged . . . Democracy has been the dominant factor."[47]

If industrialism provided the material resources for modern war, democracy fueled its dynamism. In his later writings, Toynbee repeated the same anxious proposition he set forth in 1939: "In A.D. 1790 the French National Assembly was warned by the prophetic voice of Mirabeau that a representative parliamentary body was likely to prove more bellicose than a monarch. In A.D. 1792, less than ten years after the statesmanlike peace settlement of 1783, the menacing accents of a Democracy conscripted for War were heard by Goethe's sensitive ears in the cannonade at Valmy; and the *levée en masse* of a Revolutionary France swept away the eighteenth century regime in Germany." Toynbee's anxiety presents an interesting contrast to the optimism of statesmen such as Woodrow Wilson and the dominant view in Western society following World War I. It was widely believed that if democratic governments could be set up throughout the world, international peace and order would take care of themselves. Yet republics such as Venice, Rome, and Athens and parliamentary states such as England have indeed from time to time been no less bellicose than were autocratic governments. Any careful student of history knows that certain problems of diplomacy are more acute in democratic foreign policy. One of these is surely the problem of war. Toynbee seems inclined to follow Mirabeau, who stated: "Voyez les peuples libres; c'est par des guerres plus ambitieuses, plus barbares qu'ils se sont toujours distingués. Voyez les assemblées politiques; c'est toujours sous le charme de la passion qu'elles ont décrété la guerre."[48]

One vexing question which Toynbee considered at length is why the spirit of democracy has worked to mitigate the institution of slavery and merely aggravated the institution of war. He was convinced that the inner nature of democracy is "love" and "brotherhood." Therefore the strong moral revulsion against slavery in the United States can readily be accounted for. One reason for the absence of an effective drive against war might be the American

---

47. Toynbee, *A Study of History*, IV, 143; Toynbee, *Civilization on Trial*, 114–15.

48. Toynbee, *A Study of History*, IV, 143, 150–51, 150n4, 156–58.

tendency to compartmentalize action and thinking. For example, Virginia slave-owners were moved in all good faith to oppose George III while condoning their own social practices. Athenians united against the tyranny of the Persians but felt no motivation to alter the system of slavery in Athens. But a better reason for the democratic impact on war is its relation with the nation-state:

> Before colliding with the institution of War, our modern Western Democracy has collided with the institution of Parochial Sovereignty in a society that has been broken up politically into a plurality of parochial states; and the importation of the new driving-forces of Democracy and Industrialism into the old machine of the Parochial State has generated the twin enormities of Political and Economic Nationalism. It is in this gross derivative form, in which the ethereal spirit of Democracy has emerged from its passage through an alien medium, that Democracy has put its "drive" into War instead of working against it.[49]

The two fundamental changes in war for which democracy is responsible are the transformation of the political decision-making process upon which war is based and the intensification of the nature of war itself. An eighteenth-century despot would have been more likely to risk war in 1936–1937, when Hitler might have been contained, than were the democratic governments of France and England. Carefully calculated policies based on sound political principles are more difficult to expound and execute in a democracy. Even when they evolve through established political processes, the problem of public acceptance remains. Second, having to maintain public support for military strategy puts an end to tactics designed to avoid costly struggles. Now the emphasis is upon total engagement and decisive results.[50] As Vietnam made clear, sustaining a limited war is difficult if not impossible in a democracy.

The transformations in modern warfare have presented mankind with a problem of unparalleled urgency. As early as 1931, Toynbee expressed his profound concern that "even if Western Society were so fortunate as to survive this war, it could hardly look forward to surviving another war under the new conditions." He noted with sympathy an earlier statement by Stanley Baldwin to

49. *Ibid.*, 158.
50. *Survey of International Affairs*, 1937, II, 137–38.

the effect that "one more war in the West and the civilization of the ages will fall with as great a shock as that of Rome."[51] If a nation were so fortunate as to avert political destruction in World War II, it could hardly avoid the subsequent crumbling of the delicate and complicated fabric of its economy. Indeed, Britain's decline as a world economic power supported Toynbee's prophecy.

The crisis in war which has deepened over four centuries takes on the character of an epic tragedy following World War II. In *A Study of History*, Toynbee cited some twenty-odd civilizations in which war dealt each society its deathblow. Yet each passing civilization was succeeded by a new one. In 1947, for the first time Toynbee expressed doubt that this process of historical recurrence could be depended upon to continue: "The failure to solve the problem of war has been the death of most civilizations that have died since civilizations first came into existence, but hitherto mankind has always survived to make new civilizations out of the ruins. We are now faced with a situation in which the whole enterprise of civilization may come to a stop if we cannot solve the problem of war; and that degree of urgency . . . is, I think, something new."[52]

This passage accurately reflects Toynbee's deepening conviction that something must be done about war. His theory of history and his morphology of societies were not primarily responsible for his apprehension. Although war has been the scourge of society, there has been one saving feature: civilization has shambled along from the destruction of one of its specimens to the birth of another, but it has not destroyed itself. Now the prospect of general destruction calls for a new state of mind on the part of any scholar who loves humanity. It is most illuminating to compare Toynbee's outlook in the 1930s with statements made in the late 1940s. Shortly after the ratification of the Pact of Paris and following some of the early efforts at collective security by the League of Nations, he observed: "At this stage we can only be sure that in our Western World, war will now be abolished sooner or later by one means or another. If it is not abolished in the near future by the method of pacific adjustment, then it is certain to be abolished—and this in a future which may not be much more remote—by the alternative method of 'the knock-out blow,' in which a war—or a series of wars—of attrition will end in the decisive and definitive victory of

51. Quoted in *Survey of International Affairs*, 1931, p. 10.
52. Toynbee, *The Prospects of Western Civilization*, 19.

one single Power through the annihilation of all the rest." Toynbee then observed through World War II the astounding advances in weapons of destruction. That specter has haunted other observers and appears to have motivated Toynbee's statement in 1948: "We are thus confronted with a challenge that our predecessors never had to face: We have to abolish war . . . and abolish . . . [it] now under pain, if we flinch or fail, of seeing . . . a victory over man which, this time, would be conclusive and definitive."[53]

Toynbee's statement of the nature of the problem, therefore, does not differ from that of countless men of letters and philosophers who have sought to awaken mankind to its peril. Describing the problem, however, is one thing; it is quite another to comprehend its true nature so profoundly that one is able to proffer wise counsel. Most writers have assumed that the task was merely to banish war, perhaps by legal fiat. A less widely held view has been that peace, if one found it, would be not the absence of conflict but the ability to contain it. These views derive from two theories of war that merit examination.

War in our times takes on the nature of civil strife, is fired by religious motives, and is all-embracing. The first two characteristics are fuel for conflagrations without precedent in history; the third constitutes a demonic strategy which entangles everyone in the conflict. The fact that civil and religious wars are more ruthless than any other conflict serves to aggravate an already precarious problem. Since the Spanish civil war no national war has been a local war, for the fundamental conflicts within Western society have been involved. This is a most serious issue because "civil wars are waged with more bitterness and ferocity than any others."[54] In Toynbee's pattern of history, when groups external to a society have fought with the ruling factions, the conflict has been the most violent of all. This trait has been aggravated because materialistic aims have led to religious methods and forms in war. And finally, as we have seen, the most striking physical fact has been the absolute nature of wars in which all men and equipment are mobilized. These sobering aspects make the problem of war's abolition, for Toynbee, a challenge requiring greater efforts.

53. Toynbee, *A Study of History*, IV, 153–54. This is evidently the type of statement from which some of Toynbee's American followers such as William H. McNeil derive their views that Western civilization can confidently face World War III, from which the United States will probably emerge as the universal state. It is a mistake to equate Toynbee's thinking with this view, as the *Times* (London) did in a review of McNeil's writings. Toynbee, *Civilization on Trial*, 25.

54. Toynbee, *A Study of History*, IV, 487.

Certain lessons can be gleaned from the record of past attempts to achieve the goal toward which Toynbee reached. First, attempts at outlawing war have been moderately successful over wide territories and sometimes for long periods of time. According to Toynbee, for nearly two centuries after the closing of the Temple of Janus in 29 B.C., the successors of Augustus were successful in banishing war from the "heartland" of the Roman Empire. During this period, there were not more than about six years of internal strife. War was pushed to the fringe of the empire and even there, it was greatly reduced: at the boundary with the territory east of the Euphrates, there were only fifteen years of war. From the disorder which prevailed after the death of Commodus in 192 B.C. to the close of the civil war between Antony and Augustus in 30 B.C., there was a period in which a universal state had remarkable success and seemingly managed to eliminate war. A parallel development took place in China during the Han dynasty. Also, in the Indic universal state under Asoka, war seemed to have been successfully outlawed. But just as the successors of Asoka were unable to deny themselves the use of war as an instrument of policy, the Romans and the Chinese turned out to have established no more than extended armistices. Toynbee observed that universal states offer a peace which disguises, for a time, the inherent violence: "Under its serene mask of effortless supremacy the Oecumenical Peace of a universal state is fighting, all the time, a desperate losing battle against an unexorcised demon of Violence in its own bosom; and we can see this moral struggle being waged in the guise of a conflict of policies."[55]

Toynbee viewed the eighteenth century as one of the inspiring peaks in mankind's progress. What impressed him was the strategy of avoiding total engagements, despite the fact that these actions were based on cynical motives. It may be appropriate to note, however, that some scholars would take exception with his emphasis upon the eighteenth rather than the nineteenth century. In the latter period, Britain's economic role and the European balance of power were responsible for the peace that prevailed in the years from 1815 to 1914.

The third effort to do away with war which preoccupied Toynbee was the Pact of Paris. At the time, he was naïvely optimistic about it: "This enterprise was more difficult and also more hope-

55. *Survey of International Affairs*, 1928, p. 4; Toynbee, *A Study of History*, VI, 197.

ful." His confidence derived from the fact that Western civilization was still in its prime, but the Roman and the Chinese experiments at outlawing war had been made only at the eleventh hour. As crisis widened into catastrophe and general war, he grew less and less sanguine. By the 1940s, he expressed a conviction that charters and resolutions can go no further than the political forces which they reflect.[56]

As a historian, Toynbee was of course greatly interested in every past attempt to rid the world of war. As a philosopher and political scientist, he found no less absorbing the various suggestions and policies for meeting the challenge of worldwide destruction: universal democracy or world communism; domination or empire; the fear of an absolute weapon; and moral disarmament. It is possible here to indicate only a few of Toynbee's conclusions.

History does not support the assertion that democracies have consistently been more successful in avoiding war than were other forms of government. Especially in his later writings, Toynbee appeared to be more in agreement with Alexander Hamilton than with Woodrow Wilson. In 1936–1937, he was critical of the foreign policies of Great Britain and France which were based on political errors that eighteenth-century leaders would probably have avoided. Nor did he suffer from any illusions concerning the inherently peaceful nature of world communism: "One of the capital points on which the Communists differed from the Socialists was that the Communists were not pacifists." Here, he was referring to the Spanish policies of the French Socialist and Communist parties, but on other occasions his outlook was more general. So his conclusions about universal democracy or world communism bringing an end to war were decidedly on the pessimistic side.[57]

Many have suggested that war can be eliminated only through American or Soviet domination of the world. This is surely a possibility with which any contemporary historian must deal. The problem is, however, the historical fact that domination has never lasted. As early as 1915, Toynbee wrote prophetically: "If we beat Germany and then humiliate her, she will never rest till she has 'redeemed her honour,' by humiliating us more cruelly in turn. . . . Two great nations will sit idle, weapon in hand, like two Afghans

56. *Survey of International Affairs*, 1928, p. 6; Toynbee, *The Prospects of Western Civilization*, 25ff.
57. *Survey of International Affairs*, 1937, II, 137–38, 142n1.

in their loopholed towers when the blood fued is between them."[58] When he considered the history of universal states, he merely applied this principle on a larger scale.

Fear of an absolute weapon is a possible force for eliminating war. In 1932, Toynbee thought the "new terror of aerial warfare" might shock people into some kind of constructive action. In the present crisis, there may be some chance of a political settlement because both "America and Russia have a common enemy . . . and that is atomic energy." He found this third suggestion somewhat persuasive.[59]

The notion of moral disarmament is implicit in Toynbee's approval of the practices of the eighteenth century. At least in the short run, the consideration of political questions on their merits is essential. Religion and morality should not supersede politics but provide a substratum. When religions become commingled or equated with politics, great harm results. Certainly in the realist phase of his thinking, one finds little evidence of a crusading outlook.[60] As tentative solutions of the problem of war, the last two approaches are more hopeful; the ultimate solutions toward which these may carry mankind are world government, which must come in one way or another, and universal but not nationalistic religion.

58. Toynbee, *Nationality and the War*, 4.
59. *Survey of International Affairs*, 1932, p. 189; Toynbee, *The Prospects of Western Civilization*, 45.
60. *Survey of International Affairs*, 1933, p. 165; Toynbee, *Civilization on Trial*, 148.

CHAPTER III

The Forces in International Politics

T HE NEW discipline of international politics has as a primary focus the study and analysis of political forces which determine relations among sovereign nations. For many students, the most elemental of these forces and the systematic principle around which the discipline is integrated is the concept of international politics as a struggle for power. Although he dealt with this principle, Toynbee placed nationalism rather than power atop his hierarchy of forces in international politics. Nationalism as the ultimate repository of man's political and moral loyalties, as the major obstacle to world unity, and as the driving force among causes of war is at the core of international politics.

Toynbee acknowledged that nationalism is a man-made phenomenon, which in at least one respect is not new. In primitive communities the universal historian found instances of "the pagan worship of a parochial community." In Hellenic history this "paganism" was a warning sign of society's breakdown. However, the elements which made up primitive tribalism are but one side of modern nationalism. With the transition from medieval to modern Western civilization, loyalty to an ecumenical church passed to the parochial state. At the time of transition four or five centuries ago, much could be said to justify this change. By then, the old universalism was merely the ghost of a cherished legacy. In contrast, the new parochialism fostered few pretensions regarding its true nature. It symbolized the passing of Hellenic political unity. The effects upon Western civilization were felt in both the political and the religious spheres: "In politics it displayed itself in the form of a plurality of new vernacular literatures, and in the field of religion it collided violently with the medieval Western Church."[1]

Nationalism was scarcely visible in Europe during the Middle Ages. The quickening of national consciousness inspired by the Crusades prepared the way for it. Frenchmen, Castilians, Portuguese, and Catalans came into contact with one another—peoples who spoke the same language or dialect. The Crusades fostered pride in a common nationality, stirring a sense of difference from and rivalry with others. This is what present-day observers call a we-they attitude. Attachment to a locality, which as patriotism had been present for a long time, and nationality based on the spoken language were seeds from which modern nationalism grew. A psychology of nationalism also stemmed from demands by ethnic groups for a state or an independent political organization within which they could govern themselves. However, this stage in the evolution of nationalism was to await popular revolutions in the late eighteenth and nineteenth centuries.

As early as the fifteenth and sixteenth centuries, the development of nationalism was foreshadowed by the emergence of the North Italian city-states, which coincided with the breakdown of the unity of Christendom. In Florence, Milan, and Venice, "the pagan religion of Tribalism [was] evoked on Italian soil, in the later Middle Ages, in a new crop of Central and North Italian city-states." They were forerunners in microcosm of the modern nation-state, separated only by a distance as far as that which set apart the Italian city-state and the contemporary kingdom-state. The rules for politics which Machiavelli conceived for the one became accepted principles for the practice, if not everywhere the theory, of the other. These miniature city-states were laboratories for the testing of the techniques of diplomacy and power politics. Some of their leaders and publicists displayed loyalty to nationalism itself. Machiavelli himself "as the last chapter of *The Prince* reveals . . . was at heart a devotee of Italian nationalism and a would-be forerunner not so much of Metternich as of Mazzini." Some students of political theory would take exception to Toynbee's linking the Italian city-states and nationalism, but that was his early appraisal of the embryonic nationalism he found as he studied the fifteenth and sixteenth centuries.[2]

1. *Survey of International Affairs*, 1933, p. 115; Arnold J. Toynbee, *A Study of History* (12 vols.; London, 1934–61), IV, 215.
2. *Survey of International Affairs*, 1933, pp. 116, 117.

The seventeenth and eighteenth centuries were marked by a shift to a halfhearted form of dynastic nationalism, in which followers were starved of any plausible object of worship: "It is much more difficult to idolize a state that is the vested interest of a dynasty than a state that is the incarnation of a tribe; and therefore, so long as the dynastic state remained the standard type of parochial community . . . it was difficult to carry the new community-worship to extreme lengths." It seems strange that Toynbee should mention only one characteristic of dynastic nationalism. In addition to furnishing imperfect objects for worship, the rulers of these regimes had common membership in an "aristocratic international" with supranational interests. Often princes or rulers felt more sense of community than existed between a prince and his own subjects. Frederick the Great, who preferred French, spoke German like a coachman. It should surprise no one that a political system whose rulers were essentially indifferent to nationalism produced no strong nationalist sentiments.[3]

The late eighteenth and nineteenth centuries ushered in a new epoch, marked, in Toynbee's phrase, by "a revolutionary substitution of national states for dynastic states in a series of convulsions which racked the Western World from A.D. 1775 to A.D. 1918." The uninspiring figures of monarchs, such as George III or Louis XV, were replaced by the absorbing images of America, France, Germany, England, and Italy. Toynbee wrote: "These direct incarnations of national communities were idols of the same splendour as an Athena Polyuchus, or a Dea Roma; and their erection immediately inflamed the neo-pagan community-worship which neither was, nor could be, evoked so long as 'the Prince' was the official object of the cult."[4]

A national consciousness which was to become fanatical and ruthless flared up first in the harsh treatment of the Loyalists by the Americans following their victory in 1783 and then in "the French Revolutionary *levée en masse*; in the Spanish guerrilla war; in the burning of Moscow; in the German *Befreiungskrieg*, in the Belgian Revolution of 1830; in the Italian *Risorgimento*." International politics became infected with the virus of unqualified national loyalty and mutual hostility until the old forms of moderation and accommodation had disappeared. A signpost of this development is the contrast between the last moderate treaty of

3. *Ibid.*, 117–18.
4. *Ibid.*, 118, 118–19.

1866 between Austria and Prussia and the peace of 1871 between France and Germany: "In 1871, when he had to make peace with a defeated France, Bismarck was confronted with a German Nationalism that had gained such strength under his fostering hand that it had become his master instead of his servant; and, against his better judgement, he was compelled by this masterfully recalcitrant anti-social force to inflict a rankling wound on the French national consciousness by tearing away Alsace-Lorraine from the French body politic."[5]

This ferment of nationalism clearly was not confined to the West. In Southeast Europe it presented the Hapsburgs with a major problem they proved unable to solve. Spreading for almost a century through Central Europe, Hungary, and the Balkans, the movement was climaxed by sweeping reforms in Turkey, where nationalism had been kept alive after 1909 by a handful of enthusiasts in Salonika. But even in Orthodox Christian civilization, to use Toynbee's terms, nationalism made its appearance in the early nineteenth century. What were the factors which facilitated its growth in both East and West at this time?

It may be helpful in addressing this question to begin by proposing a conceptual framework comprising three categories under which the elements of nationalism can be examined: the political or territorial, the objective, and the subjective concepts of nationalism. The first assumes that a nation is a group of people living under a common system of governance and subject to the same law. The second holds that even if government is lacking, a nation can exist if a people are bound together by language, custom, tradition, and territory. If a group has an objective community of interests, this is the only prerequisite for becoming a nation. The third concept, in contrast, is based upon the sense of belonging or consciousness of being a nation over and above the existence of government or common traditions and interests. This new pattern came into being with the French Revolution and transformed the character of modern nationalism. One hesitates to place Toynbee's outlook wholly in one of these general classifications. It is fair to say, however, that he emphasized primarily the second and third. In essence, nationalism is national consciousness: "Like all great forces in human life, it is nothing mechanical, but a subjective psychological feeling in living people." But the material forces which this dynamic feeling uses are "a common country, espe-

5. Toynbee, *A Study of History*, IV, 165–66.

cially if it is a well-defined physical region, like an island, a river basin, or a mountain mass; a common language, especially if it has given birth to a literature; a common religion; and that much more impalpable force, a common tradition or sense of memories shared from the past." Such factors, however, may be present in groups which can hardly be called nations and may sometimes be absent among peoples who consider that they constitute a nation. Germany is a state but it lacks a common religion and tradition and for much of its history has had uncertain boundaries. If the test is geography and tradition, Wales and the Highlands share British nationality, but not if the test is language. The Armenian nationality has its own language and religion but no common territory. Nationalism is more than the sum of its elements, yet they are central to any evaluation of it.[6]

Language has always been considered one of the primary cultural elements of nationalism, and most modern nationalities have been so founded. An English nationality appeared almost simultaneously with the language, which grew out of a fusion of Anglo-Saxon and Norman French. Similarly, when the Franks and Gauls had drawn from the Latin a new and common language, French, that nationality was born. Language is important because of the habits and attitudes it encourages. A noted historian and scholar of nationalism has written: "Uniformity of language tends to promote like-mindedness, to provide an inclusive set of ideas as well as of words, and like-minded persons tend to develop group-consciousness, to experience a sense of common interest, to constitute a tribe or nationality." Individuals who speak the same language think of themselves over time as a group separate from those with an alien language. Moreover, language provides the medium through which past achievements and trials and tribulations are stamped indelibly upon each generation's consciousness.[7]

There is one negative feature, however, in the influence of language upon nationalism. Following the breakdown of any civilization, one of the forces of archaism which reunites and reidentifies the present with the past stems from the classical forms of a language which revive, or attempt to revive, ancient literature. The great works in Greek literature, produced in the period from 480 to 320 B.C., were written by Athenians in the same dialect used in their daily life. A second body of literature, which dates from the

6. Arnold J. Toynbee, *Nationality and the War* (London, 1915), 13, 14.
7. Carlton J. H. Hayes, *Essays on Nationalism* (New York, 1926), 16.

last century B.C. to the sixth century A.D., was written in the same vernacular but was little more than a shameless and servile imitation. Contemporary and modern forms were ignored, and the writing and thinking of the group from the intervening "Hellenistic age" was passed over or destroyed. Thus the period from 320 B.C. to the last century B.C. was dominated by the curious blending of Hellenistic patriotism with the language of an earlier people. Men of letters became "indifferent to the preservation of Greek books which were not either the Attic originals themselves or else ultra-modern neo-Attic imitations of them."[8]

A second element of nationalism is history and tradition. Men have a sense of time and a capacity to remember, both of which nationalism uses to strengthen itself, especially in times of crisis. In primitive groups, a well-recognized body of officials and elders serve as custodians of the legends and epics of the past. Youths become full members of society only when such mysteries are disclosed to them. Nationalism thus becomes a personal and dynamic force having a life and spirit uniquely its own: "History provides a body of ideas which serves to unify the attitudes of the individuals of a nation toward their common country. . . . In every land . . . the historian has been the hearth at which the soul of the country has been kept alive. . . . Not only has history writing awakened peoples to a consciousness or nationality; it has prompted them to action by inciting hopes for the future."[9]

History is in one sense not so much a cause of nationalism as a means of preserving and sustaining it. This is the function of those Toynbee names "the historical pastors and masters" of any generation. By eagerly promoting the study of national history, a community seeks to assure itself of the absolute loyalty of its members. The struggle for power and independence by Greek nationalists in Cyprus, for example, crystalized in demands that local education systems be open for the dissemination of Greek history and, some said, Greek propaganda. Schoolteachers and historians serve as missionaries in promoting a national cause. Paradoxical as it may seem, an enthusiasm for the past often provides the basis for an increased interest in the immediate present. Even in cases such as the emergence of Turkish nationalism from the ashes of the Ottoman Empire, this fundamental principle comes to light: "An archaistic or 'romantic' nationalism was one of the

8. Arnold J. Toynbee, *Civilization on Trial* (New York, 1948), 45.
9. Frederick J. Teggart, *Theory and Processes of History* (Berkeley, 1941), 28–29.

characteristic features of contemporary Western society, in which it served as a psychological counter-weight to the rapid and bewildering changes in the material circumstances of life. . . . It was no accident or inconsistency that certain Islamic peoples, particularly the Osmanli Turks . . . were beginning to display a new interest in and care for the literary, artistic and architectural monuments of the Ottoman past, at the very moment when they were shaking themselves free from the dead hand of the Ottoman tradition."[10] The revival of historical legends and myths plays a crucial role in the making of a vital nationalism. It does this, however, at the expense of objective and scientific history, since no student can record the full meaning of history from but a single national perspective.

A third element of nationalism is race. Nations have been disposed to prove, as have royal families, their descent from ancestors of unique achievements. Toynbee reflected on the tragicomical spectacle of "half of the people of modern Europe industriously striving to prove their descent from the Barbarians of the Volkerwanderung, in the mistaken belief that these casual war bands from no-man's-land were pure races."[11] As a historical fact, however, Toynbee summarily dismissed the reality of race. He had little interest in certain of the more recent anthropological findings based on a people's stature, type of hair, and cephalic indices. What is apparent is that anything corresponding to a pure race cannot be found, and therefore the level on which race functions is that of myth and legend. People "imagine" they possess moral, physical, and intellectual traits which are hereditary. Only in this way does race bring together attitudes and assumptions, and contribute thereby to nationalism.

A fourth element is territory and government. It is often assumed that possession of a well-defined geographical area or of unity within political boundaries is essential to national consciousness. For France this was true: people whose language was Flemish or Basque or German were no less inspired by the Revolution than were their French-speaking fellow citizens. If France had been typical, the consequences of the spread of nationalism could hardly have been so volatile and tragic. In most cases, however, national movements were devoted less to preserving a common territory or government than to securing new territory or a

10. Toynbee, *Civilization on Trial*, 5; *Survey of International Affairs*, 1931, p. 376; *Survey of International Affairs*, 1928, p. 213.
11. Toynbee, *A Study of History*, I, 61.

new political framework. This comes about "either by making a schism in the body politic of some pre-existent state or by merging the identities of a number of pre-existent states in a body politic embracing them all." The founding of the United States is an example of the two developments occurring as a single political act.[12]

Numerous exceptions exist to the rule that nationalism depends upon a "natural" territory and government. In Catalonia, for example, a national movement was frustrated in its attempt to achieve political unity. In the Soviet Union, Armenia, the Ukraine, and Kurdistan do not have the political means for the full expression of their nationalism. Toynbee summed up his conclusions on the relationship: "If national movements did all duly conform to the pre-existent pattern of state territories and inter-state frontiers, then the havoc wrought by Nationalism would be much less extensive than it has actually been."[13]

A fifth element of nationalism is the community of interests of a people. Materialist and scientific studies of nationalism have emphasized the role of common social, political, and economic aims in stirring men to an appreciation of their nationality. Objective conditions, in other words, provide the foundation on which nationalism is built. This aspect received less attention from Toynbee than it merits. His attitude was probably consonant with his greater emphasis on psychological factors as they relate to individuals and groups.

The last element of nationalism is some form of religion or ideology. The traditional rival of nationalism has been the independent church, which it has often supplanted. Bismarck saw as his first task the replacing of the Catholic church with the spirit of a new religion. The architects of the restoration of the imperial government in Japan similarly viewed the Mahayana Buddhist church. Indeed, this is the most far-reaching change, for "in our modern Western World the spirit of religious fanaticism and the spirit of national fanaticism are manifestly one and the same." This is also true in the Soviet Union, where diverse nationalities are held together by "the common spiritual possession of the Stalinist-Leninist-Marxian ideas and institutions." Even the nations with ties of race and language are now grounded in an ideology or secular religion. " 'The Third Reich' is not only German but National Socialist; Italy is not only Italian but corporative; France not only

12. Toynbee, *A Study of History*, IV, 186.
13. *Ibid.*, 185.

French but a child of 'the ideas of 1789'; and, in the nationalism
... of the British Commonwealth, parliamentary government and
the liberty of the subject are more important ingredients than either the 'Anglo-Saxon' race or the English language."[14] When Nazi
Germany, Fascist Italy, Revolutionary France, or British parlia-
mentarianism expanded into areas abroad, the qualities of their respective secular religions were manifest.

Toynbee has sometimes been criticized for considering only the
negative and tragic aspects of nationalism. Someone might reach
this conclusion from the judgments he made about the future of
the West if the problems resulting from unrestricted nationalism
were not resolved. His view of a future dominated by nationalism
was in one sense unqualifiedly pessimistic. Yet Toynbee would
have concurred with another historian who wrote: "Whether we
like it or not, some form of nationalism is likely to continue in-
definitely."[15] He considered in some detail not only the vices de-
riving from modern nationalism but also its palpable virtues.

One strength of nationalism is its promotion of political unity.
Nationalism has made a notable contribution to civilization by
providing larger political units within which rivalries among
groups, classes, and sects might be contained and adjusted. New
loyalties which transcend feudal and religious ties have served to
limit these older tensions. One writer has observed: "With the rise
of nationalism private feuds, duels, banditry, and feudal, religious,
and class hostilities have tended to decline." At least this has been
true of what some scholars have called nineteenth-century "idealist" nationalism, which emphasized the right of all nations to
determine the form and character of their own political systems
based on the principle of nationality. Each also honors the right of
other nations to do likewise. These assumptions furnish a background for the theory of national self-determination which for
Toynbee and others was the guiding principle of international politics before and after World War I. Writing then, he concluded that
"peace is endangered far more by the unjust violation of the national idea than by the resentment due to the just reversal of the
injustice, even if the wrongdoer be the most potent factor in Europe and his victim the most insignificant."[16]

14. Toynbee, A Study of History, V, 160; Survey of International Affairs, 1934,
p. 371
15. Arnold J. Toynbee, Pieter Geyl, and Pitirim A. Sorokin, The Pattern of the
Past (Boston, 1949), 67–70; Hayes, Essays on Nationalism, 247.
16. Quincy Wright, A Study of War (2 vols.; Chicago, 1942), II, 987; Toynbee,
Nationality and the War, 40.

Another virtue of nationalism stems from community. Nationalism has provided the most effective means thus far of harnessing man's gregarious instincts in administratively efficient political units. We know that there are certain fundamental social impulses that may be channeled and controlled but never wholly suppressed. There is in modern nationalism an element of the instinctive; it performs both a social and spiritual function. Through it a people obtain a sense of self-respect and destiny. Individuals have a defined sphere in which social virtues can be practiced. Nationalism is a safeguard against materialism since it presents a people with ideas for which they can live and die. Through its instrumentalities, tradition and sacred memories are made a part of the living present. The Enlightenment was lacking in these things, for "the enlightened scepticism of the eighteenth century elite, as it had gradually worked its way downward . . . into the minds and hearts of the lower middle and the working class, had produced an immense and intolerable spiritual void."[17]

Finally, the ongoing institution by means of which economic welfare is given substance is the nation-state. Within the last half-century, the state has undergone a fundamental transformation. There are some indications, according to Toynbee, that "while continuing to be used as instruments of an immoral violence, these states are now also beginning to be used simultaneously as a means to social welfare. Even in the most old-fashioned communities of our twentieth-century Western World the traditional military state and police-state is now concerning itself to some extent with the promotion of health and education and employment."[18]

Toynbee observed a more general tendency which he recognized as a profound social force, not a partisan political design. Idealist nationalism, at least in theory, has sought to merge humanitarian principles with liberal democratic ideals. When its growth has been organic, natural, and gradual, as with English-speaking peoples, these aspirations have been fulfilled to a considerable degree. At one point in his writing, Toynbee assumed that there were two kinds of nationalism—the milder English type was a basically constructive force in civilization, but crusading nationalism, which sought to convert the world to its creed, was less benign. Nationalism is a cultural virus which works with a potency that is proportionate to its novelty.[19]

17. *Survey of International Affairs*, 1933, p. 133.
18. Toynbee, *A Study of History*, V, 49.
19. Toynbee, *A Study of History*, VI, 67.

The positive attributes of nationalism were, for Toynbee, only part of the story. The seeming virtues he described have been weakened if not destroyed by certain no less destructive aspects of contemporary nationalism. As the twentieth century unfolded he became increasingly aware that of all factors threatening civilization, nationalism was by far the most deadly. What caused Toynbee's deepening concern was the knowledge that other civilizations had succumbed to this same threat: "An unceasing round of internecine warfare of ever increasing intensity between deified parochial states has been the principal cause of the breakdown and disintegration of some, and perhaps most, of the civilizations that have already gone the way of all flesh." The new nationalism, which some have called integral nationalism, has harnessed the humanitarian and spiritual elements to the needs and aspirations of sovereign states in an unhumanitarian world. This potent force has been used for aggressive and authoritarian ends in international politics. Toynbee saw integral nationalism as the besetting sin of Western civilization.[20]

The second vice of modern nationalism is the obstacle it places in the way of economic world unity. This economic nationalism can "be defined as an exploitation of the apparatus of a parochial state for the purpose of promoting the economic interests of the population of that state at the expense of the rest of mankind." Economic rivalries were evident among eighteenth-century mercantile groups seeking control over new markets and raw materials. In the new era of economic nationalism, however, nations have become self-contained economic units which vie with each other not for luxuries but for the means of preserving industries and populations in times of war and crisis. A nation prepares for all eventualities by erecting high tariff walls and by stimulating in countless other ways economic self-sufficiency. Nationalism drives a people in the direction of autarchy at the expense of seeking a wider community of interests.[21]

A third defect is the deterioration of common moral standards in international affairs. It becomes difficult if not impossible to hold a nation responsible for aggressive actions which a representative government plans and endorses. Once policy is executed, nationalism welds whole populations into a phalanx of fervent supporters. At the time of the Japanese rape of Manchuria, Japanese

20. Toynbee, *A Study of History*, V, 189.
21. Toynbee, *A Study of History*, IV, 175.

spokesmen declared before the League of Nations that sixty-five million Japanese could not be wrong. They argued that dissenting voices would have been raised within Japan if there were not good reasons for the action. The totalitarian nature of modern nationalism has made moral distinctions between just and unjust policies almost meaningless. The defense of all acts of aggression becomes essentially the same everywhere, that "sixty-five million people cannot suddenly have gone mad."[22]

The fourth vice of nationalism is the exaggeration and absolutizing of the principle of national self-determination. Hitler could invoke this concept in justifying Germany's claim over the Sudeten Germans in Czechoslovakia. What in 1915 appeared to be a valid base for judging the claims of separate peoples for national self-government, now becomes a crude rationalization for grand imperialistic adventures.[23]

The final and most demonic evil of modern nationalism is its dire influence upon the nature and conduct of war. The fond expectations that war could be abolished have been superseded by the knowledge that "the struggle for existence between absolute governments has merely been replaced by a struggle between nationalities equally blind, haphazard, and nonmoral, but far more terrific, just because the virtue of self-government is to focus and utilize human energy so much more effectively than the irresponsible government it has superseded."[24]

The essence of modern nationalism, then, is its religious and crusading character. Throughout history, plurality has been the striking feature of men's loyalties. In the Middle Ages the individual was devoted to church, feudal lord, and emperor. In modern times, there are still multiple loyalties, but in an unprecedented manner the individual has become disposed to sacrifice church, family, and friends to the paramount call of nation and nationality. This tendency has been aided by the substitution of a political creed for a philosophy of skepticism, the heritage of the eighteenth century. All of the habiliments of a once dominant traditional religion now grace the new secular religion. The land becomes one's god, its aims emerge as sacred missions, a flag serves as the chief symbol of faith, national holidays become distinctive holy days, and a theology grows out of a body of precepts from the "fathers." Soviet communism has its holy prophet in Marx, its high priests

22. *Survey of International Affairs*, 1933, p. 496.
23. *Survey of International Affairs*, 1932, p. 182.
24. Toynbee, *Nationality and the War*, 9.

in Lenin and Stalin, and its sacred text in Communist writings. In earlier civilizations, this idolization of political institutions has signaled deterioration. Another student of religion and history described its dynamic in present civilizations in these terms: "Nowhere is the temptation to idolatry greater than in national life. The nation is so much larger than the individual that it not only naturally claims to be the individual's god but naturally impresses the individual with the legitimacy of this claim."[25]

The first example of a political religion about which Toynbee wrote was fascism. In 1929 he observed that fascism "had erected the National State into a kind of pagan political divinity . . . which was to be worshipped in the same spirit by good Fascists as the Christian Godhead was to be worshipped by 'good Catholics.'" The theory and practice of fascism, however, are an exaggeration of Western political institutions. Toynbee discovered that both nazism and fascism were mere consummations "of a politico-religious movement, the pagan deification and worship of parochial human communities, which had been gradually gaining ground for more than four centuries in the Western World at large, and which had a still longer history behind it in the medieval city-states of Central and Northern Italy." What this means for international politics is that political struggles have taken on a religious character. The restraining traditional forces of religion have been absorbed into the new molds of political fanaticism. The problems with which diplomacy deals have been intensified. Nationalism in Toynbee's view is not only a false religion. By the intransigence it has imposed upon international politics, it threatens the destruction of the nation-state system itself.[26]

Despite nationalism's menacing qualities, Toynbee came to have fewer and fewer illusions about its early disappearance. The spectacular successes of nationalism, when historians had prophesied its conquest by universalism, have made it the most powerful force in the contest for men's loyalties. Writing of Kemal Atatürk's institution of nationalism, he observed: "One of the most remarkable signs of the times . . . is the emphasis with which the Turkish Republic has repudiated the tradition of Islamic solidarity."[27] There are nevertheless three comments on transcending

25. Toynbee, A Study of History, IV, 303ff.; Reinhold Niebuhr, Beyond Tragedy: Essays on the Christian Interpretation of History (New York, 1937), 85.
26. Survey of International Affairs, 1929, p. 438; Survey of International Affairs, 1933, p. 111.
27. Toynbee, Civilization on Trial, 210.

nationalism which Toynbee put foward and which should be noted.

Historically, parochialism has been transcended mainly in those spheres where it has not yet gained a people's complete devotion. On the boundaries of the Greek city-state constellation, for example, "the Roman Empire had not won a complete ascendancy." World empire was most successful at "the borderline between the city-state cosmos, which was the brilliant heart of the Hellenic World, and its pre-city-state penumbra."[28]

Another method for transcending nationalism can be seen in Soviet policy. Stalin recognized at an early date that one of the most formidable threats to the triumph of the Marxian ideology was nationalism. To avert this danger the people have been given "so wide a scope for the satisfaction of nationalist proclivities as to reduce to a minimum the danger that nationalist grievances may be used as a 'red herring' to draw the people's feet away from the path of Communism." Political centralization has been joined with cultural pluralism for the various ethnic groups in the Union of Soviet Socialist Republics. This was Toynbee's view in 1939.[29] He could hardly have foreseen the postwar crisis which was to confront the Soviet Union in Afghanistan.

A final method of transcendence is through power itself. If a world state is established, it will be buttressed by the strength of some "Great Power." This need not be world empire, but even for a cooperative world organization, the facts of power must take priority over principles of organization. Toynbee turned to this consideration increasingly in his last years of writing and reflection.

Beyond the subject of nationalism, a large part of A Study of History is devoted to an appraisal of the divergent trends of localism or parochialism and universalism or ecumenicalism. Toynbee described the former as the tendency to glorify the part rather than the whole; politically, the importance of the member states of a society tends to be magnified at the expense of the whole society. In Greek history, this was expressed in the adulation of the city-state. In our own day, it takes the form of the political religion of nationalism. Universalism, on the other hand, is the view that a civilization or religion is itself a unity. One such form was realized in the Roman Empire; another was typified by medieval Christendom. What forms of universalism can be found in Western civili-

28. Toynbee, A Study of History, IV, 310.
29. Toynbee, A Study of History, VI, 110.

zation today? Some say there is a political universalism embodied in the United Nations; others point to signs of the humanity and basic needs shared by all. By contrast, Toynbee held firmly to the view that the most impressive universal force in the twentieth century is "Westernization."

Certain writers on international politics deal with this force on another level. Usually something called "industrialization," part of the background of international politics, affects but does not determine the nature of the political forces. Most scholars discuss a society's change stemming from socioeconomic factors as economic development. Westernization, however, has affected non-Western societies as well—China, Russia, and the Near East, for example. It is more profound than "industrialization," for the borrowing of one habit or technique by a more primitive society has presaged the eventual unconditional surrender to the whole alien force of Westernization. Indeed it seems likely that "future historians will say . . . that it [Westernization] was so powerful and so pervasive that it turned the lives of all its victims upside down and inside out—affecting the behaviour, outlook, feelings, and beliefs of individual men, women, and children in an intimate way, touching chords in human souls that are not touched by mere external material forces—however ponderous and terrifying."[30]

Three fundamental aspects of Westernization distinguish it as a force in international politics. First, it is worldwide—to the extent that Western economic forms have spread throughout the world. Second, it has had the effect of combining all contemporary civilizations into "a single great society." It "has swallowed—and in some degree digested and assimilated—at least eight alien societies: the Mexic, the Andean, the Hindu, the Iranic, the Russian Orthodox Christian, the Japanese Far Eastern, and the main bodies of the Far Eastern and Orthodox Christian societies in China and in the Near East. The number of victims rises from eight to ten if we reckon in the Yucatec and Arabic societies, which their Mexic and Iranic neighbours had respectively succeeded in devouring."[31]

As a consequence, the old distinction between internal and external proletariats, or threats to the civilization from within and from without, has disappeared. All the non-Western civilizations and their people are absorbed into a massive internal proletariat. So the remaining civilizations—such as the Orthodox Christian,

30. Toynbee, *Civilization on Trial*, 214.
31. *Ibid.*, 196; Toynbee, *A Study of History*, V, 89.

its Russian offshoot, the Hindu, and the two Far Eastern civilizations—became in at least certain respects incorporated in the one vast Western civilization.

Third, its predecessors, most notably Graeco-Roman civilization, were ultimately challenged in their ventures of expansion and unification by counterattacks. Graeco-Roman culture extended its influence as far as India, the British Isles, China, and Scandinavia. Only the Central American and Peruvian societies were untouched. But the developments of greatest significance for us are the responses to this penetration. The counterattacks against "Hellenization" began with the Jewish armed resistance in Palestine, included the Parthian and Persian successes, and culminated in the Islamic victories of the seventh century that liberated the Middle East from Graeco-Roman domination. A nonviolent counterattack resisted the dominance of this movement in a different and even more telling manner. The new religions audaciously set about conquering the minds of men. Missionaries and leaders, in delivering their challenge, became the chief adversaries of Graeco-Roman domination in regions that had once been attacked and conquered. We must anticipate a repetition of these counterattacks if Westernization as a movement conforms to the pattern of its forerunners.[32]

It is perhaps more illuminating to examine Westernization as a force in particular countries. Its impact has nowhere been exactly the same, but certain common elements can be observed in Turkey, China, and Russia. The first thin wedge of Western influence penetrated Ottoman life in the eighteenth century with the creation by Sultan Selim III of a Western-model army. The immediate cause for this was the shocking defeat in the Russo-Turkish war (1768–1774). But the most far-reaching changes in Turkish life came with the government of President Mustafa Kemal: "The Turks . . . not only declared a republic and abolished the Caliphate but . . . disestablished Islamic religious institutions, abandoned the last vestiges of Islamic dress, and ceased to use the Arabic Alphabet."[33]

The response of Far Eastern society to the impact of Western forces was remarkably similar to that of the Turks. The same traces of revolutionary violence and social ferment were present; there were the recurring problems of adjusting to the times. In China the

32. Toynbee, *Civilization on Trial*, 217–18.
33. Toynbee, *A Study of History*, III, 48; *Survey of International Affairs*, 1928, pp. 188–89.

direction of education was away from the classics of Confucius to the study of the physical sciences. Young men received technical training abroad in science and engineering and returned with the aim of building and repairing roads, railways, and irrigation canals. Instead, most remained unemployed as the Chinese system of public works continued to deteriorate. Fundamental social and political changes which the new movement introduced were too turbulent for the fabric of a medieval Far Eastern society. In circumstances of political anarchy, China was unable to deal effectively with such problems as public works.[34]

Peter the Great visited Western Europe in 1697 and returned to launch a campaign to supplant traditional Russian life. He drew inspiration particularly from Germany, Holland, and England. One of his first efforts was to replace the Strelitzy, or "old guard," with a new and Westernized army. The public service was thrown open to all classes in society, and the special privileges of nobles, or boyars, were restricted in practice. The whole broad arena of social life and manners was transformed by provisions making compulsory the wearing of Western dress. In Russia, as was not the case in Turkey, certain of these provisions applied only to the upper class. Also in Russia, the church became a docile instrument of the state.[35] As history was to demonstrate, the changes fell short of transforming those areas which remained a feudal society.

Westernization can hardly be said to have been an unmixed blessing. The extension of Western influence and domination throughout the world has had its price. Among the more costly aspects of technical progress have been its effects upon native peoples and the misguided outlook it fostered among Westerners concerning the "native." So-called primitive peoples such as the Polynesians have suffered as profound a shock as if they had been the victims of military invasion. They have been subjected to the ravages of new and contagious diseases and have been spiritually alienated from society. They have suffered from "the profound devitalizing influence which the Westerner's very spiritual presence exerts upon the Primitive who suddenly comes into social contact with him." More disquieting is the moral and intellectual blindness that has characterized the Western outlook toward the "native." As Toynbee observed: "The following extract from the New English Dictionary speaks for itself: 'Native, Substantive. . . . One

34. Toynbee, *A Study of History*, IV, 50–51.
35. Toynbee, *A Study of History*, II, 181n2.

of original or usual inhabitants of a country, as distinguished from strangers or foreigners; now especially one belonging to a non-European and imperfectly civilized or savage race.' "[36]

More paradoxical still, even Toynbee, seeking in principle to refute this widely held point of view, succumbed inadvertently to the philosophy he opposed. At one point he stated: "The superiority of the colonists over the 'Natives' in arms was only one manifestation of a *superiority all round* which extended to other branches of social activity." This is surely a mild expression of the dominant Western viewpoint, especially when contrasted with Buckle's assertion that "it is in Europe that everything worthy of the name of civilization has originated."[37] I am reminded of a statement by a former teacher that he knew of no Islamic country which had a culture. Nonetheless, Toynbee's comment is a particular illustration, from an unexpected source, of the condescending attitude which has characterized the Westerner's conception of non-Westerners for much of the past century. The most likely cause is the spectacular triumph of Western economic and political techniques outside its own area. In dealing with non-Western peoples, and especially the imponderables of their societies, colonial powers in particular have repeatedly made this tragic mistake. It blinds both masters and indigenous peoples to the creative customs which inhere in native cultures and undermines the contributions they might themselves make to the mitigation of new social difficulties. For example, the Islamic recipe for easing racial tensions through teaching a radical egalitarianism has sometimes been superior, as have "native" remedies for certain other problems. Perhaps the signal example of the failure of Westernization has been its dismal record in this regard.

Nevertheless, the spread of more effective Western techniques and the extension of a more dynamic Western culture are often accepted as inevitable and self-evident. Toynbee, however, insisted upon tracing these events back to their logical causes. One key to the successful movement of the West is plainly sheer military and political power. In the offensive against primitive societies, Toynbee observed, extermination or eviction or subjugation has been the rule and conversion the exception. In the instance of the North American Indians and again of the African Negroes, the fate of non-Western peoples has been decided through force of arms.

36. Toynbee, *A Study of History*, III, 282–84, 3n4, I, 151.
37. Toynbee, *A Study of History*, III, 51; Henry T. Buckle, *Introduction to the History of Civilization in England* (2 vols.; New York, 1925), I, 47.

The second key, however, lies in the inner nature of the challenge with which non-Western societies are confronted. To effectively restrain the onward march of Westernization, they must borrow those selfsame techniques and methods through which the West gained its supremacy. But in so doing, they in effect appropriate the economic structure and organization of the West. No society thus far has been able to follow this line of action without in the end falling under the domination they sought to resist. Whether by force or imitation, then, Westernization is a pattern indelibly stamped with the markings of Western civilization.

Yet the "Westernizers" ought to remember that other historical movements have evoked reactions which ultimately proved their downfall. The Roman colonies, an imperfect parallel to the regions of the world which have been Westernized, "degenerated into parasitic growths which were eventually swept away by a proletarian revolution." It is not surprising, therefore, that one can already discover examples of resistance and profound reaction to Westernization, now the most far-reaching worldwide social and political movement. Toynbee found two fundamental and abstract forms this reaction may take. The first is that of the "Zealot": the likely victim buries his head ostrichlike in the sand and continues stubbornly to make use of outmoded forms of production and trade, as Abyssinia did from the early nineteenth century until Italy's invasion of Ethiopia (1935–1936). The second is "Herodianism": a society confronts the new forces, calling to its service their own weapons and techniques. The one obvious weakness of this response is its uncreative character.[38]

The outstanding example of a latter-day reaction against Westernization is Russia, which after two centuries was "seized by a revulsion which gradually gathered strength below the surface until it broke out in the Bolshevik Revolution of 1917—a catastrophe that abruptly reversed in Russia the long process of 'Westernization' and, in the name of a Western revolutionary creed, impelled the peoples of the U.S.S.R. along a new course towards an unknown goal." In fact, the Russians extracted the Western-born philosophy of Marxism, transformed it into a system uniquely their own, and now are using it for their own ends to prod and challenge its creators. This strategy is characteristic of most anti-Western movements today. Threats which are even more disquieting in the long run are evident in India and China, which in Toynbee's opin-

38. Toynbee, A Study of History, V, 321, 47.

ion, "seem likely to produce much deeper effects on our Western life than Russia can ever hope to produce with her Communism." Other cultures which need only to free themselves of superficial signs of Westernization are beginning to stir. Revolutions in Latin America will surely continue, and countries such as Mexico may before long be able to shake off the "top-dressing" of Western culture.[39]

When one contrasts, however, the pace of Westernization with that of the spread of the West's spiritual heritage, then it becomes plain that there must be a spiritual void in many "native" societies: "The frail customary institutions of the primitive societies which were formerly at home in the land have been shattered to pieces by the impact of the ponderous Western machine, and millions of 'native' men, women, and children suddenly deprived of their traditional social environment, have been left spiritually naked and abashed." It is a law of history, or at least a principle approaching a law, that although economic and political forces may be transplanted successfully, social and cultural heritage can rarely be exported. Indeed, introducing an alien culture may lead to destruction, as colonial experiences make dramatically clear. The more intelligent statesmen and administrators have sought to restore native institutions which had been overthrown. Anthropologists in particular call attention to the problem, and some have encouraged sweeping changes in the practice of colonial administrations.[40]

It seems somewhat strange in this connection that Toynbee should analyze so fully the spiritual and cultural problem and so inadequately the political problem. Western influence has spanned the globe through technology, but to assume that there has also been a comparable political influence and unification may constitute a grand illusion. The mere existence of institutions of representative government tailored by outsiders to a society's needs frequently has less to do with underlying political community on a global scale than with an existing economic world unity. Toynbee should have treated this in more detail. Political community is lacking in the world despite the community of economic interests in an interdependent world. Both India and the United States are democracies, but the divergence of their national interests has

39. *Survey of International Affairs*, 1928, p. 189; Toynbee, *Civilization on Trial*, 221.
40. Toynbee, *Civilization on Trial*, 207.

made for conflicts and mutual suspicion or the absence of community.

Another profound and far-reaching world force is sovereignty, yet it remains one of the most misunderstood forces in international politics. The general confusion which has characterized the Western outlook is reflected in Toynbee's fragmentary comments on the subject. Modern writers have frequently denounced in moral and rational terms the satanic role which sovereignty plays in the "tragedies" of international politics. Only a handful of scholars have attempted to appraise realistically its function in terms of the actual structure of the modern state system.

There are certain attributes of sovereignty, elemental to the theory we are examining, which Toynbee did seriously address. It is dependent upon a sufficient "quantum of territory" so that a people's independence can be maintained. The papacy, for example, has insisted upon its right to a given area within which it is supreme. Similarly, virtually every sovereign state holds and exercises, within its own territory, the supreme law-making and law-enforcing power. These attributes have been augmented by increasing across-the-board powers of the modern state. In this respect the dynastic states of the eighteenth century were in a happier position than are their successors. A new vitalism and fanaticism have been pumped into the forms and structures of sovereignty today, making it "a more formidable evil than it had been at any time before in the modern period of Western history." Because popular sovereignty ascribes to people rather than princes the safeguarding of territory and the function of law enforcement, the problem of peaceful change has become more complicated. In the eighteenth century, ways and means for changing the political map were widely recognized and used. Peaceful change was facilitated and sovereignty consolidated through bargains among princes and dynastic marriages. Toynbee commented: "This tendency, which was prevalent in the eighteenth century, to treat international politics as the private family affairs of dynasties, and not as the public business of peoples, undoubtedly turned international politics into something rather petty and rather sordid; but at least it performed one socially beneficial negative service. It 'took the shine out of' patriotism; and, with 'the shine,' it took the sting."[41]

41. Toynbee, *A Study of History*, IV, 221n; *Survey of International Affairs*, 1937, I, 3; Toynbee, *A Study of History*, IV, 159.

A concrete illustration for Toynbee of this new situation concerned the pressure brought to bear upon Heinrich Brüning at the London Naval Conference of 1930. The leaders of the opposition in Germany, who included Hitler and Hugenberg, wired Brüning on July 21, 1930, that "they would not recognize as binding any agreement that might be reached at the Conference if, in their opinion, such agreement involved any French encroachment upon German sovereignty." This effectively handcuffed the leader of the Weimar Republic. At each major diplomatic conference during the interwar period, the same problem became an obstacle to successful negotiations.[42]

The formulation of the nature and extent of the problem of sovereignty is the first step toward critical analysis. Some writers go on from here to examine the practical and political significance of sovereignty for the conduct of international relations. Others are more interested in designing constitutional forms for abolishing state sovereignty. Toynbee as a rule held to the orthodox viewpoint which is based on the proposition that sovereignty is divisible. National constitutions have allocated some sovereignty to the central government and some to local units. On the international level, commitments such as those to the League of Nations were assumed to represent a limitation upon the sovereignty of states. The creation of the Permanent Council of Foreign Ministers in the 1930s within the Little Entente was a further example: "Although this Council's decisions were still to be governed by the unanimity rule and were not to be taken by a majority vote, the contracting parties did, in certain other ways, make important ramifications of their individual sovereignty for the benefit of the triple common weal. They each bound themselves thenceforth to conclude no fresh treaties and take no fresh unilateral action of international import without the Permanent Council's unanimous approval; and they further bound themselves to coordinate and unify their existing treaties with third parties as far as possible."[43]

There are precedents for divided sovereignty in those empires and states characterized by dual citizenship. In the Seleucid Empire, the new Greek cities were given a status halfway between full sovereignty and mere subordination. The British method of devolution adjusted national power by granting dominion and Crown status, thus dividing sovereign powers among the states in the empire.[44]

42. *Survey of International Affairs*, 1931, p. 89.
43. *Survey of International Affairs*, 1933, p. 204.
44. Toynbee, *A Study of History*, IV, 312n4.

Probably Toynbee's clearest expression of this popular if misguided view of sovereignty can be found in his examination of the
successor states of Eastern and Central Europe as independent
units. He decided that they were not and stated: "Either they might
surrender their untenable title to sovereignty voluntarily and partially, in a non-revolutionary way . . . [by] pooled sovereign rights
. . . or alternatively they would lose their sovereignty in a more old-
fashioned and familiar way through being annexed or enslaved by
some aggressive Great Power." The first alternative is one to which
Toynbee frequently returned, particularly in his earlier writings.
It is assumed that when nations give up their sovereignty they can
do it halfway. This remains one of the most arguable points in
Toynbee's theory of international politics.[45]

How, then, can sovereignty be modified in practice? The failure
to transcend the patterns of sovereignty, as in the history of the
Greek city-states, has meant the destruction of civilization. Mitigating absolute state sovereignty must surely be more difficult
than simply dividing it. Imposing unity upon independent states
obviously cannot be brought about merely by constitutional fiat.
The minimum sacrifices of sovereignty which Toynbee insisted
were necessary to thwart the advances of nazism in the early 1930s
were not forthcoming. Although in principle divided sovereignty
is possible, this has seldom been achieved for any considerable period of time.[46] A related concept is the balance of power.

The balance of power is discussed in almost every treatise on international politics, but its place and significance depend upon
which of two philosophies the writer or publicist has accepted. One
assumes that statesmen can choose policies based either upon the
balance of power or on morality and justice. The other holds that
"any given system is perpetually subject to that play of political
forces which is known as the Balance of Power." A fundamental
social principle of relations of politically independent units pro
vides that stability can be achieved through a tendency of the separate units to establish and reestablish some kind of equilibrium.
Although such equilibrium at best is precarious, a rough stability
is from time to time achieved. This social law can be formulated
in terms that are broader than international politics: "If one species happens to vary in the direction of greater independence, the

45. *Survey of International Affairs,* 1934, p. 345.
46. Toynbee, *A Study of History,* IV, 208–209.

inter-related equilibrium is upset and cannot be restored until a number of competing species have either given way to the increased pressure and become extinct, or else have answered pressure with pressure and kept the first species in its place, by themselves too discovering means of adding to their independence."[47]

Toynbee did not leave any doubt as to which of these positions was superior. The balance of power was at work during the development of the North Italian city-states, precursors of our contemporary multiple-state system. Pressures and balances operated to preserve the independence of individual states and prevent their domination by any would-be conqueror. Moreover, one can extract from this episode principles and laws which will be evident in other political constellations.

When circumstances are favorable for the operation of the balance of power, one law which comes into play provides, according to Toynbee, that "the Balance of Power operates in a general way to keep the average calibre of states low in terms of every criterion for the measurement of political power: in extent of territory and in head of population and in aggregate of wealth." As Quincy Wright asserted, "Stability will increase as the parity in the power of states increases." Much of the anxiety over contemporary problems has been produced by an awareness that this condition has been destroyed by the emergence of the superpowers.[48]

Another law asserts that a balance of power policy can be most effectively applied at the periphery rather than at the center of a political system, where the pressures which resist the necessary adjustment are intensified. The job of a diplomat is therefore more difficult when he deals with resentments over small plots of territory at the core of an established state system. Toynbee concluded:

This extreme unevenness in the distribution of political pressure prescribes a law of the Balance of Power which can be formulated as follows: If a given society is articulated politically into a multiplicity of mutually independent local states, with the result that the Balance of Power has been introduced into the dynamics of this society's political structure; and if this society proceeds to grow in civilization, with the result that it radiates its culture out abroad and thereby enlarges its own geo-

47. *Survey of International Affairs*, 1930, p. 134; Julian S. Huxley, *The Individual in the Animal Kingdom* (London, 1912), 115–16.
48. Toynbee, *A Study of History*, III, 302; Wright, *A Study of War*, II, 755.

graphical ambit: then the states that occupy the heart and
homeland of this civilization will sooner or later be dwarfed and
overshadowed and dominated by the rise, around the periphery
of the expanding constellation, of a whole new order of Great
Powers with an overwhelmingly greater average calibre.

A consequence of this law which Toynbee emphasized is the
emergence of certain "Great Powers" at the boundaries of any civilization. This is a thesis on which the universal historian is by
training disposed to dwell. Examples are legion—the expansion of
Macedon throughout the Greek world; the universal state of Rome;
the conquests of the Italian states by France and Spain four centuries ago; and the recent emergence of great "rimland" powers in
Japan, the Soviet Union, and the United States.[49]

A corollary of this theory states that conflicts of power are most
effectively settled in political "open spaces" away from the territories of the dominant powers. What is of interest here is the political and diplomatic significance of Toynbee's thesis. Africa has
traditionally provided "open space" for the European powers, as
have Afghanistan, Siam (Thailand), and sometimes Latin America. Within Europe the buffer states "precariously protected by the
equilibrium of the vast masses around them preserve their poise
by maintaining a rigid neutrality." Such was the pattern of European power politics between 1871 and World War I. Toynbee,
however, gave primary attention to the long-run problem of the
growth of powerful states on the periphery rather than to the short-
run and practical issue of limiting tensions within or inside the
system.[50]

According to a third law, the purpose of power is to maintain a
given international order and safeguard the independence of member states within a political system. If this is our guide in evaluating the balance of power, then its record has been quite successful. Especially until the Partitions of Poland at the end of the
eighteenth century, the principle was broadly effective. "In all the
warfare between French and Spanish Armies, and French and Austrian Armies, that met in battle on Italian soil in the course of
nearly four centuries of European contests from the days of Charles
VIII to the days of Napoleon III, no combatant, from first to last,
ever dealt his adversary a mortal blow." These achievements were
possible in part because of a moral and political climate which has

49. Toynbee, *A Study of History*, III, 302–303.
50. *Survey of International Affairs*, 1926, pp. 18–19.

since disappeared. The moral consensus to which Gibbon pointed in 1781 was primarily responsible for the nature of European politics during the four centuries of "temperate and undecisive" warfare. The balance of power was ideally suited for its principal task under these conditions, for, as Gibbon observed, it would "continue to fluctuate, and the prosperity of our own or the neighbouring kingdoms may be alternately exalted or depressed; but these partial events cannot essentially injure our general state of happiness, the system of arts and laws and manners."[51] It must be acknowledged that if international peace instead of order is the yardstick for the balance of power, then its history becomes far more melancholy. For it cannot be said of the balance of power, any more than it can of international law or international organization, that it preserved the peace on any permanent basis.

A final law is a concise statement and summary of all the others. It contends that the balance of power is a universal instrument of foreign policy for any nation seeking to preserve its independence. From Henry VIII to Winston Churchill, it has been the first principle of British foreign policy. Its ubiquitous character is also revealed in Greek politics—leagues were formed against Athens, Sparta, and Thebes when each in turn constituted the dominant threat. Moreover, the Phoenicians and Etruscans combined to defend their vital interests against the Greeks. In the Roman Empire, under Christian emperors and under pagans such as Julian, there was mutual toleration based on an equilibrium of power rather than on common moral principles: "During those years the material strength of the Christians and non-Christians in the Roman Empire was approximately equal, so that, for the time being neither party could attempt to suppress the other with any hope of success." When the Christians' power increased, the policy of toleration was abandoned.[52]

In international administration, the balance of power can be observed in certain technical arrangements. Thus Toynbee found that "the new Tangier settlement [1924] was an attempt to express a diplomatic balance of forces between four European Powers."[53] The territorial settlements which provided for joint occupation of regions are other examples. Within certain limitations, the boundaries or lines of demarcation of these formal arrangements are

51. Toynbee, A Study of History, III, 311 (the quotation of Gibbon is also found here).

52. Toynbee, A Study of History, III, 121, IV, 226.

53. Survey of International Affairs, 1929, p. 198.

roughly the same as the distribution of power that underlies the postwar divisions of Korea and Germany. So the balance of power is equally present in administration and politics and in historical epochs from 500 B.C. to the present.

The balance of power has at certain times been effective because one nation played the role of balancer. Toynbee wondered which nation, if any, could take up this task. Churchill pointed out that although Britain had often been the "balancer," to do so again would be "an academic dream in an age in which Great Britain had been welded to the Continent by links of air."[54] Modern technology has destroyed the foundations on which such a policy rested.

Despite his convictions about the balance of power, Toynbee was not so sure this policy was the best one even in earlier centuries: "The English, again, were not really unaware of the fact that England had never, at any time in her history, been able to keep out of any major European conflict that might conceivably end in Europe falling under the military domination of some single Power." This statement was written in the early 1930s when Toynbee was opposing Churchill's policy. At the time of the Manchurian Crisis he wrote in more strident tones, criticizing the British Foreign Office for seeking "to finesse in the manner of those eighteenth century diplomatic virtuosi who sought to save their own countries and to 'preserve the Balance of Power' by deftly playing off one neighbour against another." For moral and technical reasons, there was little chance that England could continue to fulfill its traditional role—nor for that matter could the British Commonwealth. He answered the question regarding the latter's ability to act as a "balancer": "On a bare statistical test, yes; on a geographical and political test, no!"[55]

From time to time in the postwar era, Western Europe as a united confederation in world politics has been proposed as a "Third Force" in the cold war. Toynbee remained unconvinced, for only a Europe such as existed under Hitler could possibly challenge the superpowers. The destruction of the Nazi enterprise indicated that achieving such a design was unlikely. With the separation of Eastern Europe and Western Europe, it became an outlandish vision. If not Europe, then are there others which might play this historic role? Suggestions have included India, China, and as put forth by

54. Winston S. Churchill, *The Second World War*, Vol. I, *The Gathering Storm* (Boston, 1948), 208.
55. *Survey of International Affairs*, 1933, p. 170; *Survey of International Affairs*, 1934, p. 324; *Survey of International Affairs*, 1932, p. 540.

General De Gaulle, France. Toynbee, however, rejected them all.[56]

For many years, as Toynbee, speaking of the major balance of power, observed, "this particular balance did not transcend the limits of Western and Central Europe. For example, no Islamic countries entered into it until the General War of 1792–1815, and no Far Eastern countries until the conclusion of the Anglo-Japanese Alliance a dozen years before the outbreak of the General War of 1914–18." Since the beginning of World War II, however, the principal weights have been primarily non-European and the scales have been transplanted to the United States and the Soviet Union. All other local or "inferior" balances have become mere functions of the dominant world system.[57]

Toynbee had confidence that one could estimate the weights already on the scales of the balance of power. Most of the nations which appreciably affect the worldwide distribution of power were committed to either the Soviet or the American bloc. Thus there is less uncertainty about the strength of the major protagonists. The chances of fresh reserves being thrown in at the eleventh hour have been greatly diminished. This is true especially for the immediate future. What interested Toynbee in 1948 was that on this basis the United States and the West were "so much stronger than the Soviet Union that, short of attempting to wrench out of her rival's grip some country upon which the Soviet Union has already fastened its hold, it is apparently possible today for the United States to assert her own protectorate over any country she chooses in the no-man's-land between the Soviet Union and herself." And the United States did that, extending its influence to Turkey and Greece, on the threshold of the food granary in the the Ukraine and the Caucasus. Thus in 1948, with its immense superiority in technology, the United States seemed to have the advantage. Toynbee cautioned, however, that a dynamic and simple communist ideology, by missionary appeals and political penetration, might whittle away America's preeminence. Only a program of social transformation and political reform could compete with such a revolutionary ideology. And he wondered how far the world could be attracted "by the present rather conservative American gospel of out-and-out individualism." What might Toynbee's reactions have been in the 1980s? A world settlement today would be less favorable to the West than when Toynbee wrote—unless one assumes that social

56. Toynbee, *Civilization on Trial*, 138, 140, 124.
57. *Ibid.*, 142.

and political factors in the developing world are of minor importance compared with military statistics.[58]

In general Toynbee maintained with consistency that there are no clear alternatives to the balance of power. Even his conception of the world state was revised and "politicized" in recognition of the fact that the "Great Powers" or some combination of powers would serve as its cornerstone. In the idealist period of his writing, Toynbee seemed to share the misconception that statesmen and politicians could choose between balance of power policies and a new and better kind of international relations. He criticized Neville Chamberlain's "Munich" policy as an attempt to make the passage to a newfangled British foreign policy, one based on a collective system of international security within the framework of the League of Nations, from an old-fashioned policy built on the balance of power. In his study of the history of Islam, he deprecated the policy of Nasir, who, during his reign from the late twelfth century into the thirteenth, sought to check the imperialist adventures of any of the "successor states" which threatened to become too strong. He wrote: "This hazardous play with an unstable Balance of Power was less statesmanlike than the simultaneous efforts that Nasir made to rehabilitate the Caliphate by peaceful means."[59]

On the surface, such statements appear to be a thoroughgoing repudiation of the political principles basic to the balance of power. In fact, however, there is evidence that these statements were not representative even of Toynbee's idealist thinking. At the time of Munich, he referred to the argument that the balance of power was unreal, saying: "That is comforting; I can go to sleep again. All the same, I rather mistrust this argument that such a thing as 'the balance of power' does not exist."[60]

He went on to show, in language reminiscent of the famous memorandum of Sir Eyre Crowe, that Great Britain has always confronted any political situation which threatened the European balance of power. Was Munich this kind of situation? According to one school of thought, no threat existed since Gemany had for centuries dominated Central Europe. This viewpoint was unacceptable to Toynbee. He properly distinguished between domination by a unified Germany in the 1930s and by a disunited Germany in the past. A powerful imperialist state which has united

58. Toynbee, A Study of History, I, 28; Toynbee, Civilization on Trial, 144, 145.
59. Toynbee, A Study of History, III, 212n3.
60. Survey of International Affairs, 1936, II, 479.

eighty million people in a world mission poses a threat unlike that of a loose confederation of princes and petty rulers. The same policy which had been used against Louis XIV, Napoleon, and the kaiser had to be employed. As Toynbee wrote in 1939, "We have generally resisted the domination of Europe by a single Power when there seemed a possibility that the Power would use its domination of the Continent to threaten the independence of the British Isles and the interests of Great Britain overseas." He saw no reason for abandoning this tradition. Surely such an attitude leaves little room for a conception of foreign policy based on alternatives to the balance of power.[61]

The source of Toynbee's contradictory statements about the balance of power was probably his conviction born of the times that the new system of collective security was a step beyond previous techniques for preventing wars. If Toynbee's fervor was extravagant, so were the sentiments of most of his fellow interpreters. Obviously his remark in 1939 more closely reflected his continuing viewpoint on the balance of power, made as he was crossing from the idealist to the realist school of thought. Within or outside a collective security system, the balance of power remains one of the persistent forces in international politics.

Someone has said that ideologies are those beliefs for which large groups of people are willing to commit their lives or sacrifice themselves. In international politics, ideologies have served as driving forces for political or military action or as tools or weapons through which nations have justified their foreign policies. The idealist school of thought has emphasized the compelling and dynamic character of ideologies in themselves. The "realist" school has avowed that ideas were primarily tools or weapons with which a nation wages diplomatic war. We are concerned here with the use to which ideologies are put. This has obscured the true nature of international politics, which is not principally a contest between political ideals but a struggle for power. Instead of taking ideologies entirely at their face value, therefore, competent political observers "also look upon them as weapons in the armoury of certain Great Powers which were asserting themselves at the time." Although Toynbee suggested that political ideologies be studied in these terms, he did not deal conclusively with the subject.[62]

61. Arnold J. Toynbee, "After Munich: The World Outlook," *International Affairs*, XVIII (January-February, 1939), 9.
62. *Ibid.*, 10.

In the practice which approaches a law of politics, a Great Power seeking ascendancy must associate its aims with some ideology or religion. This has been part of the major reactions to the prevailing values of Western society. The Soviet Union is associated with communism, Germany identified itself with national socialism, and Italy with fascism. In earlier centuries, England, in somewhat different terms, stood for liberalism and parliamentary democracy, France for the propagation of Jacobinism, and Spain for the spread of Catholicism. Exploiting ideologies and counterideologies has never been practiced with more single-mindedness than by the German and Italian states before World War II. In 1936, Toynbee observed: "The first, and most valuable, trick of the 'Fascist' Powers' trade was their profession of being engaged in a 'holy war' against 'Communism' in the cause of Civilization!" The stratagem was temporarily successful in convincing some of the Western powers that however much they might dislike Fascists, they despised Communists still more. The negative bond with fascist states almost obscured the bourgeois democratic states' vision of their own national interests.[63]

In the Spanish civil war, the ideological professions of the Germans, Italians, and Russians were threadbare by the summer of 1937. It then became manifest to Toynbee and others that "this profession of a disinterested 'ideological' faith was a transparent cloak for the pursuit of material aims that were nakedly national." It appeared to Toynbee that no nation could afford to state frankly that its policies were based on the pursuit of political power.[64]

At the same time, political ideologies have sometimes obstructed the successful conduct of national policies. One clear example is the conflict between the objectives of the Soviet state and those of the Third International. In the 1920s, the political relations between the Soviet government and the British, who had only recently recognized the "bolshevist" state, were seriously jeopardized by the so-called Arcos affair. In this incident, employees of a Russo-British trading concern were suspected of spreading Comintern propaganda and its purposes in London. As a consequence, British recognition was withdrawn and Soviet foreign policy suffered a major diplomatic setback.[65]

In another event, prewar Germany and Japan were gravitating

63. *Survey of International Affairs*, 1936, p. 30.
64. *Survey of International Affairs*, 1937, I, 37; *Survey of International Affairs*, 1936, p. 33n3.
65. *Survey of International Affairs*, 1927, pp. 250–51.

toward one another because of the coincidence of their political interests. Their affinity, however, was derailed by pronouncements in Nazi ideology of the superiority of the Aryan race. Hitler's speech on January 26, 1936, which prophesied the ultimate dominion of the "white race" over the rest of the world, drew a protest from a Japanese Foreign Office spokesman in Tokyo. "By an ironical freak of fortune, three of the nations toward whom 'the Third Reich' was drawn by a community of political interests—namely the Japanese, the Magyars and the Finns—were speakers of 'non-Aryan' [i.e., non-Indo-European] languages; and the Nazi authorities at Berlin did their best to get over this stumbling-block by dubbing these three friendly nations 'honorary Aryans.'"[66]

Finally, political crusades founded upon ideologies have intensified the nature and magnitude of warfare and made more difficult its prevention. Wars of ideas and political faiths are traditionally the most ruthless. It is not surprising, therefore, that some form of ideological disarmament has repeatedly been proposed as a means of averting such tragic conflicts. Political tensions as well as economic problems might be eased if such disarmament were achieved. Toynbee counseled: "What the world needs above all now is to get the issue of free enterprise versus socialism off its ideological pedestal and to treat it, not as a matter of semi-religious faith and fanaticism, but as a common sense, practical question."[67]

In recent times, a few precedents exist for moral disarmament in international affairs. On February 26, 1934, an agreement was reached between German and Polish representatives responsible for press and propaganda releases. A system of exchange visits for newspapermen was instituted. Restraint marked the views printed in both countries, and this arrangement lasted for some time.[68] Another precedent, perhaps less convincing, is the temporary cessation of Soviet propaganda in 1933 when the United States finally recognized the Soviet Union. These examples at least suggest the possibility of ideological disarmament.

66. *Survey of International Affairs*, 1936, pp. 384–85n3.
67. Toynbee, *Civilization on Trial*, 148.
68. *Survey of International Affairs*, 1935, I, 204.

PART THREE

International Peace and Order

CHAPTER IV

Approaches to International Peace
and Order

I NTERNATIONAL government and international law have been
the remedy for war and anarchy most widely discussed in the
aftermath of World Wars I and II. The idealist school of international relations has emphasized international government as the
one overarching instrument able to prevent war and strife. The
question becomes, then, the practical one of how this goal can be
achieved. Idealists as a group, however, have tended to pay less attention to the means by which government could be created than
to the end being sought. Perhaps because of the movement in his
thought from idealism to realism, Toynbee dealt at length with
both the theoretical rationale and the practical foundations for international government.

We may begin by observing that government may be established either through cooperation and consent or through conquest and domination. The latter, though less discussed by idealist
thinkers, is more typical of the way in which governments have
actually appeared on the international scene. Alexander the Great
attempted to create an international government in this way. In
modern history, the military empire of Napoleon was a form of international government which lasted for decades. Other civilizations have witnessed comparable attempts. For example, the Emperor of Khatti successfully united the Hittite civilization through
pressure and conquest. Charlemagne established an international
government but proved unable to turn back the resistance of the
Lombards and Saxons.[1]

1. Arnold J. Toynbee, *A Study of History* (12 vols.; London, 1934–61), IV, 111.

The broad sweep of history shows that larger political units are usually created through conquest and subjugation, not through voluntary federation. In the fourteenth and fifteenth centuries, approximately eighty North Italian societies were thus formed into ten city-states. A single powerful city-state conquered six or eight less powerful ones. For example, Toynbee found that the "Grand Duchy of Tuscany was the outcome of the conquest of Fiesole and Volterra and Arezzo and Pistoia and Pisa and Siena by Florence. The Venetian dominions on the continent were built up by the imposition of Venetian rule upon Treviso and Padua and Vicenza and Verona and Brescia and Bergamo. The Papal State was . . . reconstituted by . . . the former city-states of Bologna and Ferrara to the status and style of 'the Legations.'"[2]

These various dominions often resulted in oppression by the conquering state. Both victor and victims tended to become "garrison-states." The imperial power frequently suffered the loss of liberty which is often the price a conqueror pays for his exploits. As Toynbee explained: "Imperialism required a professional army of mercenaries; and a mercenary force required in its turn a despotic government with the twofold function of keeping the mercenaries in order and organizing the city's resources to maintain them."[3]

The Hellenic world provides two notable examples of unity through conquest. One of them is well known, for who would think of omitting mention of the Roman Empire? The other example, however, concerns only a segment of Greek society: "In Hellenic history, the analogue of the . . . territorial consolidation in the history of modern Italy is to be found . . . in the colonial domain of Hellas in Sicily and Magna Graecia." In the fifth, fourth, and third centuries B.C., two powers in particular were as spectacularly successful in their conquests as Florence and Venice were in Italy. The "Venice" of Magna Graecia and Sicily was Tarentum; the "Florence" was imperialist Syracuse. In both cases, political unity was first achieved and then destroyed by military conquest.[4]

There are also, however, enough examples of international government by consent to support the conclusion that here is a second approach to political unity. As early as ancient Sinic civilization, nations whose security was endangered by hostile powers on the fringe of society banded together in a confederacy. This unity

2. Toynbee, A Study of History, III, 355–56.
3. Ibid., 356.
4. Ibid., 37n1.

was a key factor in Sinic relations for nearly two and one-half centuries. Within any balance of power system, security for small states at the center in relations with the powers on the periphery can depend on their achieving some form of collective unity. The Greek city-states, the Italian city-states, and the Sinic states confronted essentially the same problem with which European states such as France and England have had to deal in our own times. In such circumstances, there is but one alternative, according to Toynbee, and that is political union.[5]

Two intractable obstacles exist, however, to the creation of central government at the heart of a system: "The . . . geographical position [and] . . . the general effect of the Balance of Power is to keep the average size and strength of the states . . . low; and the play of forces, producing this effect, operates much more powerfully at the centre of a system than at the extremities." In addition, the deadweight of history stands athwart the achievement of political unity. The writers of the American Constitution, for instance, overcame the particularism of the separate states. A task of far greater magnitude after World War II confronted the architects of Western unity seeking to erase the allegiances of European states. Toynbee asked: "What arts or statesmanship could overcome the particularism of an England or a France or a Sweden or a Spain and persuade their peoples—living, as they lived, in surroundings which reminded them daily of a long and glorious national history—to merge their separate national lives in a single commonwealth of Europe?"[6] This question regarding international government by consent remains unanswered even in the 1980s.

Toynbee found especially intriguing two experiments illustrating the achievement of "integration" on a limited scale. In writing about chances for a more inclusive international government, he observed: "If this discovery is ever made, the laboratory of political experimentation where we may expect to see it materialize will be some body politic like the British Commonwealth of Nations, which has mated the experience of one ancient European national state with the plasticity of a number of 'new countries' overseas; or else it will be some body politic like the Soviet Union, which is attempting to organize a number of non-Western communities into an entirely new kind of polity." Although these are not simple unalloyed instances of government by consent, they provide thought-

5. *Ibid.*, 313n3.
6. *Survey of International Affairs*, 1930, pp. 134, 135.

provoking modern examples of a second way of establishing inter-
state political unity. Toynbee would agree with another historian
that "pure force or pure consent . . . simply [does] not exist on this
planet." Yet the abstractions of conquest and consent are useful in
distinguishing the limits within which government is founded. In
any event, more of the element of consent is present in international communities such as the British Commonwealth than in a
world empire brought about by conquest.[7]

The question then may be posed, are there any rules or helpful
guidelines everywhere applicable to the creation of international
government? What features of a society are essential if a government is to come into being? Writers on international government
and society have grappled with this question especially since World
War II. Again Toynbee never formulated a systematic theory. He
did refer repeatedly to three conditions which in different ways
have facilitated the formation of governments: the economic interdependence of local units; the absence of strong local traditions; and the existence of a measure of community, which sometimes is brought about by the threat of an external enemy. First,
economic ties serve as a basis for subsequent political unification
or for relations out of which political harmony may grow. Thus in
the Balkans, particularly in the early 1930s, "where economic needs
were sufficiently urgent to override political animosity, it was
possible for the 'satisfied' and the 'dissatisfied' states of Central and
South-Eastern Europe to work together in comparative harmony
for the attainment of a definite object. Ancient Greece, following
an economic revolution in the sixth century B.C. under Solon and
Peisistratus, possessed the necessary foundations for political
unity. There was, however, a problem: "The challenge of being
called upon to create a political world-order as the framework for
an economic world-order is bound to confront any society that has
accomplished the economic change from a locally self subsistent
and 'extensive' economy to an 'intensive' and oecumenically interdependent economy." The same challenge has been produced
in Western civilization by the "march of technical progress." Revolutions in trade and communications call for revolutions in politics. Within an earlier international government, the framework
for the Delian League can be found in the impact of "Attic trade

7. Toynbee, *A Study of History*, IV, 320; Crane Brinton, *From Many One* (Cam-
bridge, Mass., 1948), 21.

and seapower."[8] Similarly, the forces released by the Industrial Revolution made possible the emergence of the British Commonwealth, the Soviet Union, and the outstanding experiments in international government, the League of Nations and the United Nations.

The second condition of international government is the absence of intense loyalties to a locality. Sometimes wider government becomes possible only after parochial sentiments have broken down. Napoleon, for example, established French departments not only in the Low Countries but in Germany and Italy as well. This system "did effectively obliterate the pre-existing political landmarks, and thereby . . . cleared the ground for the erection of a united Italy and a united Germany." Centuries earlier, the city-states most loyal to the Delian League were those which had been under the domination of the Achaemenian Empire. Their participation in the league was voluntary and faithful from the beginning. In contrast, the two states which had to be coerced into joining the new intercivic organization were Scyros and Carystus and "neither of them ever lost their independence to the Achaemenian Empire." The same was true of the members who were the first to attempt to secede. Yet the strong and crusading spirit of local units is sometimes crushed by an iron-fisted conqueror.[9]

When local sympathies have never existed, the problem of creating international government is different. The patterns of unity in Greek civilization provide illustrations. Despite the existence of economic foundations for political unity, neither Athens nor Sparta could escape their own parochial traditions and accept a superior political authority. "On the other hand, the new Greek city-states founded on Asiatic soil by Alexander and his successors had no cherished tradition of independence which inhibited them from allowing themselves to be banded together." Their participation in the Achaean and Aetolian leagues is understandable on these grounds. In this one respect, the "parvenu," or the society or political unit without deep-rooted political traditions and experience of its own, is in a better position to join in forming larger political units.[10]

8. *Survey of International Affairs*, 1931, p. 326; Toynbee, *A Study of History*, III, 364n1; *Survey of International Affairs*, 1935, II, 5; Toynbee, *A Study of History*, II, 41.
9. Toynbee, *A Study of History*, VI, 109, II, 41.
10. Arnold J. Toynbee, *Civilization on Trial* (New York, 1948), 120.

The third condition for the creation of international government is international community which, for national government, modern historians call "national self-consciousness." Some
degree of common tradition, loyalties, history, and language must
exist in the world or some part of it before a superior political authority can be successfully established. This was true of the American Republic; it has also been true of other political unions. Toynbee said, for example, that the Scandinavian union formed at
Kalmar in 1397 "had been preceded by tentative experiments in the
direction of an All-Scandinavian union in the course of the fourteenth century."[11]

Since 1815 the tendency has been to shift attention from the substance of international relations, as manifested in foreign policy,
to the forms and institutions of international government. As a result, international peace and order have been seen as depending on
the existence and especially the universality of an international
organization, to which member states' policies have been subordinated. And thus international organization has been viewed as a
practical alternative to foreign policy.
    With the possible exception of views expressed in the idealist
phase in his writing, Toynbee shared few if any of these illusions.
His appraisals of the League of Nations and the United Nations
were formulated largely in terms of foreign policy. The League offers a particularly striking example of the importance of studying
international government in relation to foreign policy. Its decline
was attributed oftentimes by Americans to its lack of universality
and particularly to the defection of the United States. In recent
years, however, writers have focused on the policies of the major
powers within and outside of the League. It is important not to
emphasize some flaw in its organization or the comprehensive-
ness of its membership alone but to concentrate on the divergent
policies of France and England and their opposing conceptions of
the status quo after World War I.[12]
    In the Surveys and elsewhere, Toynbee wrote about and re-
viewed the events of the period from 1919 to 1939, placing primary
emphasis on foreign policy. He analyzed France's policies at the
time of the Ethiopian affair. Why did France not apply sanctions
against Mussolini? One simple answer was that France lacked good

11. Toynbee, A Study of History, II, 175.
12. See Arnold Wolfers, Britain and France Between Two Wars (New York, 1940).

faith and was not firmly enough committed to the principles of the Covenant. Another answer depended upon an evaluation of France's traditional foreign policy. Germany was France's perpetual foe. Here the threat to peace came from the wrong direction. Italy was a possible ally, and as Toynbee wrote in 1935, "while France had recently been drawn towards Italy by the conclusion of the Franco-Italian Pact of the 7th January, she had still more recently been alienated from Great Britain by the signature, on the 18th June, of the Anglo-German Naval Agreement." French foreign policy had two major objectives, security (*sécurité*) defined in uncompromising terms and maintenance of the status quo. These determined its policy within the League of Nations. Therefore, "the essential function of the League, in French eyes, was to mobilize the rest of Europe in support of France in the event of France again being attacked by Germany." Indeed, the French were inclined to think of the League in political rather than ideological terms. It was primarily an extensive alliance which was qualitatively no different from other alliances. Thus Aristide Briand, the French foreign minister, proposed in the autumn of 1929 a European federation, a program stemming from the same fear and anxiety which had prompted earlier French demands for territorial guarantees by the British and Americans. In addition, André Tardieu at the World Disarmament Conference asked for a permanent international police force and international control of aviation; both proposals were seen as singularly appropriate to the threat with which France was confronted.[13]

Some analysts, disputing the validity of national interest as a test of foreign policy, have asserted that France pursued one policy early in the history of the League and then adopted an opposite one in 1936 and 1937. However, Toynbee discussed this question in the language of political realism:

> In 1919 the League had been forced upon the attention of the French as a quasi-religious and wholly fantastic Anglo-American project of much the same order of foolishness as the Tsar Alexander I's Holy Alliance. In 1937 the French were clinging to the Covenant while the British "Governing Class" were showing signs of impatience to banish this piece of Anglo-Saxon bric-a-brac to the lumber-room. The truth was, no doubt, that in the interval the French, without swerving from the pursuit of their own national interests, had come to perceive how

13. *Survey of International Affairs*, 1935, II, 38.

the League might be pressed into the service of these [goals].

Thus both France and England pursued policies within the League based upon national interests. When conflicts between those interests and the League were not successfully adjusted, the League's death knell was sounded. In 1937, Toynbee voiced his conviction that international government was in practice the mere image of the foreign policies of influential states: "For the French the League signified, in the last resort, an 'ideological' facade that lent an air of principle and virtue to the military alliances between France and certain other European states on Germany's opposite flank which had as good reason as France had to dread and resist the process of Germany's resurgence."[14]

In yet another sense, international government can be understood by studying the foreign policies of its members. In the 1920s and 1930s the small nations tended to give more support to the League's collective security policy than did the Great Powers. Toynbee was careful to ascribe this to political reasons: "Morally, the unqualified loyalty to the League which was displayed by the smaller states might have to be discounted by the consideration that, for states of this calibre, the League was the one possible shield and buckler." Whatever the reason, he discovered an important qualitative difference between the loyalties of the "Small Powers" and the Great Powers: not only do the "Small Powers" confine themselves to limited objectives; they had learned from experience that their own security was best safeguarded by the collective action of the League.[15]

Toynbee somehow assumed that the staunchest supporters of collective security within the League were, in both word and deed, the "Small Powers." At the same time, however, he recognized the peculiar status enjoyed by these states. For example, he was quite aware that "Switzerland's permanent neutrality had been confirmed by Article 435 of the Treaty of Versailles, and she had been allowed at the time of admission to membership of the League, to contract out of the obligations imposed upon members by Article 16 to take part in warlike operations." Other small nations which gave nominal support to the League were for one reason or another incapable of supporting effective enforcement action. It is surprising that Toynbee should not have given more attention to the capacity as well as the willingness of nations to support collective

14. *Survey of International Affairs*, 1937, I, 26–27.
15. *Survey of International Affairs*, 1935, II, 491.

action. Salvador de Madariaga in another context distinguished between the producers and the consumers of collective security. One might have thought Toynbee would say more about Great Power responsibilities as contrasted with those of small nations, given his understanding of their motivations in supporting the League.[16]

His silence suggests one of the chief flaws in his view of international government and foreign policy. Despite his realism, moralistic and utopian conceptions crept in, sometimes obscuring the historian's perspective and causing him to ignore the hard facts of foreign policy. In 1935 he deprecated attempts to define Britain's vital interests, insisting that any such limitations under the Covenant would require that the League be " 'reformed' out of all recognition." He was also critical of Austria's acceding to Italy's Ethiopian policy in return for the promise of protection: "From the nakedly Machiavellian point of view . . . it would have been better if Austria had relied on the protection of the League." He assumed that the League would have been willing and able to provide such protection, but that assumption rested on the belief that more powerful nations such as France and England would protect Austria. Toynbee's critics would argue that important issues demand careful scrutiny of foreign policy interests. They can hardly be disposed of through pious incantations about international organization.[17]

It is nonetheless clear that "Great Powers" inevitably occupy unique positions within an international government. In some cases, they have been responsible for the breakdown of superior authority before government was successfully launched. Athens and Sparta effectively destroyed the embryonic political unity within the Hellenic world when "in the critical year 228 B.C., Athens refused to join the Achaean Confederacy and Sparta went to war with it!" As a rule, however, the Great Powers have viewed international organization as a changing field of action in which they could pursue their own national interests. In 1938, realists such as Churchill sensed that Great Britain was not strong enough to ensure its own security. Allies should be sought within the League, they urged, as a way to build up a proponderance of force. Tragically, this counsel was not accepted, "for most of the British

16. *Survey of International Affairs*, 1937, I, 352n1.
17. *Survey of International Affairs*, 1935, II, 458, 89.

statesmen and publicists . . . concurred with one another in presenting 'the Genevan institution' as a new departure which was not part and parcel of the historic tissue of international life."[18] However, in analyzing its possibilities, the clear-eyed observer of international government must begin by appraising its role in the context of power. The nature of international relations and the disparities in the power of its member states ensure that for the foreseeable future the "Great Powers" will dominate an international organization.

There is another sense, however, in which those nations which are not "Great Powers" have seen their influence augmented and strengthened by the existence of an international government. England and the Western European countries count for little today in the United Nations, on the basis of pure power potential. However, "in an even semi-parliamentary international forum, the political experience, maturity, and moderation of countries like these will weigh heavily in the balance alongside of the grosser weight of Brennus' sword." Experienced diplomats from Britain and various European states have played a decisive role in the U.N. A Norwegian, a Swede, and an Austrian have been among its first secretaries-general. Also the influence of Third World nations has expanded, with the rise of groupings such as the Committee of 77. Nevertheless, the special position of the Great Powers was for a long time reflected in the appointment of officials to the Secretariat of the League of Nations. The staff was at first chosen on grounds of competence. Then it became apparent that permanent officials were wielding considerable influence: "The result was a virtual competition between the Powers to secure the highest posts for their own nominees, and the nomination of diplomatic candidates when vacancies occurred." Not only did appointments come under Great Power domination, but the appointees were important diplomatic figures who saw themselves as ambassadors for their native country instead of as international civil servants. World leaders such as Salvador de Madariaga and Edvard Hambro expressed mounting concern, but the influence of the Great Powers was inescapably the outgrowth of political forces that spread across the League's operations.[19]

By far the most significant fact about the Great Powers is their

18. Toynbee, *A Study of History*, III, 341; *Survey of International Affairs*, 1937, II, 24–25.

19. Toynbee, *Civilization on Trial*, 137; *Survey of International Affairs*, 1928, p. 137.

influence upon sanctions: no effective enforcement action can be taken by international government against the will of a Great Power. The Council of the League of Nations, in fact, could be effectively blocked by the abstention of one Great Power. There were permanent seats on the Council for the five powers which had presided at the Paris Peace Conference. The Convenant also provided that permanent seats would be granted to the other surviving Great Powers, Germany and Russia. Toynbee issued a criticism: "It is a very great evil that statesmen should set their hand to obligations which they cannot . . . carry out. . . . It tends to breed contempt for all international obligations, just as in the United States the passage of laws which cannot be enforced breeds contempt for all law."[20] Yet another example of a constitutional provision for the role of the Great Powers in international government is the inclusion of the veto in the Charter of the United Nations.

In Western civilization, more specifically, two broad forms of supracivic or supranational government have emerged, the federal and the unitary. The first combines advantages of variety and devolution with the possibility of unified action where this is required. The United States is perhaps the most spectacular example, but Toynbee pointed to national experiments with a federal form of government such as "the United States of Brazil, the Republic of Mexico, the Chinese Republic, the nascent polities of India and Pakistan." He also discovered that in nature and membership "the Swiss Confederation and the United Netherlands are counterparts of the Aetolian and Achaean Confederacies." The Western experiment with federalism and its Hellenic counterparts represent a type of political architecture in which great diversity is maintained in the parts which make up the whole. In the case of Switzerland, city-states and cantons coexisted; in the Netherlands, there were city-states, clusters of city-states, and provinces. And these diverse units enjoyed some degree of autonomy within a federal system.[21]

In contrast, the unitary form has characterized the organization of the majority of states. Toynbee used Great Britain, France, and Italy as principal examples to present questions about international government through dealing with the types of political organization instituted by modern nation-states. On the interna-

20. *Survey of International Affairs*, 1926, p. 20; *Survey of International Affairs*, 1931, p. 506.
    21. Toynbee, *Civilization on Trial*, 116; Toynbee, *A Study of History*, IV, 316.

tional level, the only type of organization established by consent is the confederation. Toynbee cited the United Nations as an example, adding that it represents the maximum cooperation now possible between East and West. Only world empires provide illustrations of the unitary form and in every case thus far, they have been achieved through force and conquest.

Toynbee singled out for more systematic analysis three major attempts to form more comprehensive international governments in modern times: the Holy Alliance, the League of Nations, and the United Nations. He of course pointed to their forerunners, one of which was in the Sinic civilization: "In 681 B.C. the pygmy states in the heart of the Sinic World had organized themselves into a Central Confederacy under the presidency of the eastern Great Power, Ts'i, with the object of opposing a collective resistance to the pressure of the preponderant and aggressive southern Great Power, Ch'u." The struggle between them only ended when they temporarily assumed the joint presidency. This was accomplished at a memorable conference in 546 B.C., only five years after the birth of Confucius in the neighboring state of Lu.[22]

Greek history provides notable experiments, the Delian League in the sixth and fifth centuries B.C. and the Achaean and Aetolian leagues in the third century B.C. After freeing themselves from Persian domination through the defeat of Xerxes in 479 B.C., the Greek victors founded in 478 B.C. the Delian League. It was modeled on the Persian pattern with which the Greeks had become familiar and rested on the dominant force of Athens. It was centralized to the degree that members had to make financial contributions, which were transmitted to the federal treasury at Delos. The limited central powers of the league could be maintained because of the residual effects of Persian control. This experiment, however, became solely an instrument for Athenian policy, and by 431 B.C. its decline was complete.

The Achaean and Aetolian leagues were undermined by the negative character of Athens' role and Sparta's undependable contributions. The inability of the Greek city-states to create some lasting form of organization was an invitation to the Roman Empire to accomplish by force what the Greeks had failed to achieve by consent.

The first modern experiment in international government was the Holy Alliance and the Concert of Europe. An informal system

22. Toynbee, *A Study of History*, VI, 292, 293.

grew out of the peace treaties at the time of the Congress of Vienna, which helped to create the rudiments of a true international system. After previous wars, plans for international government had been advanced, but the first launching of an actual organization did not occur until the end of the Napoleonic Wars. Toynbee observed: "The two earlier general wars in the modern Western World had given birth to projects which had remained entirely academic. The Abbé de St. Pierre's project had been the aftermath of the General War of 1672–1713, and Sully's project the aftermath of the warfare resulting from a widespread resistance to the ambitions of Philip II."[23]

One reason that the Holy Alliance came into being was the prevailing influence of a common code of manners, which Toynbee described as "a generally recognised standard of honour in the conduct of international transactions and the observance of international undertakings; and though this standard might not be very high, a Great Power could not depart from it, such as it was, without disagreeably 'losing face.' The Great Powers were bound together by a certain solidarity of feeling." Although Toynbee used *Holy Alliance* as the term for the cooperation of the Great Powers after the Napoleonic Wars, it actually refers to a treaty (September 26, 1815) proposed by Czar Alexander I. The signatories, all European rulers except the prince regent of England, the pope, and the sultan, declared that their sole guide in their political relations would be Christian principles.[24]

There was, however, a rudimentary international government which existed between 1815 and 1822. This was based on the Quadruple Alliance among Austria, England, Prussia, and Russia (November 20, 1815), and in 1818, France was admitted. Because of this working agreement, several congresses met and committees were created to deal with international issues. After this alliance ended at the Congress of Verona in 1822, there was established the Concert of Europe, a system of informal cooperation. Toynbee once called this "a euphemism for an exclusive cabal of the European Great Powers." Although the League of Nations as an effective body lasted less than eighteen years, the Concert of Europe was far more successful: "When 'the Holy Alliance' had collapsed within the first decade following the close of the Revolutionary and Napoleonic Wars, the European heart and danger-

23. Toynbee, *A Study of History,* II, 2n1.
24. *Survey of International Affairs,* 1937, I, 6–7.

zone of the Western World had still been kept in some kind of peace and order for the next ninety years by a certain measure of co-operation between the European Great Powers; and this 'Concert' had achieved an imperfect yet by no means unsubstantial success in virtue, not of any formal constitution, but of a practical community of interest and outlook." Toynbee's emphasis upon the realistic features of the Concert of Europe was a clear sign that his idealist phase had ended.[25] This collective system was essentially international government by the Great Powers and its success resided in their working relations and a certain measure of international order and peace.

Toynbee's conception of the League of Nations was from the outset fairly explicit and often idealistic. In 1930 he explained: "The League of Nations represented an attempt to reconcile peace with growth, security with elasticity, treaty law with international equity." The League was an introduction of "new methods of reason, debate and conciliation" onto the international scene. It took the place of traditional secret diplomacy which "was morally discredited and officially excommunicated, so that its secret supporters always had to eat their words." It was an alternative to power politics, and having accepted its premises, no state could return to the "old dispensation." Indeed "to suggest to states [which were] members of the League a course which was an alternative to the application of the Covenant, was really to suggest that they should break their pledge to act as was prescribed in the Covenant." Only with the breakdown of the League did states return to power politics. The aim of the new organization was the "pacific, even though belated, abolition of War through a free agreement and voluntary co-operation between all the fully self-governing states in the contemporary world." By "the 30th June, 1930, it looked as though the ultimate triumph of the League, and of what the League stood for, was assured."[26]

Toynbee qualified his singularly unpolitical if not utopian conception of the League only occasionally during this early period. He appreciated the need for Great Power unanimity on questions of enforcement: "The executive organ of the League could not be

25. Survey of International Affairs, 1935, II, 79; Survey of International Affairs, 1937, I, 6.

26. Survey of International Affairs, 1930, pp. 10, 7; Survey of International Affairs, 1935, II, 281; Survey of International Affairs, 1937, II, 132; Toynbee, A Study of History, IV, 153; Survey of International Affairs, 1930, p. 7.

sure of being able to carry out its decisions if one or more Great Powers . . . offered active opposition."[27]

Then competition developed as various nations sought to gain greater power and prestige within the framework of the League. The Great Powers achieved a preponderance of representation in the Secretariat. The "Intermediate Powers," demanding recognition of their higher standing over the rank and file of "Small Powers," claimed one of the permanent seats on the Council. Regional arrangements were worked out to supplement the deficiencies in the security provisions of the Covenant: "The eventual conclusion of the Locarno Pact in October 1925 offered a practical solution to concrete difficulties, creating a sense of security where it was most urgently needed, and at the same time keeping the door open for measures of wider application to be taken at a later date." Positions such as these made concessions to the "old diplomacy" and its time-honored devices.[28]

Members viewed the operation of the League of Nations from a variety of perspectives. In German eyes, the League was but one more way to maintain an unjust peace settlement imposed by the victors on the vanquished states following World War I. In this view the Convenant was "a kind of device for roping in people like the Scandinavians, the Dutch and the Swiss who had kept out of international affairs during previous centuries and had gone in for neutrality to keep the peace settlement as the French and British wanted it kept. It is a device . . . for enlisting as many people against any attempt at revision, either violent or peaceful, on the part of the formerly defeated states at whose expense the settlement was made." At the opposite pole was the American view, as expressed by President Woodrow Wilson. "For President Wilson, and for Wilsonians in Europe and overseas, the League is an association of democratic, unaggressive states organised for the purpose of establishing a reign of law and order in the international sphere of social relationships which was formerly so anarchic. The League is an attempt to introduce into international relations a law and order and a reasonable measure of justice such as has already been achieved to some degree in the national social life of the more advanced countries of the world to-day."[29]

27. *Survey of International Affairs*, 1926, p. 20.
28. *Survey of International Affairs*, 1925, II, 79.
29. Royal Institute of International Affairs, *The Future of the League of Nations: The Record of a Series of Discussions Held at Chatham House* (New York, 1936), 8.

These varied conceptions, which were politically and not constitutionally based, resulted in the differing emphasis given to particular aspects of the Covenant. To the democratic powers, stability was so important that peaceful change was underestimated. The defeated powers, led by the disarmed Great Power, Germany, and including Italy, Austria, Hungary, and Bulgaria, saw the League increasingly become an instrument of the status quo and of repression. In the opposite camp, a heavily armed Great Power, France, stood at the head of a number of successor states, among which were Poland, Czechoslovakia, Yugoslavia, and Rumania. For them, the League was an instrument of international law and order.[30]

The Soviet attitude in its earliest manifestations was somewhat different. As Toynbee saw it, "They regarded the League as a net treacherously spread to draw them back into a European city of destruction out of which they had just made good their escape at the cost of being seared by the flames of the apocalyptic conflagration." At the same time, the Bolsheviks perceived the League as a conspiracy by the victors in World War I who happened to be the surviving pillars of capitalism. In this double sense the League was a sinister construction from birth, and Soviet fears were hardly relieved when the Germans capitulated by applying for membership after the signing of the Locarno Pact.[31]

This was the attitude of the Soviet government in January, 1920, when the principal threat to its security appeared to be the Allied powers who had joined together in establishing the League of Nations. By 1933, however, the threat was no longer France or England but Japan and Germany, which gave notice of their intention to withdraw from the League. Immediately the Soviet position was reversed—the powers hostile to the Soviet Union were now outside of the League and those nations toward which the Soviets were gravitating, drawn by the common fear of Germany, were the bulwarks of the collective system within the League. "Accordingly, it is not surprising to find that, in the course of the year 1933, the public references to the League, in the mouths of prominent Soviet Statesmen, reveal a profound change of outlook."[32]

Finally, France's viewpoint with regard to the League was based on concern for its national interest. For Frenchmen, more than for Englishmen, the League was principally a large-scale multiple alliance which would be strengthened as soon as it created military

30. *Survey of International Affairs*, 1932, p. 186.
31. *Survey of International Affairs*, 1934, p. 388.
32. *Ibid.*, 39.

power and freed itself from ideological assumptions. The League was the chief guarantor of the sanctity of treaties and of the principles of international law. This viewpoint differs in only one respect from the British attitude. British statesmen approved the role of international law, but they also displayed "a willingness to make effective arrangements for peaceful changes in the existing state of the law or in the existing state of affairs." If the British view had prevailed, the League of Nations would have been considered as an instrument both of law and of peaceful change.[33]

Another question which has preoccupied all students of international relations who have written on international government concerns the reasons for the failure of the League. Toynbee offered three major reasons for its decline, although he never analyzed them fully or offered explanatory principles. The simplest explanation was that the League was "honoured by the lips of statesmen whose hearts were very far from being moved to serve the League in deed and in truth by modifying any of their national policies or renouncing any of their national assets." If an institution could have lived on verbal tributes, the League of Nations would have survived for many years.[34]

The second reason was the creation of a "counter-Covenant" in the form of an anti-Comintern pact, which "was designed to insure aggressors against defeat by the 'sanctions' which the Covenant was intended to impose." This pact, one analyst explained, was designed to make the world safe for aggression. This challenge, although merely negative in character, was based on strength and purposes which sought the destruction of the existing international order. It represented the first great reaction against Western civilization, and that civilization was unable to deal with it solely by means of the League.[35]

The third reason for the breakdown of the League was the conflict between foreign policies, particularly of France and England. And a final reason, which is implicit in much of Toynbee's analysis but which he did not emphasize to the same degree as did American writers, was the great weakening of the League by the absence of the United States.

Toynbee regarded the United Nations as the third experiment in international government. In the Western world, two view-

33. *Survey of International Affairs*, 1930, p. 13; Royal Institute, *The Future of the League of Nations*, 14.
34. *Survey of International Affairs*, 1933, p. 224.
35. *Survey of International Affairs*, 1937, I, 46.

points have predominated in discussions of the U.N. since 1945. For idealist writers, the United Nations, a new institution separate from any of the traditional forms of conducting international relations, has ushered in a brave new era when nations would abandon power politics. The other looks on the United Nations as providing a framework within which nations through give and take are able to work out their destinies. It is fair to ask which of these views Toynbee held.

In the years following World War II, Toynbee gravitated more and more toward the second philosophy, as is seen in what was perhaps his most conclusive statement on the matter: "The United Nations organization may fairly be described as a political machine for putting into effect the maximum possible amount of cooperation between the United States and the Soviet Union—the two great powers who would be the principal antagonists in the final round of naked power politics." Some postwar writers insisted that the United Nations fell short of a genuine world government, and only for this reason was there an absence of law and order. If the people of the world would meet in constitutional convention, they argued, a real world legislature could be established, thus eliminating power politics once and for all. I find little support for this kind of utopianism in Toynbee's thinking. In his view, effective government must be based upon a community of interests and beliefs, and under the present pattern of international politics a loose confederacy has been the most that East and West have been willing to accept. If Toynbee had lived to observe the functioning of the United Nations in the late 1970s and 1980s, he would surely have seen this outlook confirmed.[36]

Nevertheless, one of the more hopeful features of contemporary international organization has been the activities of the U.N. Specialized Agencies. Their efforts over time may create a network of social and economic ties which may ultimately contribute to a greater measure of community. As Toynbee viewed their work: "The economic and technical activities of the United Nations, though the least conspicuous, are not the least important. Regional organizations may sometimes be necessary and useful but success for the U. N. is the goal towards which we ought still to strive with all our might." Thus Toynbee's latter-day views on the United Nations corresponded with those of realist defenders of international organization. Because their expectations were less ex-

36. Toynbee, *Civilization on Trial*, 135.

travagant, they were able to defend its somewhat more modest record.[37]

If we turn to international law, the tendency in Western society has been either to claim too much for it or, alternatively, to deny its very existence. Some jurists have equated international with municipal law and assigned it the qualities of a complete legal system. In his more utopian moments, Toynbee flirted with this view, as we have noted, when he said that "this supreme British interest [in law and order] was also the supreme interest of the whole World." Some writers argued that a foreign policy could be an international law policy. For example, it was said that "the maintenance of the reign of law in international relations, of which the Covenant was the instrument, was the supreme interest of the British Empire." The opposing view was that international law was nothing more than international morality—a collection of vague and amorphous sentiments and clichés which could not be enforced in practice. Sometimes Toynbee seemed to range himself alongside the moralists rather than the legalists. Thus he proclaimed that "the resort to the use of poison gas on Italy's part [in Ethiopia] was a sensationally shocking piece of wickedness."[38] His outrage led him to condemn national behavior as he would an individual's wickedness.

Nevertheless, in the long sweep of history something corresponding to international law has emerged whenever central authority has broken down. That is to say, international law has in effect grown up on the ruins of empire. It is as though there were a revulsion against the absence of law, and societies which have freed themselves from one political authority refuse to dispense with all forms of interunit law. Often this law is imposed by the threat of force and coercion. Writing of the ancient Greek world, Toynbee explained:

> This Athenian attempt to establish a Pan-Hellenic common law and a Pan-Hellenic jurisdiction on an Athenian basis would have been impossible if the Athenians had not possessed, and employed, the means of coercion; this coercion was only thinly veiled by the network of treaties, between Athens and her associates in the Delian League, on which the process of judicial centralization was formerly grounded; and this expedient of

37. *Ibid.*, 115.
38. *Survey of International Affairs*, 1935, II, 456.

conjuring into existence an oecumenical system of law-and-order by compelling the city-states to enter into a network of treaties, wholesale, was demonstrably borrowed by the Athenians from their Achaemenian predecessors in the dominion over the Asiatic Greeks.[39]

However, Toynbee discovered other examples, such as the League of Nations and the United Nations, in which the element of consent was given priority. Whether through coercion or consent, the groups involved discovered that it was in their interest to fashion a body of rules and laws on which they could depend. Such groups included the traders of Athens, the church in the Middle Ages, royalty in the eighteenth and nineteenth centuries, and business and commercial people in the nineteenth and twentieth centuries.

What relation, then, do the principles of foreign policy bear to the successful application in practice of international law? In the first place, international law and international agreements will be observed only if they are in the national interest. Toynbee was keenly aware in the 1930s that a policy of international law was in harmony with England's maintaining its postwar position. At the same time he was quick to point out that such a policy was also "in the true interest of the whole of Mankind." He took special pains to acknowledge: "Yet the fact that it was in harmony with British interests was no proof that it was not also a correct rendering of the verdict of history." Germany in particular, in its weakened and demilitarized state, should have recognized that its interests were no less in harmony with the practice of international law. Toynbee announced: "This was the sensible policy for Germany, even on the shortest and narrowest view of her national interest in the circumstances, since she had no prospect of being able to repudiate the treaty and no expectation that within the framework of the treaty, the utmost ingenuity of her experts would find means of restoring her to the rank of a first-class naval and military power."[40]

In the same way, Toynbee construed Japanese foreign policy as violating not only the Covenant and the Pact of Paris but Japanese interests as well. In 1931 one neutral observer who commented upon Toynbee's essay on collective security was sharply critical of

39. Toynbee, A Study of History, IV, 213.
40. Survey of International Affairs, 1935, II, 46, 17; Survey of International Affairs, 1929, pp. 60–61.

his tendency to overlook the hard facts of political situations such
as the Manchurian affair: "Of course Japan signed the Covenant,
the Pact. . . . But even if she knew in her heart that in vital matters
she would never defer to the League, what actually could she have
done in 1919 and after? To my mind there *never* was a question of
her following League standards in Manchuria. The standards she
has followed are, I suggest, more or less comparable to ours [Brit-
ish] at the heyday of our imperial days at the beginning of the century." For Toynbee, however, the Japanese in Manchuria were bra-
zenly disregarding law and order, and their actions could not be
interpreted as anything other than a grave and unprecedented
crime. He also took exception to the theory which compared British and Italian imperialism: "The Italian thesis that 'what was
lawful for my neighbour yesterday is lawful for me today' was assuredly untenable."[41]

French foreign policy, with its accent on the status quo and on
the sanctity of treaties, came closest to being an international law
policy. France sought to guarantee not only that part of the peace
settlement directly affecting its own territory but also those treaties pertaining to Eastern Europe: "In itself, this doctrine was neither bad morals not bad politics." The French were convinced that
the American and British refusal to undertake commitments was
morally wrong and politically shortsighted. Toynbee answered this
criticism: "French consciences were more eloquently prompted
than British or American . . . by manifest considerations of national self-interest, since the post-war situation of France—with
Germany still her immediate neighbour on the Continent—was
appreciably nearer to the situation of Poland or Czechoslovakia
than were the situations of the English Speaking Powers."[42]

For international law to be effective, it must be based on political realities. Nations accept international commitments principally because they thereby improve the prospects of their security.
Portugal, for example, a colonial power with an interest in preserving the status quo, based its policy in Europe and Africa not on
a particular set of moral virtues but rather on its own political position. Toynbee explained in a sentence the connection between
cause and effect in Portugal's foreign policy: "In general, they set
store by the vindication of principles of law and order in international affairs as against *Faustrecht* and *Machtpolitik*; and in par-

41. Quoted in *Survey of International Affairs*, 1931, p. 508; *Survey of International Affairs*, 1935, II, 17.
42. *Survey of International Affairs*, 1932, p. 309.

ticular they were anxious to see it established that the title-deeds to colonial possessions should be respected even when the holder was in no position to defend his titles by force."[43]

China's respect for its obligations under the Covenant and the Pact of Paris at the time of the invasion of Manchuria was dictated in part by its aim to enlist the sympathy of neutral nations and of "world public opinion." If China breached any treaties, its legal position would be equated with that of Japan. The influence of political factors on legal commitments can also be seen in the objective situation of those nations which bound themselves to observe the optional clause of the Permanent Court of International Justice. Of the sixteen nations which initially recognized the Court's jurisdiction as compulsory, only one was a Great Power. That was Germany, and its position was then in question. The other states were Abyssinia, Austria, Belgium, Bulgaria, Denmark, Estonia, Finland, Haiti, the Netherlands, Norway, Portugal, Spain, Sweden, Switzerland, and Uruguay. Within the British Commonwealth, the policies of member states likewise reflected particular interests. Australia and New Zealand asked that reservations be made to the Court's jurisdiction on disputes over domestic issues such as immigration. The Irish Free State asked for ratification without any reservations at all, hoping thus to take away from the Judicial Committee of the Privy Council matters which by treaty had been placed under British jurisdiction. A broader review of the positions states have taken on concrete legal issues would doubtless substantiate still further the primacy of political considerations in such decisions.[44]

In any realistic assessment of international law, one has to take account not only of domestic jurisdiction but also of three major limitations imposed, according to Toynbee, by reservations, local interpretation, and political disputes. The first was manifested when England was considering the optional clause of the Permanent Court of International Justice. In 1924, Toynbee's opinion was that the Labour government then in power would be willing to sign but would insist upon at least one reservation: "They would probably feel obliged to make a reservation in order to ensure that the British fleet should remain subject to British maritime law if it should be called upon to take action in accordance with the terms of the Geneva Protocol." For other nations, similar matters of suf-

43. *Survey of International Affairs*, 1937, II, 207.
44. *Survey of International Affairs*, 1931, p. 423; *Survey of International Affairs*, 1929, pp. 72, 75–76.

ficiently vital interest could not be entrusted to judicial determination.[45]

The second limitation not only affected the extent of judicial action but raised the fundamental question whether England should in any way commit itself by signing the optional clause. International law was interpreted and precedents were established by local and national courts, or at least by jurists of a particular nationality and background. In certain cases, this could conceivably be disadvantageous: "It was also frequently pointed out that there were two schools of thought in regard to international law—an Anglo-American and a Continental School—and since the majority of Judges who composed the Court had been trained in the Continental School, the fear was expressed that there might be cases in which the Court's decision would run counter to British ideas of justice." On questions of maritime law, this conflict existed not between English and Continental courts but, more significantly, between members of the British Commonwealth.[46] In the 1940s and again in the 1980s, American political leaders were to voice a similar concern. This reached a crucial point in the decision of the Reagan administration to deny jurisdiction to the International Court of Justice in Central American matters involving the U.S. for a given time period.

The third limitation on international law is the distinction nations have drawn between political and justiciable disputes. The former have generally been withheld from adjudication on the grounds that strategic and vital interests are at stake. On September 26, 1928, the Assembly of the League of Nations passed and approved the General Act for the Pacific Settlement of International Disputes, one of the purposes of which was to facilitate the implementation of the Pact of Paris. In Toynbee's opinion, it was wise to recognize that all states, or at least a majority of them, were not yet prepared to accept general legal obligations without qualifications. They would be unwilling "in particular, to bind themselves, in the last resort, to submit disputes of a political nature to arbitration." It was stipulated that nations might accede to the General Act, or to Chapters I, II, and IV, or to Chapters I and IV. These dealt primarily with conciliation, arbitration, and reservations, whereas Chapter III set forth provisions regarding justiciable disputes.[47]

45. *Survey of International Affairs*, 1929, p. 73.
46. *Ibid.*, 74.
47. *Survey of International Affairs*, 1931, p. 247.

Toynbee drew his examples of the role of international law as practiced from the international law of peace and the international law of war. The law of peace evolved in response to the interests of people even in the absence of international legislatures and courts. The "Law of Rhodes," which sought to normalize trade coming into this famous island in the Aegean, was one example. Laws of "jettison" and "fair divide" regulated the losses which merchants suffered if some part of their cargo was thrown overboard because of limited shipping space. The law of peace provided specific rules of commerce. In Greece in the fifth century B.C., as archaeological discoveries have established, bilateral agreements were signed safeguarding the person and property of merchants in alien cities. Oeanthea and Chaleum, two city-states on the western shore of the Crisaean Gulf in northwestern continental Greece, made such an agreement. They represented a backward colonial area in Hellenic society, and so the practice of similar negotiations must have been widespread: "The type of treaty of which this surviving treaty between Oeanthea and Chaleum may be taken as a late and unimportant example, is a bilateral agreement between two city-states for the enactment between them, *ad hoc*, of a rudimentary code of international law to govern their economic relations." These arrangements were, however, limited to local "Riverain Powers" and accounted for only a fraction of the shipping in the area. Moreover, such trade was only a small part of total Hellenic trade. The great deficiency in this type of law was its lack of universality, according to Toynbee.[48]

It is surprising that Toynbee should have had so little to say about Roman law. He refers to it only in passing or by way of more general illustrations. Most of his examples, though, establish the point that Roman law was also subordinated to political considerations. The episode which intrigued him was the deportation of Polybius and some fellow Achaeans to Rome because, it was alleged, they had been hostile to the Roman cause during the Third Macedonian War. When the deportees arrived in Rome, the Senate protested that it should not be expected to pass judgment on the action of citizens of other states already tried by their own governments. The Achaean government promptly dispatched an envoy to point out that the Romans should either try the deportees or send them home for trial there. The Roman Senate, unwilling for political reasons to permit Polybius to return, used the pretext of an in-

48. Toynbee, *A Study of History*, IV, 209–10.

terstate juridical irregularity to justify its holding the deportees. That the Roman appeal should have been made at all suggests that even universal Roman law was decentralized in practice.[49]

The vast body of rules and principles of the international law of peace, developed in the nineteenth and twentieth centuries, seldom gained popular recognition but in practice was widely adhered to. It included extradition treaties, maritime law, claims and rights of aliens, copyrights, patents, migratory birds, and sponges. International agreements sometimes are negotiated by states on issues of immigration, which is generally considered a primarily domestic concern. By the Immigration Acts of 1921 and 1924, the United States closed its coastal frontiers to the free entry of alien peoples. An exception was the immigration across land frontiers of "native-born inhabitants of the adjoining American countries." However, a European or an Asiatic attempting to enter the United States through Canada or Mexico, without having a place in the annual quota assigned to his country, was excluded. The United States Bureau of Immigration adopted the British Admiralty's doctrine of "continuous voyage."[50]

Toynbee also found a significant collection of rules of warfare given at least nominal recognition in most civilizations. Their violation was the exception occasioning comment by modern historians. The ancient Sinhalese society in Ceylon, which was the cradle of Hindu civilization, broke down when alien mercenaries from southern India deliberately cut the irrigation canals, breaching the bonds which supported the system. A sharp distinction was drawn in warfare between civilians and combatants in Hellenic civilization. In a conference at Malis just prior to the "Second Romano-Macedonian War," charges were brought against King Philip V of Macedon by the Romans' Greek allies fighting under the banners of the Aetolian League. They "complained that Philip was neither making peace sincerely . . . nor in the habit of making war honourably when war was the order of the day." The method of warfare in which towns and property were burned and pillaged was in direct opposition to the practice of sovereigns from Alexander the Great to Pyrrhus. Toynbee said: "To destroy the objects of contention in the war while leaving the war itself in existence was the act of a madman."[51]

The high point in the observance of the international law of war

49. Toynbee, *A Study of History*, III, 315n1.
50. Toynbee, *A Study of History*, I, 72n1.
51. Toynbee, *A Study of History*, IV, 147n1.

came in the eighteenth century: "The punctiliousness of . . . eighteenth-century soldiers towards one another was matched by the
consideration which they usually displayed towards the civilian
population, and by the care which they usually took to avoid inflicting serious injury upon the permanent capital equipment of
social life in the war-zone." Military leaders were moved to genuine indignation at flagrant breaches of the rules of warfare such
as the destruction of the Palatinate by Louis XIV in 1674 and 1688
and the atrocities at Neumarkt and at Cüstrin in 1758 for which
the Russian army was responsible. The French action produced a
moral shock throughout Europe, but there was a tendency to view
the Russians' lapse into barbarism as the acts of a primitive group
only recently accepted in polite society. In another instance of observance of general rules of warfare, Napoleon reportedly executed
some of his own soldiers who broke into private homes in Egypt.[52]

The clear lines of demarcation between war and peace, so painfully worked out over centuries, were obliterated in the twentieth
century. The Western world reverted from the temper of its Vol-
tairean epoch: for political religions, the strategy and the stakes of
war became total. In 1935, both Italy and Abyssinia were guilty of
violations of laws of land warfare. Individual Abyssinian soldiers
made use of dumdum ammunition, although the practice was
surely less widespread with them than with the army bringing civilization to a barbarous people. Dutch Red Cross units treated
hundreds of Abyssinians who were victims of unrestricted warfare. This trend reached its culmination in World War II, and
Toynbee held no illusions about the influence of international law
if World War III were to break out.

One of the sources of profound misunderstanding throughout
Western thinking on international law stems from popular assumptions that treaties are merely glorified business agreements.
Nations are sometimes classified as those who display "good faith"
and can be depended upon to fulfill their international commitments and those who are the traditional lawbreakers. Toynbee
quoted from a speech by Ramsay MacDonald in the House of
Commons on April 13, 1933, illustrating this viewpoint: "It is no
use talking about disarming by agreement, it is no use talking about
pacts, it is no use talking about co-operation for peace unless you
have had some experience which justifies you in accepting the word

52. *Ibid.*, 147; Toynbee, *Civilization on Trial*, 83.

of those with whom you are to co-operate." Other observers have maintained that some nations adhere to the dictum *pacta sunt servanda* ("treaties ought to be observed") while there are those which are incapable of the slightest measure of "good faith" in their relations.[53]

This moralistic conception of international law has sometimes been invoked to regulate and influence particular aspects of international affairs but it cannot deal with important political issues. The assumption here is that nations observe treaties out of friendship for their allies or out of gratitude. Yet history is crowded with examples in which just the opposite has been true. Roman intervention liberated Capua from Samnite domination, but then Capua opened its territory to Hannibal's troops on the eve of the Battle of Cannae, when the security of Rome was hanging in the balance. The Samnites, on the other hand, who had been conquered by Rome, remained loyal to Rome with the exception of one canton.[54]

Another less commonly understood viewpoint regarding treaties postulates that nations keep their agreements only when it is in their interest to do so. Common interests and enemies provide the bonds which prevent treaties from breaking asunder: "The history of international relations showed that there was no cement of friendship so efficacious as a common object of hostility." One striking example was the history of the Little Entente. In the early 1930s, evidence appeared that the alliance of Czechoslovakia, Rumania, and Yugoslavia was beginning to crumble. Then in 1933, with the Nazi ascent to power in Germany, the three parties became aware that "with the great new factor of uncertainty . . . it would be more than ever unwise . . . to leave open any rift in their own solidarity." The real test of the durability of treaties is functional, whether the circumstances in which they have been established provide a firm basis for their continued existence. The test is a political, sociological, and psychological one—treaty observance is not exclusively a moral issue.[55]

Indeed, when the common aims and interests upon which treaties are based disappear, it is unlikely that they will continue to be observed. International law recognizes this in its doctrine of *rebus sic stantibus* ("circumstances change obligations"). Wartime alliances break up when the enemy is defeated. The Triple Entente, eventually a worldwide association, had during World War I the sole

53. *Survey of International Affairs*, 1933, p. 169.
54. Toynbee, *A Study of History*, II, 19.
55. *Survey of International Affairs*, 1933, pp. 178, 198.

objective of meeting the military threat of Germany: "It served this purpose in the War; but even before the War had ended in the overthrow of Germany the fabric of the anti-German coalition, including the European nucleus, had begun to dissolve." Shifts in loyalties within the Little Entente appeared as early as 1926, and it was inevitable that each member "should enter into fresh relations with neighbouring states in accordance with its own interests." France's relations with Poland and the Little Entente were weakened not because of the evil nature of any of the partners but because "France was no more natural a partner for Poland and the Little Entente countries than Italy was for Austria and Hungary."[56]

A more specialized question remains—that of accounting for treaty violations. In a very real sense, all treaties are subject to a process of legal misinterpretation. Toynbee found that the French had a kind of genius for whittling down their legal commitments and concluded: "It is hardly necessary to enter into the controversy . . . whether these differences of interpretation arose out of genuine misinterpretation or whether France was in fact making a new claim." Although he had in mind the special case of France's demand for replacement tonnage in the naval dispute with Italy, one can safely say that his conception of French policy and of foreign policy in general was that international obligations which conflict with the national interest will be set aside.[57] American negotiations with the Soviet Union in the postwar era point to a similar trend in Soviet observance of treaties.

From a different perspective, an important factor in limiting the tendency of states to violate their obligations has been the balance of power. As we have seen, the play of forces in any system of independent states is strongest at the center of that system, and there are pressures not to violate the independence of states within it. "While the Powers of modern Europe were exhausting their strength in preventing one another from acquiring some single city or province, a Russia or a United States was able to extend its domains, unhindered and almost unnoticed, across the whole breadth of a continent." Where the balance of power can restrain shifts in the status quo, treaty observance is stimulated and enhanced. International law, therefore, depends on the balance of power.[58]

Frequently, domestic conditions are responsible for a nation's

56. *Survey of International Affairs*, 1920–23, p. 58; *Survey of International Affairs*, 1926, p. 147; *Survey of International Affairs*, 1934, p. 341.
57. *Survey of International Affairs*, 1931, p. 273.
58. *Survey of International Affairs*, 1930, p. 134.

violation of its international agreements. Germany's actions in 1937 were based at least partly upon the German leaders' observation that "the domestic situation on the eve of another winter was felt to demand some gesture which would reassure the German people that their sacrifices were making their country strong enough to impose her will upon other nations." Italy's aggressive actions had similar roots.[59]

In the final analysis, Toynbee explained, "no state could claim to be guiltless in the matter of treaty-breaking." There were merely differences in degree, important as they might be, between French occupation policy, "the entry of German troops into a portion of German territory without taking a single life or inflicting any material damage upon another country," and Italian and Japanese aggression. Toynbee said: "The Japanese apologia for the military occupation of Manchuria as a necessary and therefore legitimate act of self-defense against attempted violations of Japanese treaty-rights was in fact more convincing than the similar French apologia for the military occupation of the Ruhr." The alleged German violations to which the French pointed were merely passive, such as nonpayment of debts; the Chinese, however, were reportedly making "a deliberate assault upon Japanese treaty-rights." Viewed in this light, treaty violation becomes a far more complex issue. Violations of agreements—no less open to question if all nations are guilty—must be interpreted within a political context. Treaty violation is a manifestation of contemporary international politics rather than a reaction against it.[60]

What is the character of those treaties and political settlements which have proved most durable? Toynbee nowhere analyzed this question in a single treatise on international law or diplomacy. However, he formulated his views on the approach to diplomatic negotiations in rather terse and unequivocal terms: "The vast issues which the war has opened up have all to be disposed of summarily and simultaneously in a peace settlement, instead of being grappled with one by one and being settled in the fullness of Time."[61] From the vantage point of the 1980s, a great historian could hardly have offered wiser counsel to a civilization whose major representatives, balancing precariously on the edge of universal destruction, seem oblivious to the immense risk of frag-

59. *Survey of International Affairs*, 1937, I, 377.
60. *Survey of International Affairs*, 1936, p. 277; *Survey of International Affairs*, 1932, p. 522n2.
61. Toynbee, *A Study of History*, IV, 300.

menting fundamental political problems and even negotiations on armaments and leaving outstanding disputes unresolved.

Toynbee also discussed certain practical questions in international law. Few issues have greater importance for Americans than the problem of recognition, which some tend to see as a favor granted to a state whose conduct is morally acceptable. By contrast, traditional international law views recognition as a practical means of facilitating relations among states. The American position on recognition was formulated at the time of the French Revolution, when Jefferson insisted that despite the violence and brutality in France, it was in the interests of the United States to put into place the machinery for doing business with that nation. Moreover, he reminded his many critics that not too far back in history, Americans had been engaged in sanctifying a revolution of their own. With certain exceptions, Jefferson's policy was pursued down to 1913, when, in the era of Woodrow Wilson, recognition was withheld from governments established by means of armed force. Another policy change occurred on September 13, 1930, when Secretary of State Henry Stimson instructed American representatives in Argentina, Peru, and Bolivia to resume normal diplomatic relations with those governments. The secretary was satisfied that there was no continuing active resistance to them, and the governments also gave assurance that they would abide by international agreements. Toynbee observed: "Thus, the United States Government returned . . . to their traditional policy, which they had followed down to 1913, of recognizing *de facto* Governments when and where they succeeded in establishing themselves."[62]

In 1933, in one of its most controversial acts of recognition, the United States recognized the Soviet Union. American policy had been in striking contrast to that of most European nations—Germany had recognized the Soviet government in 1922 and the United Kingdom and Italy did so in 1924. The reason given, especially in the United States, for the change in policy was that American business would benefit. Through private citizens, however, the United States had conducted trade with the Russians that compared favorably with that of Germany and Japan. On July 2, 1933, it was reported that an extensive contract had been signed between Amtorg Trading Corporation and the Reconstruction Fi-

62. *Survey of International Affairs*, 1930, pp. 362, 367.

nance Corporation. Moreover, "American commercial relations with Soviet Russia had been conspicuously free from 'incidents' of the kind which both the Germans and the British had experienced." The popular refutation of the economic-interests argument was that "it was improper for the United States to recognize officially a Government that had shed innocent blood, confiscated private property, persecuted religion and repudiated debts."[63]

Toynbee maintained that these popular arguments, though interesting, provided little foundation for a change in policy. He argued that the primary reason, barely mentioned in public discussion, was the need for redressing the balance of power in the Pacific. The United States at this time, through the initiative of Stimson, was proposing to vindicate the system of collective security and to contain Japanese aggression in Manchuria. This action required the support of the largest possible number of states with interests in the Pacific. The most logical Great Power for Washington to turn to was the Soviet Union. But here American diplomacy found itself hamstrung by devices of its own making. It had stubbornly refused to recognize and to enter into diplomatic relations with its most natural ally in this crisis. And hence the change in policy:

> A mere comparison of dates suggests that the question of the balance of power in the Pacific was an important consideration in the United States Government's mind; for President Roosevelt's message of the 10th October 1933, to the President of the Central Executive Committee of the Soviet Union, Monsieur Kalinin, which opened the Americo-Russian recognition negotiations, was despatched less than eight months after the Geneva verdict of the 24th February, less than six months after the announcements, on the 1st May, of the United States Government's decision to allocate a sum of $46,000,000 for naval construction from the Federal Public Works Programme, and at approximately the same interval after the serving of the Japanese notice of intention to secede from the League of Nations.[64]

The Soviet Union from the beginning "made no secret of the fact that, in their mind, the political consideration was uppermost." They emphasized that a rupture in diplomatic relations was hardly an appropriate method for settling disputes. They attributed the growing crisis in the Far East mainly to the fact that not all states

63. *Survey of International Affairs*, 1933, pp. 533–34, 533.
64. *Ibid.*, 535.

with interests in the Pacific had sustained diplomatic relations with one another. The balance of power had shifted heavily in Japan's favor, and only through effective countermeasures could this situation be redressed. Whether acknowledged or not, these same political considerations, in Toynbee's opinion, "also played an important part in the private counsels of the Administration at Washington."[65]

Toynbee gave examples of other instances of obstacles being placed in the path of diplomatic relations. In 1930, the local Chinese government at Mukden was directly involved in the problem of the Chinese Eastern Railway, which concerned primarily the actions of the Russians. The situation might have been dealt with more successfully if diplomatic relations between Nanking and Moscow had been restored or if the local Chinese government could have negotiated directly. Since neither alternative proved practicable, the Russians were able to reestablish their control over the railway.[66]

These illustrations from the diplomatic histories of the United States and China demonstrate the theory of recognition to which Toynbee gave his support. It was that theory which also led him to criticize the United States for standing almost alone in its maintenance of nonrecognition until President Nixon normalized relations with China. Toynbee believed that the United States and the world would pay a high price for lack of diplomatic contact. American experience in Korea and Vietnam tended to confirm his prophecy. Another area where stakes are high is disarmament.

The problem of seeking limitations on armaments in modern international politics has inspired ever wider popular concern since World War I. The case for disarmament is based on assumptions underscored in varying degrees by different proponents: the threat of universal destruction, the risk of economic disintegration, and the hazards of a diplomacy inspired and directed by selfish and evil men such as munitions makers. The first of these arguments is the one given priority in present-day international society. Far-reaching technological changes have made it possible, as it was not possible before, for men to destroy first cities and now nations and civilizations. The old ratio of one shot to one casualty was gradually altered as military science evolved toward the "absolute

65. *Ibid.*, 533, 537, 533.
66. *Survey of International Affairs*, 1930, p. 359.

weapons." The fateful trend found its first expression with the revolution in aerial warfare, about which Toynbee wrote as early as 1932: "The momentous and urgent choice between getting rid of war and committing suicide by the perhaps unavoidable use, in any future war, of unprecedentedly destructive weapons was summed up and symbolized, in a shape which the simplest and least well-instructed lay mind could apprehend, in the new terror of aerial warfare." Yet this was only a pale reflection of atomic war.[67]

The second argument for disarmament is based on a practical calculation that the continued diversion of great sums of money for military expenditures will sooner or later exhaust the national resources of even the richest country—a trend Toynbee pointed to in most civilizations. In the early 1930s, the League Secretariat calculated the average military expenditures for sixty-one countries over a period of the last four years, and the figure "reached 'the immense sum of 4,000 million dollars a year.'" According to Arthur Henderson of Great Britain and other delegates to the World Disarmament Conference in 1932, such expenditures could only lead to grave economic crises and eventual bankruptcy.[68] For this reason, disarmament was a compelling necessity then, and with worldwide military expenditures reaching $800 billion to $900 billion a year in the 1980s and 1990s, it is even more so now. Significantly, an American president with a military background, Eisenhower, issued a similar warning.

The third line of reasoning in support of disarmament attracted public attention in the 1920s. Then it was assumed that private munitions makers' zeal for profits led them to promote arms races which increased the prospects of war. The same individuals, active participants or lobbyists at various disarmament conferences, contributed materially to the breakdown of negotiations. They were powerful because of their influence upon military and diplomatic representatives and because of their control of the American press. The theory here was that men fight because they have weapons and, as a corollary, that when arms were abolished, warfare would cease. Shades of all three arguments appear in Toynbee's philosophy of international relations at various points in time. In his last years, he spoke with greater fervor about attaining disarmament to avert universal destruction.

67. *Survey of International Affairs*, 1932, p. 189.
68. *Ibid.*, 195.

The major political and strategic problem which has confounded nations seeking to restrict or eliminate armaments has
been their divergent interpretations of which weapons and how
many should be limited. This was particularly the case after World
War I. Toynbee pondered these questions, and it may contribute to
an understanding of the problem of disarmament to outline the
conclusions he reached about particular nations.

France's policy with regard to disarmament in the interwar period mirrored its foreign policy: national security was the primary
concern. At the World Disarmament Conference, for example, the
American delegate Hugh Gibson proposed that aggressive weapons such as tanks, mobile guns of greater than 155mm, and gas be
outlawed. Toynbee observed: "In the French press, Mr. Gibson's
proposal was generally criticized as an attempt to prohibit the types
of armaments which were of interest to the military Powers like
France, while leaving untouched the naval armaments with which
the United States and Great Britain were principally concerned."
In addition, the unexpected Hoover Plan, providing for overall one-
third disarmament, raised questions concerning concrete actions
the United States was prepared to take if the Pact of Paris was
breached. Gibson's inability to offer any guarantees merely confirmed France's suspicion of the plan.[69]

In 1932 it was expected that the French would display greater
sympathy toward disarmament when Edouard Herriot came to
power. The delegates soon discovered, however, that French policy was not dependent upon the individuals who were its spokesmen: "Security, however, was still to be the determining factor;
and Monsieur Paul Boncour (who represented France in the conversations at Geneva, while Monsieur Herriot spent most of his
time at Lausanne) could not hold out the hope of any substantial
concessions in the absence of further guarantees of security."[70]

The policy of Great Britain at successive disarmament conferences was based upon its own national interest. British delegates
were well aware that their proposal for restricting the construction of submarines "which would suit their special needs . . . was
entirely unacceptable to the smaller naval Powers under the existing conditions of relative naval strength." The British nevertheless continued to emphasize this issue, for the nation would hardly
be willing to sacrifice key elements in its own naval strength for

69. *Ibid.*, 296–97, 217, 243–44.
70. *Ibid.*, 237.

minor concessions by the smaller naval powers. One principle introduced by Lord Cecil approved specific budgetary limitations on armaments. In defense of this approach and in opposition to the German proposal for direct enumerated restrictions, the British argued that concealing machine guns and rifles was easier than concealing total military expenditures.[71] It may be of some significance that a former Rhodes scholar, Dean Rusk, was to make similar proposals in the 1970s.

The American delegation found itself in accord with the British policy on submarines. Although this conflicted directly with the interests of small naval powers, it was unlikely to injure the relative position of the United States. On other issues, however, American proposals diverged from those of the British. Hugh Gibson was the chief opponent of a policy of budgetary limitations, and a political analyst could hardly ignore this reflection of the superior wealth of the United States. In its place, Gibson suggested publishing all details of military expenditures. Finally, the fact that the ill-fated Hoover Plan was introduced without any warning shortly before a crucial domestic election must also be considered in appraising American disarmament policy.[72]

On the policies of Germany, Hungary, and Austria, Toynbee observed: "The states which had been unilaterally disarmed by the Peace Treaties had a common interest in securing the widest possible measure of general disarmament, and Austria and Hungary . . . generally followed Germany's lead in such matters at the Assembly." Germany proposed, for example, the inclusion of trained reserves among effectives and the limitation of overseas forces assigned to adjoining countries. Since Germany possessed no reserves or overseas forces, this agreement would not have reduced its existing power. France, on the other hand, with elements of strength in each category, would have suffered a substantial loss.[73]

Another German proposal called for the prohibition of certain offensive weapons, broadening the definitions to include heavy artillery, tanks, and all classes of military aviation which might in any way constitute a threat to other nations. Toynbee commented: "It will be seen that the intention of these German proposals was to obtain the equality of states which Germany de-

71. *Ibid.*, 209; *Survey of International Affairs*, 1930, p. 106.
72. *Survey of International Affairs*, 1930, p. 106; *Survey of International Affairs*, 1929, p. 29.
73. *Survey of International Affairs*, 1930, p. 94; *Survey of International Affairs*, 1933, p. 262.

manded by applying to all countries the system which had been applied to Germany and her former allies by Peace Treaties."[74] Germany sought to bring others closer to the level of disarmament imposed on it after World War I.

Toynbee saw in Japan's policy between the two world wars one more illustration of the tendency for proposals advanced at the disarmament conferences to be based on the national interest. "During the Washington Conference of 1921–2, Japan appears to have abandoned as impracticable those dreams of sole supremacy in the Far East and the Pacific." In subsequent conferences Japan assumed the role of arbiter and made an effort to encourage some form of agreement which might keep political tension low. Of Japan's disarmament policy after 1928, Toynbee remarked: "In pursuing this sober policy, Japan was considering her own national interests as well as serving the general cause of peace; for it became apparent . . . that the role of a Great Naval Power, even on the 5/5/3 ration, was imposing upon Japan a financial burden which she would find it difficult to bear in perpetuity." Realism dictated that Japan follow certain policies regarding disarmament.[75]

Russia's role in disarmament also deserves mention here, even though it will be a major focus in the later discussion of the cold war. In a circular note, the czar, concerned about the dangerous nature of modern weapons, proposed a disarmament conference. His initiative resulted in the first Hague Peace Conference of 1899. And during the interwar years, when the Soviet delegation arrived in Geneva in 1927, Litvinov made an eloquent plea for total and universal disarmament.

Despite the enormous efforts of nations, the success of virtually every major disarmament project has been impaired by incompatible national interests, the fallacy of seeking a definition of offensive-defensive weapons, and the necessary attainment of security as a precondition. We have already observed the impact of the opposing claims by various nations with regard to particular weapons. Each nation construes as defensive those weapons in which it enjoys a supremacy and as aggressive those unsuited to its needs and which it has no intention of constructing. England and the United States maintained that the battleship was a purely defensive weapon and that the only vessel that was clearly aggressive was the submarine. For Japan, neither battleships nor submarines

74. Survey of International Affairs, 1932, p. 204n2.
75. Survey of International Affairs, 1927, pp. 22, 23.

were offensive weapons but aircraft carriers, which were a possible threat to Japanese security, were classified by the Japanese as aggressive. All small naval powers considered large battleships offensive; and Germany maintained that all vessels forbidden to Germany by the Versailles Treaty were offensive. "Pocket battleships," which Germany had been permitted to retain, it considered defensive in character. Salvador de Madariaga summed up the situation in a fable and related it particularly to the Russian proposal for universal disarmament. Toynbee quoted it with approval: "The animals had met to disarm. The lion, looking sideways at the eagle, said: 'Wings must be abolished.' The eagle, looking at the bull, declared: 'Horns must be abolished.' The bull, looking at the tiger, said: 'Paws, and especially claws, must be abolished.' The bear in his turn said: 'All arms must be abolished; all that is necessary is a universal embrace.'"[76]

The second obstacle to disarmament results from the assumption that offensive and defensive weapons can be clearly distinguished, an assumption which has been renewed in proposals in the 1980s for a "Strategic Defense Initiative." This approach had then and has now the merit of relative simplicity and appeals, therefore, to world public opinion. In addition, disarmament of this type was already part of an experiment inasmuch as it was used in restrictions imposed upon Germany following World War I. Its great weakness was the basic divergence in national views regarding particular weapons. For this reason, what was simple and appealing in principle proved in practice to be unworkable.[77] It is sobering in the 1980s to ask if history will repeat itself.

The final difficulty was the question of which had priority, security or disarmament. In the British view, as repeatedly expressed by Arthur Henderson, the two were interlocked and progress in one inevitably facilitated achieving the other. Toynbee in 1930 seemed to lean toward this formula. In the French view, as Aristide Briand stressed, there were successive stages to the disarmament problem: arbitration, security, and disarmament. Under this formula, disarmament was not a technical but a political question dependent upon prior attainment of security. Rumania, for example, in reply to a League questionnaire explained that it presently lacked those armaments necessary for security in light of its geographical position. Any disarmament program would have to be postponed

76. *Survey of International Affairs*, 1932, p. 208n5.
77. *Ibid.*, 210.

until security had been attained. Other nations offered similar replies. Despite Toynbee's early preference for the British formula, it was the French approach which prevailed in practice. Rather impressive evidence regarding foreign policies and disarmament can be arrayed in support of the latter formula, even though American foreign policy has for long periods down to the present appeared to accept the former.[78]

Disarmament conferences as such are of course not a novelty in relations between political societies. In Hellenic and Sinic civilizations, there is historical and archaeological evidence of such conferences being held. Toynbee spoke of one in Sinic history which was "attended by representatives of fourteen states, in 546 B.C." That conference broke down, as have the vast majority of endeavors since.[79] Postwar approaches to disarmament provide additions to a growing list of failures. Why have these attempts so consistently miscarried? What errors in theory or in practice on the part of statesmen and politicians account for these failures? We have already enumerated some of the ill-fated practices which Toynbee emphasized. Four factors, in ascending order of importance, bear repetition and underscore Toynbee's main points.

First, there is the element of absolute national loyalty: "On the one hand, the experts were being instructed to consider how the organization of peace might be rendered most efficient, from a technical standpoint. . . . But at the same time, each national group of experts was still being instructed to consider, in narrowly national terms, how a reduction of armaments could be arranged with the minimum diminution of their own country's war-power in the event of the statesmen agreeing upon a substantial reduction of national forces." Toynbee evaluated this cause of the disarmament dilemma in terms which were sometimes idealistic and sometimes moralistic. In the early 1930s he virtually implied that statesmen had a real choice of basing their actions on national or universal interests. As to whether these alternatives were equally attainable, however, Toynbee seemed to have had a change of heart as his thinking developed and matured.[80]

Second, disarmament talks have broken down because of inadequate preparation, a weakness which experienced statesmen and diplomats from various national backgrounds have emphasized.

78. *Survey of International Affairs*, 1930, pp. 94, 96; *Survey of International Affairs*, 1931, p. 284.
79. Toynbee, *A Study of History*, I, 89.
80. *Survey of International Affairs*, 1932, pp. 179–80.

Americans in particular have had a tendency to introduce a new policy into full conference proceedings without any prior warning or preparatory discussions of what might be expected. The Hoover Plan is one example, and there have been others, earning the United States a none too favorable reputation for engaging in such practices. As Toynbee observed: "Mr. Henderson attributed the failure of the Conference [of 1934–1935] to the lack of adequate political preparation as well as to the political complications which arose after the Conference had begun its work." Nor should this comment be limited to disarmament conferences, as all prewar and postwar diplomacy has from time to time been thus hampered.[81]

The third factor was the absence of genuine and serious negotiation. The demands put forth by both France and Germany reflected a certain rigidity of thought. France requested security and limited disarmament; the German proposals were for general disarmament. In practice the majority of nations might have supported the French plan but the consequence if there were no real negotiations would be "a new Balance of Power in Europe." The consequences within Germany would be no less far-reaching because "the definitive rejection of Germany's case by the Preparatory Commission would strengthen the hands of the 'Nazis' still further, and bring new recruits into the ranks of those who had returned to the belief that Germany would gain nothing except by force." New threats raised new issues which the conference was obliged to consider. Yet the action taken was designed principally to preserve specific disarmament programs instead of seeking to grant protection against the rising threat to peace in Germany, Italy, and the USSR.[82] Where serious negotiations are excluded, diplomacy becomes a "dialogue of the deaf."

The fundamental cause of the disarmament debacle was the basic misunderstanding regarding the whole nature of political settlement and agreement. Many of the delegates assumed that disarmament could be built upon foundations of political division. The British in particular maintained that security and political settlement would proceed simultaneously once a formula for disarmament had been approved. The French position was more realistic in asserting that disarmament was necessarily dependent upon security. A few minority voices were raised in England and elsewhere: "In pursuing security through agreements, we will get round

81. *Survey of International Affairs*, 1935, I, 57n1.
82. *Survey of International Affairs*, 1930, pp. 98–99.

the problem of trying to discover some means by which America and ourselves can come to an agreement."[83] The few settlements that have lasted, such as the Rush-Bagot agreement between the United States and Great Britain, have been based on some form of prior political accommodation. Otherwise, no disarmament formula, however ingenious, can be expected to succeed. Toynbee in his last years became increasingly aware of this timeless principle of international politics. He was to apply it specifically in his vision of the requirements for peace between the United States and the Soviet Union.

83. Quoted in *Survey of International Affairs*, 1927, p. 80.

CHAPTER V

Diplomacy and the Laws of International Politics

I T SHOULD NOT be surprising that Toynbee would attempt to formulate a theory of diplomacy. On the main issues of international politics, he wrote from firsthand experience, having been an observer of two wars and two major peace conferences. He demonstrated that no student of contemporary world affairs who deals realistically with the subject can write convincingly on problems of peace if diplomacy is omitted. Foreign policy, someone has said, is not like an eight-day clock that can be wound up and then forgotten. The only way foreign policy can be carried on and implemented is by diplomats who pursue their tasks from day to day. The conduct of foreign policy is the task not of legislators but of diplomats. Diplomacy is simply the centuries-old way in which nations do business with one another. It is a laborious and serious business, one which lacks most of the evil and mysterious features the public has sometimes ascribed to it. Inspired by such assumptions, Toynbee approached his analysis of diplomacy.

Thinking on international relations in contemporary Western society has frequently been based upon a belief that there were two patterns of conduct which nations were free to follow if they chose. The "old dispensation" was power politics and international anarchy, symbolized by Machiavelli. The new order would be one of law and the absence of conflict, and Grotius became the symbol. Idealists assumed that society can, if it will, transfer its allegiance from Machiavelli, whose precepts are evil, to Grotius, whose principles are good and will ensure peace, law, and justice. Toynbee set forth his views on these contrasting orders: "There is a sharp contrast . . . between the situation in which there are a number of local states in conflict with each other and the situation in which the whole of a society is politically united in some form, and I do feel that it is characteristic of the former of these two situations that, so long as it lasts, Machiavelli always gets the better of Grotius. There are . . . things to be said for this, to me odious, international anarchy. It is more stimulating as well as more destructive and wicked than the universal state dispensation." If this analysis is accurate and if the present order is a Machiavellian one, then a student must ask, what are the techniques most appropriate for adjusting divergent claims? The answer given by both Machiavelli and Toynbee is that traditional diplomacy provides the one proven method. Diplomacy has endured the test of time: "We infer the maintenance of diplomatic relations between two Great Powers from the pictures of envoys from people called the Keftiu that appear in wall-paintings in Egyptian tombs of the first half of the fifteenth century B.C. The clothes which those envoys wear and the presents which they carry are recognized as being characteristic of Crete in 'Late Minoan II.'"[1]

Diplomacy's roots shape its capacity for dealing with both secular and sacred disputes. A striking example was the negotiations in the late 1920s between Pope Pius XI and Mussolini. Both had claims and practical interests which were essential to their influence and power. The pope sought a concordat with Italy to remedy the existing conflict between a major Catholic country and himself; formal recognition of the territorial sovereignty of the Vatican enclave; and "a substantial revenue which would be absolutely secure in perpetuity and absolutely under the Pope's own control, in contrast to 'Peter's Pence,' which fluctuated according to the means and the disposition of the Roman Catholic community all over the world." To realize its objectives, the papacy was willing to grant recognition to the new Fascist state and assurance against outside intervention. For Toynbee, the relation between one sacred and one secular sovereign was a classic example of the practical use of diplomatic means for adjusting outstanding differences: "Neither the Fascist Party nor the Papacy could compromise . . . upon questions of principle . . . but upon a realistic division of power over the lives and activities of the inhabitants of Italy . . .

1. Arnold J. Toynbee to Kenneth W. Thompson, September 10, 1949, in possession of the recipient; Arnold J. Toynbee, *A Study of History* (12 vols.; London, 1934–61), I, 94.

this revolutionary faction and this supernatural autocracy found it possible, without sacrifice of principle or loss of 'face,' to come to a political agreement with one another."[2]

In modern times the tendency has grown to substitute for diplomacy not only the techniques of Grotius but also supremacy in military might. With more and more power in the hands of fewer and fewer states, militant leaders promote the illusion that all rivalries can be resolved through brute strength. France between the world wars believed that temporary military supremacy made less urgent the need for seeking new political arrangements with Germany. Toynbee viewed Britain as having decided that rearmament made alliances and spheres of influence on the Continent unnecessary. As in the past, diplomacy was frequently the last resort of smaller states, and it is no accident that they were the home of some of the most skillful United Nations diplomats. Toynbee observed that such states "could not yield to the illusion—so seductive, though perhaps also deadly, to the Great Powers—that armaments could be made to do duty for statesmanship." The dread illusion of those who would build ever stronger arsenals is that military strength can assure success in diplomacy. Yet historically certain nations and city-states have achieved national power through the quality of their diplomacy. Toynbee found that Venice's greatness was principally "the reward of a clear-headed and unslumbering statesmanship." A small state, or indeed a state reduced to inferiority, can still keep its footing in international relations with the Titans only through masterly diplomacy. Even the Great Powers are in the long run dependent upon diplomatic capacities if their resources are not to be squandered.[3]

A primary reason for the neglect by nations that are strong and by those which cherish grand moral principles is the belief that diplomacy is essentially immoral. Diplomats' practices have been associated with questionable bargains and stratagems which have brought on war. The image of Perfidious Albion has spread beyond British diplomacy. Hugh Gibson told of a well-known public figure who proclaimed "that [if] every diplomat in the world could spend a day or two at the fighting fronts . . . this mess would soon be over." Whenever conflicts require explanation in the simplest terms, viewpoints of this kind are always available. The limited achievements of diplomats are contrasted unfavorably with the

2. *Survey of International Affairs*, 1929, pp. 439–45, 445, 439.
3. *Survey of International Affairs*, 1936, p. 2; Toynbee, *A Study of History*, IV, 277.

notable successes of businessmen and soldiers. Even Toynbee occasionally disparaged diplomacy, as, for example, in his idealist
days in 1931: "Official diplomacy showed to less advantage in this
emergency than private enterprise in the handling of international
affairs; for, while the statesmen hesitated and fumbled, a private
international organization, the Institute of Pacific Relations, succeeded in holding a nonofficial conference at Shanghai on the 21st
October–2nd November at which Chinese and Japanese met in
roundtable conferences and exchanged ideas like rational beings at
a time when, elsewhere, their respective countrymen were flying
at one another's throats." Furthermore, diplomacy must deal with
immense difficulties. In Germany, even under a government sympathetic to Western diplomacy, a crisis state of mind existed: "The
coexistence . . . of this German temper with the French and Italian
tempers . . . [was] a dangerous conjunction of psychological forces."
To Germans and Italians, French insistence on security implied a
policy of keeping Germany and Italy permanently subdued. In
French eyes, the German and Italian policies of equality threatened to undermine French security.[4]

In the 1980s the psychological foundations for diplomacy are
surely no better. Because this is true, most Western governments
have been shy about the use of the second string in the bow of traditional diplomacy. The first has always been collective defense and
armaments, which the West has come slowly but strongly to approve. The second string, the companion of the first in any world
where Machiavellianism is dominant, is the judicious use of instrumentalities such as buffer zones and neutralized areas, spheres
of influence, and political settlement. If these forms of accommodation are to be realized, they can emerge only through the pursuit of genuine diplomacy.

The diplomatic settlement between Pope Pius XI and Mussolini was, as we have seen, a division of power. It was also influenced by the law of the balance of power. Both church and state
had common enemies whom they feared, the Freemason and Liberal groups and the Socialist party. Avowedly to redress the balance of influence, both Fascists and Papists took up the challenge.
When rival groups threatened to become too strong, church and
state united.

The business of the diplomat is to act in the self-interest of his

4. Hugh Gibson, *The Road to Foreign Policy* (Garden City, N.Y., 1944), 32; *Survey of International Affairs*, 1931, pp. 398–99n5; *Survey of International Affairs*,
1930, p. 29.

state, and the paramount aim of the state is self-preservation. Historically the best means of ensuring the independence of the state has been the maintenance of an equilibrium of power. When nations or cities have been equal or when the Great Powers have balanced one another, their self-preservation more often has been assured. In the ancient world, Toynbee discovered an important example:

> Petra and Palmyra each rose in turn to greatness by finding places for themselves in the interstices between the dominions of mutually hostile Great Powers whose hostility was too great to admit of their coming to a direct understanding with each other, while it was not great enough to drive them into forgoing the advantage of doing business with one another indirectly through the agency of commercial go-betweens who would also serve as political buffers. Petra rose in this way in an interstice between the Seleucid and the Ptolemaic "successor-state" of the Achaemenian Empire; Palmyra rose in an interstice between the Roman Empire and the Arsacid Power. Petra was doomed when the Roman Empire supplanted both the Seleucid and the Ptolemaic Power alike; Palmyra was doomed when the decay of the Arsacidae left Rome momentarily without a rival in this quarter likewise—pending the rise of the Sasanidae.[5]

Until recent times, the diplomat's success depended in part on his ability to preserve local or so-called inferior balances of power. In the early period of modern international relations, these existed in Northern Europe, among the Italian city-states, and in other regions in Eurasia. Gradually they were integrated into a general European balance of power and in our day into one that is worldwide. Between the two world wars, Italy and France found themselves aligned against one another on several specific points of dispute. Moreover, they carried this rivalry into their interests regarding Southeastern Europe, where the two Great Powers were wont to maintain some kind of equilibrium. Local, regional, and worldwide balances of power have provided the framework within which diplomats must operate.

The methods of the diplomat are the arts of negotiation. Direct diplomacy and negotiation have been the traditional way of doing business on the international stage. Privacy and gravity of talks

5. Toynbee, *A Study of History*, II, 11n3.

have been peculiarly adapted to the slow task of achieving compromise. Participants deal directly with underlying political problems, shielded from the spotlight of public attention. Direct diplomacy is less likely to lapse into meaningless "formulas" designed for domestic consumption. One illustration involved American recognition of the Soviet Union: "The negotiations between Monsieur Litvinov and President Roosevelt at Washington, which lasted from the 8th November 1933, to the 16th, were both strenuous and cordial, because both parties were determined to achieve success; but they were not facile; for there was also a strong determination on both sides to handle and dispose of the real difficulties and not to be content with a paper settlement which would slide over the practical obstacles and would thereby threaten to breed disappointments and recriminations at a later stage."[6]

However, direct diplomacy has been the exception rather than the rule since World War I. The disarmament conferences during the interwar period were primarily diplomacy in open forums. Certain respected diplomats and statesmen proposed, however, that particular questions be dealt with through private negotiations. For example, Arthur Henderson, who presided at the World Disarmament Conference, "was reported to have made the suggestion that it might facilitate the task of the General Commission if the European 'Great Powers' were to attempt to clear the ground in private conversations." Hugh Gibson was also aware of the importance of such discussions. In 1928 after a deadlock in the League of Nations Preparatory Commission for the Disarmament Conference, Gibson proposed that "nothing further could be accomplished in public meetings until after an effort had been made by direct negotiations between various Governments and between groups of Governments to find a way, through mutual concession, to eliminate existing divergencies." Yet the Hoover Plan was an example of "diplomacy by storm," and "the somewhat lukewarm reception which was accorded by the General Commission to Mr. Gibson's statement perhaps reflected a certain amount of resentment against what was felt to be a typically American proceeding." The use of crash diplomacy by Americans "had neither been forgotten nor forgiven."[7]

A second form of diplomacy involves conferences, which rep-

6. *Survey of International Affairs*, 1933, p. 536.
7. *Ibid.*, 238; *Survey of International Affairs*, 1928, p. 61; *Survey of International Affairs*, 1932, p. 242.

resent one of the great technical achievements of Western society. Delegates and their corps of experts from almost all of the self-governing countries of the world convene in one center while remaining in constant touch with their own governments. When, however, political leaders appear on the scene, to carry out their diplomatic responsibility and to advance political interests at home, success in one sometimes requires sacrifice of the other. Hugh Gibson pointed out:

> Political leaders . . . are busy men and cannot settle down long enough to do a thorough job. How often at Geneva, or elsewhere, have we seen a meeting called to order with the statement that we must press forward to reach a solution of this or that question because the French Foreign Minister is obliged to leave on Thursday morning. You may well ask what relation there is between these two statements. The solution need not be reached before the Minister leaves Geneva. It could be reported to him. . . . But that is just the catch. The politician simply cannot go home with the press trumpeting the fact that he did nothing more important than sit in at the beginning of the discussion. He must have his little triumph.

A similar problem arose during the April, 1932, discussions held at Geneva. Henry L. Stimson arrived on April 16, 1932, and was joined by Ramsay MacDonald and André Tardieu on April 21. Heinrich Brüning and Dino Grandi were present, but on April 22, Tardieu and Grandi returned to their countries for the election campaigns then in progress. After their departure, conversations went on, but suffered from the distinct handicap of long-range communication with the two absent participants.[8]

A further negative feature of diplomacy by conference is the tendency to revert to false face-saving devices such as the diplomatic "formula." When a conference has been deadlocked, a political leader presents a harmless formula upon which everyone can agree. This gives an illusion of substantial agreement, and delegates can return home pointing with pride to a major settlement. At the World Disarmament Conference a strategy of this sort was worked out: "The time was rapidly approaching at which the Conference would have to be adjourned for a summer vacation, and it was felt desirable that the delegates should be able to produce some concrete results of their labours before they dispersed." Thus Sir

8. Gibson, *The Road to Foreign Policy*, 83–84; *Survey of International Affairs*, 1932, pp. 224–25.

John Simon's draft was the basis for a resolution by Eduard Beneš, the *rapporteur*.[9]

Also, in diplomacy by conference, a tendency exists for delegations to present their policies as ultimatums, and the Americans did this at various interwar disarmament conferences. Toynbee commented that "the immediate reaction of the Coolidge Administration to the work of the Geneva Conference of September 1926 was to treat the refusal of the Conference to accept the fifth reservation [regarding membership in the Court] without further negotiation as though it were a definitive rejection." Political considerations are often involved, but it is undeniable that in diplomacy by conference policies are often presented on a take-it-or-leave-it basis.[10]

A third style of diplomacy, by parliamentary procedure or majority rule, has its basis in the belief that all questions can be worked out within open assemblies, just as local and national questions are resolved. In practice, the most troublesome problem internationally has been obtaining agreement on a compromise when each nation's policy is set forth and then reported instantaneously throughout the world. Once this occurs, concessions become difficult and sometimes impossible. A nation's prestige, not a diplomat's first trial proposal, is at stake. France's policy between the wars was inflexible because of its obsession with security, and on all major issues, France's views had been made public. Once on the record, there could be no retreat: "Monsieur Flandin . . . declared that France could not and would not negotiate until Germany had restored the *status quo*."[11]

These difficulties, serious enough in themselves, have been aggravated by other conditions. Democratic diplomacy has introduced new factors in international politics which have contributed to the awkward character of diplomacy. There is, for example, the risk of pursuing policies which are wise internationally but not acceptable at home. Sometimes delegates must press for points in the world forum which are essential to perpetuating their government in office but which may be at odds with the principal task of adjusting international conflict. Toynbee discovered an example of this in France's policy in 1932: "Monsieur Tardieu felt, no doubt, that any appearance of defeat at Geneva would react unfavourably upon his Government's prospects of success in the elec-

9. *Ibid.*, 246.
10. *Survey of International Affairs*, 1929, p. 83.
11. *Survey of International Affairs*, 1936, p. 283.

tions." So no major concessions were made until it was too late.[12]

There is a similar problem in the importance of having like-minded groups simultaneously in power in various countries. "Yet it was too much to expect that, in the political life of every one of these 'Great Powers,' the currents, at any given moment, should all flow in a single direction." There was a perversity to post–World War I history which prescribed that whenever conservative governments were in power in one major nation, liberal governments with opposing viewpoints were in power in the countries with which cooperation was essential.[13]

A final weakness of democratic diplomacy is that delegates must deal with political pressures from forces in their own countries. Gibson, Lord Cecil, and others wrote about how frequently diplomats were called home just when agreement was in sight. Many times, changes in domestic policy or intra-cabinet politics were responsible for the unexpected policies which statesmen introduced in the international forum. Or continued pressures required a drastic shift in policy. In 1927 the British delegate Lord Cecil was recalled from the Three-Power Naval Conference for internal political reasons. He himself was most discouraged and issued a statement: "I was very much disturbed. Agreement seemed to me to be in sight." In one precipitous action taken on the home front, days of hard-won agreement abroad were wiped out.[14]

No one has described the responsibilities of the diplomat better than Hugh Gibson has: "Diplomacy is a grim business with the underlying objective of getting as much as you can for your own country. The unfailing courtesy which should characterize it is not based, as is so generally assumed, on a spineless desire to make yourself agreeable to foreigners and give everything away. It is a reciprocal recognition that current negotiation is a mere incident in a continuing relationship: that both parties to any controversy will have an unending series of matters to be settled in the future and that agreement will be facilitated by maintenance of good temper and good feeling." The diplomat must be blessed with a sensitivity that blends cynicism and courtesy. For every profession, the nature of the task determines the human qualities that are most essential. The military man must be able to focus his attention narrowly and sharply on given concrete problems. He must

12. *Survey of International Affairs*, 1932, p. 220n1.
13. *Ibid.*, 177.
14. *Survey of International Affairs*, 1927, p. 64.

pursue victory and avoid defeat. In contrast: "The task of peace-making demands the intellectual gift of seeing all round a problem, leaving no element out of account, and estimating all the elements in their relative proportions, and the moral gift of an aptitude for cautious conservatism, ripe deliberation, taking long views, and working for distant ends."[15]

The mute tragedy of contemporary international politics stems from the fact that diplomats who have been replaced by military men in warfare have continued in their accustomed pattern at the time of the peace settlements. Toynbee observed: "The perversity of peace settlements is proverbial."[16] The deadly blindness of men who have excelled in the organization of victory but who suffered defeat in grappling with the alien task of writing the peace can be accounted for in part by the strong continuing influence of the military. This distinction is surely an intriguing one but it sometimes carried Toynbee rather far afield. The genius of British diplomacy, in contrast to German diplomacy, has been its freedom from domination by military and particularly naval leaders. To this degree, Toynbee's thesis is incontestable. Some students of power politics might insist, however, that in modern diplomacy the military factor has become so important that military planners must always be on tap. Toynbee would not have contested this minor reservation, and few would question the soundness of his major thesis.

For Toynbee, Machiavelli, Metternich, and Bismarck embody the principal virtues a diplomat must possess. Machiavelli, who held several high administrative posts in the Florentine Foreign Office, acquired an even wider knowledge of politics among the Italian city-states and a clear comprehension of the true character of international affairs. His experiences at the courts of other city-states as well as in France and thoughout Europe qualified him uniquely for his later endeavor to formulate a systematic theory of politics. "With his genius for political observation, he studied and apprehended and recorded exactly those features in the political structure of the new Transalpine nation-states which were of practical interest and importance for contemporary Italian statesmanship." Machiavelli is profoundly important in the history of diplomacy because the political principles he formulated have served as a grammar for diplomats to the present day. Indeed, as

15. Gibson, The Road to Foreign Policy, 32; Toynbee, A Study of History, IV, 298.
16. Toynbee, A Study of History, IV, 299.

Toynbee reflected, "if *The Prince* had happened to inspire some living Italian princeling—if a Medici or Este or Sforza or Gonzaga had employed the author's methods to attain the author's ends— it is not inconceivable that Machiavelli might have lived to see the political union of Italy accomplished."[17]

Two other great diplomats, Metternich and Bismarck, each dealt with the problem of balance and stability in international politics. They each had to maintain a favorable balance of power and at the same time permit a reasonable amount of peaceful change. After an illuminating comparative study of the foreign policies of Metternich and Poincaré, Toynbee concluded:

> If we think of the years 1918–34 in terms of the years 1815–48, which was the "post-war period" after the General War of 1792– 1815, we shall find in Monsieur Poincaré our closest latter-day counterpart of Metternich; but the comparison is, of course, far too flattering to the Frenchman. The confrontation of these two statesmen suggests not so much a parallel as a contrast; and in this contrast we have the measure of the deterioration in the quality of European statesmanship in the course of a century. When we measure our Poincaré by a Metternichian standard, the poverty of the later statesman's ideas, as well as the crudity of his methods, becomes manifest; and the respective results of the two statesmen's endeavours are proportionate to the difference in degree of their genius. The *tour de force* of imposing fixity upon a political flux, which a Metternich managed to keep up for thirty-three years, was only kept up for some fifteen years by a Poincaré.[18]

Bismarck's skills approximated if they did not surpass Metternich's. Bismarck's political genius was his capacity for recognizing that German interests would be served by allowing, and even helping, the Third Republic in France to achieve greater power and prestige. No attempt was made to block France in its African adventures, for this was considered a fair price to pay for that government's staying in power. "By contrast Monsieur Poincaré ensured the downfall of the Weimar Republic in Germany by implacably meting out to it exactly the same measure of harshness that he would have meted out to Kaiser Wilhelm II if the latter had retained his throne."[19]

17. Toynbee, *A Study of History*, III, 306, 309.
18. *Survey of International Affairs*, 1934, p. 322n1.
19. *Ibid.*

Another type of diplomacy, of which certain British policies are notorious examples, by its very nature repudiates most of the standards of effective diplomacy. It assumes that one nation's brand of diplomacy is intrinsically superior to all others. The best English example is the conception which was popular in the new diplomacy of Lord Halifax and was practiced by those who surrounded him. Again, Toynbee's somewhat lengthy explanation speaks for itself:

> In the minds of his countrymen, peers and colleagues, Lord Halifax was regarded at this time with a certain pride and awe, not unmingled with a spice of sceptical amusement, as a characteristically English exponent of some simple but noble virtues who at the same time had the gift of charming the most outlandishly un-English "wild men" by the unconscious exercise of an intuitive art which was capable of surpassing the Machiavellian triumphs of cleverer and less scrupulous politicians. To the average Englishman's eye Mr. Gandhi and Herr Hitler were two hardly distinguishable specimens of the same species of foreigner in virtue of their being, both of them superlatively exotic; and the average member of a British Cabinet may have reasoned in November 1937 that the guileless tamer of Gandhi had at any rate "a sporting chance" of taming Hitler likewise. Were not both these political "mad mullahs" non-smokers, non-drinkers of alcohol, non-eaters of meat, non-riders on horseback, and non-practisers of blood-sports in their cranky private lives? And did not the German Führer, like the Indian Mahatma, have some bee in his bonnet about the importance of being "Aryan"?[20]

We must conclude, therefore, that the qualities of a diplomat are to a considerable extent distinct from those of the businessman, politician, and militarist. Some societies have unexpectedly had to produce groups of able diplomats to meet new situations. For example, in 1793 the Ottoman Empire faced this problem for the first time. Sultan Selim III, in establishing diplomatic missions in Paris, Vienna, London, and Berlin, could find no competent diplomats with the necessary fund of experience. It was also apparent that the former military leaders around the "Osmanlis" were unable to negotiate successfully with Western diplomatic representatives. In consequence it was necessary to call upon the empire's

20. *Survey of International Affairs*, 1937, I, 338–39.

Greek Christian subjects to serve in this new capacity. They knew Western habits and languages because of their training in business and commerce. The traditional curriculum in Ottoman schools with its accent on militarism contributed few of the qualities essential for carrying on diplomatic functions.[21]

Sometimes it has been argued that changes in the international system require a change in diplomacy. One of the most attractive slogans in President Wilson's program for a new international order was "open diplomacy." It was widely believed that World War I had been caused mainly by secret diplomacy. If there were open forums and public discussions, leaders would be unable secretly to devise schemes for political domination. In the utopian era of the 1920s, Toynbee found little reason to dissent from this new creed. He sided with the most outspoken exponent of open diplomacy, Lord Cecil, and found reason to suspect the motives of Sir Austen Chamberlain, who supported private and unpublicized negotiations. One contributing factor to the crisis in the operation of the League was the aura of suspicion which surrounded its private and technical discussions: "The problems were faced not in official meetings of the Council but in 'conversations' or 'tea-parties' of the Foreign Ministers of the 'Great' or 'Locarno' Powers. Not only were these secret in the sense that the public were not admitted . . . but of many of them no record appears to have been kept and the personnel varied according to the humour of the principal statesmen."[22]

Toynbee and Lord Cecil, in their arguments for open diplomacy, did not recognize that the policies which individuals propose tend to reflect not personal preferences as much as the interests of their states. Rather, their philosophy was that international politics had been transformed by the forces of democracy and international organization and that international questions could no longer be settled by individuals, however eminent or skilled, in private discussion. Further, according to Toynbee, Sir Austen Chamberlain took his stand "primarily and avowedly on the ground that these demands [for open diplomacy] hampered him in attempting to carry out his very difficult diplomatic tasks, but perhaps also—secondarily, and without avowing this even to himself—on the ground that such demands constituted an unwarrantable attack upon a traditional prerogative."[23]

21. Toynbee, *A Study of History*, III, 47–48.
22. *Survey of International Affairs*, 1926, p. 48.
23. *Ibid.*, 62.

Toynbee saw the controversy as "a constitutional issue between an undemocratic pretension, on the part of the Executive, to be exempt from parliamentary control in its conduct of foreign affairs and the democratic claim of a self-governing nation . . . to control Ministers' conduct of public policy in every department of public life—not excluding the department of foreign affairs." For similar reasons, Toynbee supported the action initiated by Salvador de Madariaga at the World Disarmament Conference "to counteract the tendency for important questions to be discussed on the fringe of the Conference by a few Great Powers."[24]

There was a more practical reason for Toynbee's antagonism toward secret diplomacy. Particularly in the late 1920s, one of the main obstacles to successful diplomacy was publicity. Much of the business at early disarmament conferences was conducted in technical committees behind closed doors. The proceedings of these groups were analyzed and reported in the public press, which often sought to exploit the sensational and sinister. Delegates therefore spent a great deal of time denying these false and misleading reports: "The result was an alarming rapid growth of suspicion and resentment in the public mind of all the countries concerned during the weeks while the Conference was in session—a state of public opinion which reacted upon the Governments and, through the Governments, upon the Conference itself." This objection, surely more reasonable than sweeping indictments of all private diplomacy, reflects the dominant Wilsonian philosophy which at this time Toynbee seldom opposed.[25]

In the years that followed, open diplomacy was given a fair trial by both the League of Nations and the United Nations, and competent observers came to question certain of its assumptions. Critics charge that open diplomacy, as open management in a business enterprise, is a contradiction in terms. Political leaders have tried handling international negotiations, and the results for recent generations have not been encouraging. Since World War I, therefore, attempts have been made to more precisely define secret diplomacy. Hugh Gibson stated: "Secret diplomacy, if we use the words in their real meaning, is nothing more than the established method of unpublicized negotiation. This method was evolved through centuries of human experience. It is predicated on systematic exploration of a subject in private by trained negotiators. Such ex-

24. *Ibid.*, 54; *Survey of International Affairs*, 1932, p. 235.
25. *Survey of International Affairs*, 1927, p. 74.

ploration involves the exercise of resourcefulness, patience, and good will in order to arrive, perhaps after many failures, at a meeting of minds where conflicting interests are reconciled, at least in principle, under a form of agreement involving the common denominator of understanding."[26]

Toynbee himself took a second look at open diplomacy and cautiously, reluctantly, and perhaps painfully at times, made concessions to private negotiations. In 1932, writing about democratic diplomacy, he offered the observation that "it was easier to discern the drawbacks of Democracy than to recognize its benefits." In discussing the London Naval Conference and the procedures employed there, he concluded: "This method of informal discussion behind the scenes . . . had obvious advantages, and there is no doubt that it contributed largely to the results which were ultimately achieved." Even earlier, he appraised the issues which remained after World War I: "This array of major political questions could . . . only be dealt with by direct negotiations between the Governments concerned."[27]

The inescapable lesson of past experiments with open diplomacy leads to the conclusion that the new methods of public conferences are by themselves inadequate for adjusting political disputes. The unsolved problem is that of compromise when national prestige is at stake. For hard-pressed political leaders dealing with issues on which there is no underlying agreement and for which the groundwork has not been laid, this difficulty is serious indeed. Further, parliamentary methods are frequently applied with little discrimination. Diplomacy is trial and error, and solutions are rarely forthcoming on first attempts. Yet open diplomacy often requires that political leaders achieve their objectives in a few hectic meetings, or else relinquish the confidence of constituents back home.

Experience in recent generations confirms the dangers of both secret and open diplomacy. If commitments are undertaken but then not made public, the abuse of secret diplomacy is self-evident. But if commitments negotiated privately are presented for public approval, such dangers can be averted. This leads to the formula "open covenants privately negotiated" and to the later concept of quiet diplomacy.

Those who questioned the theory of open diplomacy went on to

26. Gibson, The Road to Foreign Policy, 80.
27. Survey of International Affairs, 1932, p. 176; Survey of International Affairs, 1930, p. 36; Survey of International Affairs, 1920–23, p. 5.

point out that success in negotiations was directly proportionate to the care and thoroughness of diplomatic preparation. For them, negotiation is the last stage in the diplomatic process. As lawyers are called in to draw up the results of negotiations between businessmen, foreign ministers who sign a political agreement in fact merely sanction what has already been worked out through traditional diplomatic channels. The most successful public conferences are almost always those which convene principally to adopt what has already been negotiated.

This practice was frequently ignored at the time of the League of Nations. Before the Three-Power Naval Conference (1927), for example, there were a few informal discussions between Lord Cecil and Hugh Gibson. Yet it was Cecil himself whom Toynbee quoted in support of his point about diplomatic preparation:

> There had been no previous discussion before we met, so that each set of experts came armed with their own plan, to which they naturally were deeply attached. Indeed I believe that the first we knew of the American proposals or they of ours was when they were announced at a public meeting of the Conference soon after our arrival. . . . Thus the very thoroughness with which these concrete national proposals had been prepared, at any rate on the British side, became adverse to the success of the Conference, because it heightened the effect of the lack of any international preparation on the political plane.

The gravity of this omission was increased because during the conference no attempt was made to achieve a real basis for political understanding. Toynbee saw as most significant the attitudes with which each participant approached the discussions. Anyone who has observed recent debates in the United Nations will hardly miss the point of his explanation that "from first to last . . . the attitudes of the British and the American delegation . . . were governed by what might be called the 'combatant' as opposed to the 'diplomatic' or 'political' frame of mind." This had a clear relation to the eventual breakdown of the conference.[28] What Toynbee described has become the norm, especially with recent American representatives at the United Nations.

Even more disquieting, a similar attitude has been reflected in virtually all major efforts at diplomacy since World War I. A diplomat was formerly considered an "honest and skillful bargainer";

28. *Survey of International Affairs*, 1927, pp. 42, 75.

now the concept involves a political figure who defends his president and his national ideology with outspoken eloquence. It would be difficult to cite many examples to prove that the pattern Toynbee described has changed even now. Indeed, the situation has deteriorated further.

There is one further reason why preparation is important: contemporary diplomacy has often violated one of the first principles of traditional diplomacy. The very nature of the problems with which diplomacy is concerned requires that the successful diplomat deal with the larger political situation. On the domestic scene, institutions mesh with one another, and for this reason, isolated issues can be dealt with successfully and the effect is quickly articulated throughout the system. On the international scene, however, these integrating forces are nonexistent and political decisions in individual cases can sometimes have a negative influence. The disputes which appear on the surface comprise only a fragment of the underlying political conflicts in international society.[29] Diplomats must deal with underlying problems of power that influence the policies of states on more specific issues.

At most of the great conferences, especially those which dealt primarily with disarmament, there has been little if "any official discussion of the great problems." This was particularly the case with the Three-Power Naval Conference (1927), which dealt exclusively with the technical and material questions of Anglo-American naval competition. The conference terminated "without touching upon the political issue in which the whole significance, and almost the whole danger, of that competition resided." In the past the English-speaking negotiators had sometimes "expressed impatience at ... the unduly abstract, logical and academic way in which the problem has been approached by others." Here, the question of disarmament was discussed in an unpolitical framework.[30]

The deterioration of diplomacy can surely be ascribed in part to the manner in which diplomatic conferences have been organized and conducted. The importance of preparation is signaled graphically in the post–World War II conferences. The memoirs and letters of responsible American diplomats support, by their omissions, the thesis that the United States has generally been oblivious to that continuing need. Only in the degree to which this funda-

29. Hans J. Morgenthau and Kenneth W. Thompson, *Politics Among Nations: The Struggle for Power and Peace* (6th ed.; New York, 1985), 581–84.

30. *Survey of International Affairs*, 1927, pp. 41, 42.

mental tendency is gradually reversed can we be hopeful about the future success of American diplomacy.[31]

Diplomacy especially in the Anglo-American world has been judged not only on its success. Moral standards have been applied as well. Yet the view of the diplomat as a specialist in lies and deception has been characteristic of the Western outlook in modern times. At best diplomats are past masters of intrigue; at worst they are directly responsible for the outbreak of warfare. The question of international morality has been, where does it come into play? Some philosophers and writers have sought simple formulas, as the attempt to identify the national interest of a particular country with universal morality. In Reinhold Niebuhr's words: "The reason each nation is so certain that it possesses a higher degree of honesty than its neighbours is that what appears as hypocrisy from the outside is usually only self-deception from the inside." Another concept is more ambitious. When loyalties to the state have been expanded into a political religion, that becomes the source of all morality. The national interest and universal morality are thus interchangeable.[32]

For Toynbee, morality is relative to the tasks that diplomacy must perform. In his more mature judgments, Toynbee neither condoned the struggle for power nor imagined it could be eliminated. Therefore, any form of diplomacy has a particular job to do, that is, to secure the interests of a nation while facilitating the prospects for peace. There is a morality in international politics and diplomacy which cannot wholly be identified with the common virtues of human relations. It must rather be associated with standards which are consistent with self-preservation in the struggle for power. It is exemplified by respect and integrity, which some associate with British diplomacy; by humanitarian principles, which have often characterized the philosophy of American policy; and with other traditional virtues in the conduct of foreign affairs. The best one can hope is that morality will modify, and sometimes allow the antagonists to transcend, that ever-present struggle.

Any consideration of moral principles leads on to a discussion of objectives and purposes. The national interest has served as a guide for the diplomat in determining the objectives of diplomacy. In this connection, the importance of national security is para-

31. See James F. Byrnes, *Speaking Frankly* (New York, 1947).

32. Reinhold Niebuhr, *Beyond Tragedy: Essays on the Christian Interpretation of History* (New York, 1937), 80.

mount. Among sovereign states that may be interdependent, security is said to be attainable only by a true system of collective security. Until the close of the nineteenth century, each nation could successfully maintain its security by mobilizing its own skill and strength. Now, however, the whole habitable earth has been knit together by the effects of the Industrial Revolution. The broad sphere of international politics has been reconstituted into one "Great Society," and the old rules of diplomatic finesse have consequently been declared outmoded. One diplomat who nevertheless believed in finesse was Sir John Simon, of whom it was said: "In playing a new role of the highest responsibility, under anxious and exacting conditions, [he] employed all the vigour and subtlety of a brilliant and practised legal mind in the pursuit of a diplomacy which was perhaps more in keeping with the international conditions of a past century. . . . He emulated the virtuosity of a Talleyrand or a Metternich. . . . The ends which were actually secured . . . were a disquieting uncertainty in regard to British objectives and a corresponding mistrust of British intentions."[33]

The philosophy of universal collective security, according to its proponents, transformed the whole environment within which diplomacy must work out its objectives: "Under these new conditions the only feasible foundation for diplomatic practice was the principle that 'no man liveth to himself and no man dieth to himself'—a maxim which was not the less relevant . . . because it could claim a more venerable antiquity than Channing's." A diplomat has to safeguard his nation and its interests through the creation of a concert of power among nations with similar interests. In a sense, international organization is designed to achieve this end. The British in the nineteenth century had established a rudimentary world order and many proposed that it be protected "by putting the *Pax Britannica* into commission." Some Englishmen saw the League of Nations as an instrument for marshaling opposition to any troublemaker who threatened this system.[34]

A more difficult task of diplomacy is to estimate the interests and power of those nations which will be for or against a policy of collective security. This is not a simple and mechanical undertaking, for each case must be considered in context. It made a difference in the 1920s, for instance, whether the threat was to Eastern or Western Germany. Since Eastern Europe and Eastern Germany

33. *Survey of International Affairs*, 1923, pp. 529–30.
34. *Ibid.*, 530; *Survey of International Affairs*, 1937, I, 23–24.

were less vital to its national security, Great Britain could be expected to join less actively in collective diplomacy there.[35]

Compromise and concession, the essence of diplomacy, are dependent upon the definition of vital and secondary interests. When vital interests, that is, those seen as essential to national security, are compatible, then diplomats must seek ways of reconciling the secondary interests of their particular states. When secondary as well as vital interests conflict, diplomats confront a difficult task, for the prospect of war then hangs like a sword over the negotiators. There is in that situation an alternative—nations can yet make an effort to redefine vital interests in relation to each other. But if this fails, it is unlikely that war can be averted.

This sort of reconsideration often appears impossible, as tragically illustrated by French and German objectives between the two world wars: "Logically, the French demand for security was virtually incompatible with the German claim to equality in armaments, since an inequality in armed strength was one of the elements of security as the French conceived it." By the time French interests were redefined, however, the negotiations were being carried on with von Papen or Hitler, not with Stresemann or Brüning.[36]

At most of the disarmament conferences in the interwar period, France saw manpower as crucial: in the event of a general European War, France demanded control of the western Mediterranean to ensure unimpeded transport of French North African troops. Toynbee observed: "The command in war-time of the Western Mediterranean was as vital as the command of the North-Western Pacific was for Japan. While, however, this Japanese vital interest had been effectively secured by Japan at the Washington Conference of 1921–2, an exclusive naval command of the Western Mediterranean was not secured, and never could be secured, to France." Here, the interests of Italy and Great Britain would have to be accommodated as well.[37]

There are two problems with regard to vital interests. In a democracy, the same public opposition to power politics in general has been directed against a consideration of vital interests in particular. Second, any objective appraisal of vital interests has frequently been weakened by its counterplay with domestic policy. The best illustration of this can be seen in an episode in the history

35. *Survey of International Affairs*, 1924, p. 8.
36. *Survey of International Affairs*, 1932, p. 187.
37. *Survey of International Affairs*, 1929, pp. 13–14.

of British foreign policy. On November 20, 1936, Anthony Eden attempted to delineate those interests which were sufficiently important to national security so that Britain would fight to defend them:

> These arms will never be used in a war of aggression. They will never be used for a purpose inconsistent with the Covenant of the League or the Pact of Paris. They may, and if the occasion arose they would, be used in our own defence and in the defence of the territories of the British Commonwealth of Nations. They may, and if the occasion arose they would, be used in the defence of France and Belgium against unprovoked aggression in accordance with our existing obligations. They may, and if a new Western European settlement can be reached, they would be used in the defence of Germany were she the victim of unprovoked aggression by any of the other signatories of such a settlement.
>
> These, together with our Treaty of Alliance with 'Iraq [sic] and our projected treaty with Egypt, are our definite obligations. In addition our armaments may be used in bringing help to a victim of aggression in any case where, in our judgment, it would be proper under the provisions of the Covenant to do so. I used the word "may" deliberately, since in such an instance there is no automatic obligation, to take military action. It is, moreover, right that this should be so, for nations cannot be expected to incur automatic military obligations save for areas where their vital interests are concerned.

Eden's estimate was squarely within the time-honored tradition of British foreign policy. His formulation, interpreted in Rome and Berlin as proof that British vital interests would not be extended to Eastern Europe, was attacked in England. In response, both Eden and Neville Chamberlain declared that British interests must be construed as applying equally in Eastern and Western Europe. Eden observed: "If our vital interests are situated in certain clearly definable areas, our interest in peace is world-wide, and there is a simple reason for this. The world has now become so small—and every day, with the march of science, it becomes smaller—that sparks in some sphere comparatively remote from our own interests may become a conflagration sweeping a continent or a hemisphere." These two speeches by Eden, coming less than a month apart, reflect the influence exerted on international by domestic politics. Any state must concern itself with questions of universal collective security, for its vital interests are limited simply by virtue of its condition as a nation-state. This fact of international politics persists whatever the demands placed on political leaders.[38]

As early as 1915, Toynbee was aware of the need for recognizing the respective vital interests of important nations: "In delimiting ... our new frontier between Germany and the Russian Empire, we must expose neither country to the other's strategic initiative (otherwise we shall only accentuate their fears, and open a new era of war between them, instead of closing the era that is past)."[39] In all the discussions of strategic frontiers, the most urgent problem was to safeguard the vital interests of the parties. No intelligent theory of international relations can afford to disregard facts of international relations which are involved in the whole pattern of politics among nations.

There are certain objective conditions which facilitate the processes of diplomacy. First and foremost, the participants in world politics must view conflicts as divergencies which can be mitigated by compromise. Spheres of influence, which have traditionally permitted elbowroom for bargaining and accommodation, are no more than a formal recognition that nations have areas of special interest in which their influence is paramount. Nations which have concluded agreements regarding spheres of interest have mutually recognized each other's interests. The chances for peace are better if these respective spheres can be separated by neutralized areas or buffer zones, for they prevent the antagonists from facing each other across narrow and contentious boundaries without possibilities of strategic retreat. In Africa and the Middle East, spheres of influence helped maintain the peace over long periods of time. It is not surprising that Toynbee should make reference repeatedly to this means of preserving peace.

The United States has had its traditional sphere of influence in the Western Hemisphere, its long-term responsibilities for which were expressed in the Monroe Doctrine (1821). Some critics have maintained that since a change in policy in 1930 the United States has been less concerned with safeguarding this sphere of influence. Toynbee acknowledged that "there was a marked and avowedly deliberate change in the policy of the United States Government towards Latin America." He added: "The State Department became less energetic in championing, in *partibus pere-*

38. *Survey of International Affairs*, 1936, pp. 367–68, 317n1, 368.
39. Arnold J. Toynbee, *Nationality and the War* (London, 1915), 64.

grinis, the cause of the *Civis Americanus."* "It relaxed the political control which it had previously exercised over certain weak and backward republics in the Caribbean area . . . by keeping minoritarian Governments in power through the presence of United States marines."[40] If such direct control was relaxed under the Good Neighbor Policy, it has been reasserted by the Reagan administration in the 1980s.

Are not these steps, taken collectively, substantial evidence that the United States was in the process of abandoning its traditional sphere of influence? In Toynbee's opinion, just the opposite was true, for one of the chief purposes of its new policy was to allay "the uneasiness which had been aroused in Latin American minds by a recent tendency . . . to enlarge the scope of the Monroe Doctrine and to transform it from an instrument of national self-protection into an instrument of 'economic imperialism.'"[41] Thus the United States acted with tact and intelligence to strengthen this sphere and sought multilateral recognition for the Monroe Doctrine. Under subsequent international agreements, including the Rio treaties, its preservation became a Pan-American obligation.

Another sphere of influence arrangement involves the strategic interests of Great Britain. The configuration of European power politics would have made it more difficult to obtain formal recognition of these interests by any association of states. Still, Britain has insisted on defining its interests as concentrated principally in Western Europe. In 1936, Toynbee observed: "A majority of the Government's supporters were still in favour of limiting British commitments on a regional basis." British policy-makers have been reluctant to enter into binding commitments in Eastern Europe. When other interests have conflicted and when England has had to choose between achieving some adjustment of the German problem or turning its strength to Eastern Europe, England has always given priority to the former. Toynbee said that "a considerable proportion of the British public, including some of the government supporters in the House of Commons, would deem it to be in the interests of the British Empire to abandon Eastern Europe to its fate, if by that means the question of a redistribution of colonial territory could be shelved." Competent observers have concluded, therefore, that in most cases Britain has confined its sphere of influence to Western Europe and particularly to the Low Coun-

40. *Survey of International Affairs*, 1930, pp. 361, 362.
41. *Ibid.*, 362.

tries. Only when the European balance of power as a whole has been threatened, as in the case of the invasion of Poland, has Britain diverged from this traditional policy.[42]

In the Far East, Britain has sought to preserve a limited sphere of influence: "In 1927, for example, when the Kuomintang (at this time in Russian Communist leading strings) was sweeping across the Yangtse Basin . . . in the course of its victorious march from Canton to Peking, the British Government had sent a British Defence Force to Shanghai to ensure the safety and neutrality of the International Settlement." When Japan was expanding throughout certain areas in the Far East, the British and the Americans both attempted to protect this local sphere of influence. It is illuminating for nations such as the United States, with developing foreign policies, to remember that British interests have been limited geographically for over three hundred years.[43]

Starting with similar assumptions, Japan has insisted that it had a right to a sphere of influence in East Asia. But for Toynbee, there was a distinction between this type of regional interest and the others he had studied: "Japanese publicists made a good deal of play with the analogy which they drew between Japan's claim to hegemony over Eastern Asia and the American Monroe Doctrine, but the analogy would hardly stand close examination." The Japanese wanted this sphere of influence for purposes of expansion. Thus, for Toynbee, at least in 1936, there were good and bad spheres of influence.[44]

As early as 1924, two spheres or circles of Russian influence were seen: "The innermost zone consisted of the New European border states which, until a few years before, had been provinces of the Russian Empire." This zone was likely to be integrated successfully into the Soviet sphere. These states had some common ties of language and certain common ways of life. Other factors consolidating this zone were the antagonisms of the White Russians, Ukrainians, and Jews toward Polish rule and the dissatisfaction of the Rumanian-speaking peasantry in the Bessarabian sector with the old order. In the second sphere of Russian influence, projected to reach beyond the border states, the basis for any unity was primarily common misery. These satellites were extremely uneven in their loyalty to and identification with the Soviet planet. Be-

42. *Survey of International Affairs,* 1936, pp. 280, 281.
43. *Survey of International Affairs,* 1932, pp. 538, 539.
44. *Survey of International Affairs,* 1936, p. 54n1.

cause of the political feuds which remained after World War I, Bulgaria, Macedonia, and Croatia were most likely to succumb to Soviet attraction. "In Hungary, on the other hand, where the national disillusionment over the disastrous outcome of the War of 1914 had enabled a Communist organization to seize the government for a few weeks in 1919, there had been a violent reaction which had brought a 'White' Government into power." Czechoslovakia was another country whose position in this outer sphere was somewhat doubtful at the time, and in December, 1920, the Communists there launched a revolution, which proved a conspicuous failure. Austria, likewise, was singularly deficient in possessing a revolutionary frame of mind. Only Germany, which then as now held the key position, gave some indication of shifting to the East: "For five years the victorious Allied Powers cooperated—quite unintentionally but nonetheless efficaciously—with the Third International by driving the German people to the wall."[45]

Thus two Russian spheres of influence exist in which Soviet foreign policy has pursued its aims following both world wars. The inner sphere clearly comprises Russian vital interests; the outer zone is allegedly designed to protect those interests.

The spheres of interest mentioned thus far have, with the exception of the American, been based on political facts rather than formal recognition in political settlements. In Africa and the Middle East, spheres of influence have been based specifically on treaties and diplomatic agreements. This was the case, for example, in Abyssinia, with the Anglo-Italian agreements of July 5 and August 2, 1926. A similar agreement was worked out for Persia and it "was steadily maintained . . . on the British side from the conclusion of the Anglo-Russian agreement in 1907 down to its lapse after the fall of the Czardom ten years later." The purpose in these instances was not to obliterate the national interest of the small countries involved but to assure the alien country with commercial interests in particular regions that another alien power would not infringe upon those interests. In the case of the Anglo-Italian agreements, "what the notes did was merely to secure against Italian opposition the concession desired from Abyssinia by Great Britain, and to secure against British opposition the concession desired by Italy. In the British Government's belief the works contemplated by the Italians and the British would be enormously to

45. *Survey of International Affairs*, 1924, pp. 185, 186, 187.

the advantage of Abyssinia and would as little threaten her independence or her integrity as the railway already constructed by
French enterprise from Djibouti to Addis Ababa."[46]

Such spheres of influence and through them international peace
have been most effectively preserved when there have also been
buffer zones or neutralized areas. Between Hellenic civilization and
the realm of Eastern Orthodox Christendom was a fluctuating line
of demarcation. This area was not integrated uniformly into either
civilization, and some of the societies in the area between these
two civilizations acquired either pro-Greek or pro-Hellenic sympathies. Assyria and Egypt, especially after 250 A.D., are examples
of the latter. Other areas have resisted incorporation: "Nisibis, in
A.D. 363, refused to be ceded to Persia. The Nestorian heresy, which
flourished at Nisibis and farther East, was an Oriental reaction
against Greek influences and resisted all attempts to incorporate
it in the Western system. The Monatists of Asia Minor, also largely
Eastern in aspiration, had their Western and their Eastern branches,
the former mainly Catholic in tone and practice, the latter less
amenable to Western influence."[47]

Buffer states have often been founded upon the need among hostile powers for doing business with one another. Not being able to
arrive at a political understanding, these powers have chosen go-
betweens which also served a political function. Such areas have
had military significance as well. Acts of aggression against buffer
states are interpreted by "protector states" as aggression against
themselves. It has been a commonplace in international politics
that the best defense of a country's integrity may be found in de-
fending the integrity of a neighboring state:

> Indeed, it was almost of the essence of a Great Power's foreign
> policy that it should not contemplate submitting to the indig-
> nity of allowing its own territory to be made a target for attack,
> but should take it as a *casus belli* if its adversary ventured to
> trespass upon the no-man's-land between the two opposing
> camps. Great Britain, for example, had asserted her title to rank
> as a Great Power by thrice fighting France on Flemish, and not
> on British, soil in a war for the vindication of the integrity of the
> Netherlands as a buffer state for Great Britain, and again by
> fighting Russia in the Crimea, and not on the Indus, in a war for

46. *Survey of International Affairs*, 1929, pp. 227n2, 225.
47. F. S. Marvin and Arnold J. Toynbee, *The Evolution of World Peace* (London,
1921), 22.

the vindication of the integrity of Turkey as a buffer state for British India.[48]

The most famous instance of neutralization of a territory is that of Belgium. By a settlement in 1839 among the five Great Powers of that day, Great Britain, France, Prussia, Russia, and Austria, the frontiers of Belgium were redefined and various questions regarding waterways and transits were worked out. But the key article in the treaty provided for neutralization, rendering the case of Belgium, in terms of power politics, roughly similar to that of Austria after World War I: "In both cases the foundling happened to occupy so important a strategic position in Europe that either the *reunion* of Belgium with France in 1830 or the *Anschluss* of Austria to Germany in 1933 would be tantamount, in the eyes of the *cidevant* victors, to an overthrow of the recently established balance of power."[49]

All sides had an interest in the maintenance of this status quo, yet each interpreted the guarantee in different ways. France and England insisted that they should be permitted to send troops to Belgium if any threat to its security existed. The German agreement, on the other hand, omitted any reference to this provision. Indeed, the role of a buffer zone will in wartime be determined by considerations of power rather than formal legal commitments: "Whether, in such an event, they would sacrifice the support of France and Great Britain or the support of Germany would no doubt depend on the estimate which the Belgian Government of the day were able to make of the respective strength of Belgium's guarantors. A great apparent preponderance of strength on the German side might counterbalance the instinctive feeling (which appears to have been widespread among all sections of Belgian society) that Great Britain was the natural guardian of the independence of Belgium, and therefore her most reliable guarantor in any European conflict." Buffer states are in essence areas in which domination by one power or another is temporarily prohibited by an agreement between them. There is no expectation that buffer states will be permanent and dependable allies for one state or the other. The long life of Belgium as a neutral state attests to the fundamental soundness of this principle.[50]

48. *Survey of International Affairs*, 1937, I, 27–28.
49. *Survey of International Affairs*, 1920–23, p. 65; *Survey of International Affairs*, 1933, p. 113.
50. *Survey of International Affairs*, 1937, I, 356.

One final type of buffer arrangement which Toynbee anticipated was that which threatened to grow up between East and West
following World War I. After 1936, there was an effort by Rumania
and Poland to heal old grievances, but Poland was hostile to Rumania's ally, Czechoslovakia:

> If Rumania did take up this position her action might have a de-
> cisive effect upon the destinies of Europe; for, instead of contin-
> uing to provide a line of communication between Russia and
> Czechoslovakia, she would then be completing the process of
> insulation which Poland had begun when she had set Rumania
> the example of retiring into isolation. An insulating bloc which
> included Rumania as well as Poland would mask the western
> frontiers of the Soviet Union from the Baltic to the Black Sea
> without a break. It would mean in effect the re-establishment
> of that *cordon sanitaire* between a Communist Russia and a
> Bourgeois Europe.

In the past, a buffer zone of this sort had been desired by France in
particular as a means of preventing Russia from joining hands with
Hungary and Germany. In 1936 it would have served the opposite
purpose, preventing effective alliances among Czechoslovakia,
France, and the Soviet Union.[51]

Toynbee saw the chances for peace in our own day as proportionate to success in negotiating a settlement which would grant
the parties sufficient elbowroom in their own spheres of influence.
In 1948, for example, such an arrangement would have reflected
the immense superiority of the United States. Today, however, if
the United States and the Soviet Union are able by means of traditional diplomacy to set up spheres of influence, what are the
chances that these spheres will be separated by buffer zones?
Toynbee was very skeptical regarding this prospect: "As to my
conception of a division of the world into spheres of influence, I do
not see much prospect of keeping a neutral zone between the
Western and the Russian sphere. The pull of the United States and
Russia is so strong that I do not see how any countries could maintain anything like an independent position between them without
finding themselves having, sooner or later, to come definitely to
one or other side of the dividing line."[52]

If spheres of influence are the form through which diplomacy

51. *Survey of International Affairs*, 1936, pp. 225–26.
52. Arnold J. Toynbee to Kenneth W. Thompson, April 19, 1950, in possession
of the recipient.

seeks to establish international order and peace, political settlement is the process by which this end can best be achieved. The tendency in international politics has been to seek separate solutions to concrete political and legal problems as they have arisen. This practice has resulted in fragmenting the issues of diplomacy and ignoring the underlying political questions which must first be resolved. Some nations with effective foreign policies have succeeded in reconciling their policies with the foreign policies of others and settling outstanding political issues. In the postwar era the need for this became ever more clear. France and Germany belatedly came to the conclusion that a settlement between them was vitally important to peace in Europe. Although this could not guarantee lasting peaceful relations between the two nations, it was the first and most fundamental step in that direction.

Franco-Italian rivalry after World War I is an example of many-sided conflict. The disputes over Tunisia involved particularly the status of Italian settlers in that French territory. The Italians were dissatisfied with the limited settlements on the frontier between French North Africa and Italian Libya. Naval parity in the Mediterranean was still another source of contention. In Southeastern Europe, they both tried to win the support of the successor states of the Hapsburg and Ottoman empires. These wide-ranging differences were approached issue by issue without any serious attempt to deal with the fundamental political problems.[53]

Toynbee referred to other instances where political settlement was uppermost in the minds of leaders: "In January 1926, indeed, the Jugoslav Government went so far as to notify the Greek Government that they would be prepared to consider the conclusion of a Balkan Pact; but they stipulated that . . . outstanding questions must first be settled." The subsequent settlement paved the way for closer cooperation among the Balkan states and was followed "almost immediately by a decided relaxation in the tension between Jugoslavia and Bulgaria." Not only the principal parties but those with whom they conducted international relations were encouraged. Shortly thereafter, a comprehensive settlement between Greece and Turkey was worked out.[54]

In Western Europe as well voices were raised in support of some form of general settlement. To a limited extent, the makers of French foreign policy became more sympathetic to the idea that

53. *Survey of International Affairs,* 1935, I, 94–95.
54. *Survey of International Affairs,* 1931, pp. 146, 147.

political differences must first be settled before technical questions could be successfully debated. On May 9, 1930, Dino Grandi attempted to open negotiations with France: "To these suggestions, Monsieur Briand . . . replied that, for . . . negotiations, the procedure through the regular diplomatic channels was preferable, and that it would be advisable to wait until . . . negotiations had produced results before resuming the negotiations over the naval problem." As the German menace grew more serious, however, there was "an increasing tendency to attach importance to the success" of some kind of negotiations.[55]

A considerable price must be paid for failure to negotiate on outstanding political issues. Toynbee considered the way in which Polish and German statesmen handled the Chorzów dispute, which involved the liquidation of German property in Upper Silesia and the question of a certain nitrate factory. It was a political rather than a legal dispute and yet:

> The League of Nation's Council and the Permament Court of International Justice . . . were constantly called upon to mediate or to decide questions on which a direct settlement should have been easy. . . . There would appear to be no reason, except the absence of good will, why the agreement that was achieved by direct negotiations between Germany and Poland in November 1928 should not have been achieved by direct negotiations during the winter of 1926–7—a result which would have saved the two Governments themselves, as well as the Permament Court, from the . . . time and money . . . involved in the hearing of the case . . . on three separate occasions.[56]

There is today a pressing need for some form of political settlement. Successful negotiations depend on the privacy with which they are pursued. The idea of private discussions being broadened was foreshadowed in Chamberlain's proposal in 1937: "The ultimate object which we have in view is what is described as a general settlement. It is quite obvious that no general settlement can be arrived at merely by conversations between two or three countries, and therefore we must . . . contemplate that other countries will be brought into the conversations." In a general way, this is consistent with Toynbee's idea of the most effective form of negotiation. He would approve of negotiations at the highest level

55. *Ibid.*, 261; *Survey of International Affairs*, 1932, p. 268.
56. *Survey of International Affairs*, 1932, pp. 330–31.

conducted in privacy from which an agreement on spheres of influence might be forthcoming. Although this discounts the rights and interests of small countries in the short run, it would be the chief hope for achieving peace in the long run. It would be based for Toynbee on "situations of strength" which comprise both military and economic power.[57]

Although we have seen shifts and reversals in Toynbee's theory of diplomacy, we also have observed a common core to his thinking. In the 1930s he found certain aspects of the "old diplomacy" intolerable, particularly when he was writing within the idealist tradition of international relations, and he continued to emphasize some of its weaknesses. Likewise he criticized the operation of the "new diplomacy," which proved aimless, contradictory, and self-defeating. The striking of any balance sheet will necessarily be arbitrary and subjective; one can at least enumerate the main points which Toynbee emphasized.

First, the weaknesses of the old diplomacy are the outgrowth primarily of its autocratic and archaic character. The old diplomacy sometimes became trivial and inconclusive because it dealt only with local issues. In 1932 after the outbreak of hostilities in Manchuria, the best that British diplomats could do was to lodge protests in Tokyo against the detention at Mukden of receipts belonging to the Peking-Mukden Railway, "a Chinese concern of which the bondholders were British subjects."[58] Elsewhere, the foremost interest of traditional diplomatists was to interpret responsibilities narrowly. As we have seen, private conferences helped to create an aura of intrigue. The old diplomacy in a certain sense was the handmaiden of war, and some idealists suggested there was a causal connection. Finally, the old diplomacy was unsatisfactory because it dealt negatively and within limited geographical areas with problems that required institutions of universal collective security.

Experience since the early 1930s, however, demonstrated that in several important respects the new diplomacy was even more lacking in qualities and strengths. Democratic pressures have deflected concentration from its major objectives—political figures may fear losing an election at home or must leave a conference before their work is complete. As we have seen, differences have fre-

57. *Survey of International Affairs*, 1937, I, 34.
58. *Survey of International Affairs*, 1932, p. 542.

quently been intensified because of the preference for diplomatic victories rather than political settlements. The new diplomacy, moreover, has been plagued by shifts in the personnel of key delegations often at the most inopportune time. All these factors, together with the attempt to substitute the relative promptness of majority rule for the slow process of traditional diplomacy, which itself must create bases of agreement, have had a paralyzing effect on contemporary diplomacy.

Toynbee never drew a final tally sheet on the old and the new diplomacy. In making proposals for certain concrete problems, he chose one or the other. It may be taken as an index of his opinion that he looked principally to the old diplomacy as it adjusted itself to new realities and patterns of relationships. It remained for him the most hopeful approach in dealing with persistent conflicts in the cold war.

PART FOUR

Prospects for Western Civilization

CHAPTER VI

The West: A Political Prediction

I F TOYNBEE had been solely a historian, the topic of this chapter would probably not appear. However, Toynbee was also a philosopher of history and therefore considered such questions as where his generation stood within the stream of history and what this might mean for the pattern of the future. In doing so, he recognized that the annals of historical writing are strewn with the wreckage of innumerable ventures into political prediction.

The most common failing in appraising the present point in history has been to overestimate a people's role and assume that history has reached its climax with a single society. Such a point of view was common in England at the turn of the century. Toynbee recalled that when he was a child, a prevailing opinion was that England's history had ended with the Battle of Waterloo.[1] Conflicts were localized in places as remote and uncivilized as the United States and the Balkans, so England was free from the sacrifices of major wars. Gibbon best described this frame of mind when he wrote, in 1781, that Western society had escaped the pathos of history. Only "temperate and undecisive" conflicts continued, which were hardly destructive of normal relations. Gibbon assumed that Europe was beyond barbarism and warfare and that aliens on its boundaries lacked the skills to offer any opposition. Further, if such powers accepted European methods, they would at the same time absorb its culture and peaceful temper. This sense

1. Arnold J. Toynbee, *Civilization on Trial* (New York, 1948), 17.

of self-confidence, security, and optimism, which permeated eighteenth-century thinking, was not to reappear until toward the close of the nineteenth century. Society's ascendance from the brutality of Wars of Nationality to a recognition of common standards of politeness and cultivation was widely believed to have transformed human history and altered mankind's prospects for the future. Even countries such as Russia had become "polished nations," for in accepting military arts from the West, they had also accepted its customs and habits of peace. Yet within Gibbon's own lifetime these views were to be altered. Experience with the French Revolution hardened his evaluation of the nature of society and man. The Wars of Ideology unleashed a brutality which eclipsed the intensity of the Wars of Religion. Gibbon was compelled to flee through Europe to escape a violence he had complacently written off as an "archaism." What appeared in 1781 as permanent security and stability was seen in 1792 to be unexampled violence and brutality.

Toynbee himself enumerated the histories of ancient and modern groups who considered themselves a "Chosen People" for whom history was essentially over—indeed, he suggested, "this illusion seems to be common to all humanity." In the modern world, history had reached its culmination for the middle class in England, Germany, and the United States with the Reform Bill of 1832, the overthrow of France in 1870, and the outcome of the Civil War: "For these three batches of western middle class people fifty years ago, God's work of creation was completed." Even the wisest students who have tried to fathom the precise point in history at which the West stands have been susceptible to views of this kind. Although Toynbee himself sometimes lapsed into this popular philosophy, particularly during his idealist phase, he later saw Christianity as the final step in the quest for religious truth. Although each breakdown in civilization produced a new religion, often one with deeper spiritual insights, Christianity is the exception. Any future religious progress must express itself exclusively in interpretations of its unchanging truths: for Toynbee, Christianity is outside the history of religion since, with it, man's alienation from God is rectified.[2] Thus religion, not a nation or "Chosen People," politically provides a standard for historical evaluation.

2. Arnold J. Toynbee, *The Prospects of Western Civilization* (New York, 1947), 13, 14; Toynbee, *Civilization on Trial*, 18.

Sometimes, however, historians have looked at the future in a spirit of fatalism and have presumed to detect clear-cut symptoms of self-destruction in the course a society was following. People in 1000 A.D. believed that "the world was literally coming to an end." Instead, the eleventh century "proved to be the beginning of a tremendous uprise and advance in the history of our Western Christian Civilization." A fatalistic sense of history is just as irrational as is a philosophy of complacent self-glorification.[3]

If there had been an element of false optimism in Toynbee's interpretation of contemporary history, the events of the 1930s destroyed it. In that decade, a succession of tragedies caused people to consider seriously the possibility that Western society might break down. That prospect had been inconceivable when the discovery of ancient civilizations was regarded not as proof of the mortality of all civilizations but as a sign of important work by Western archaeologists.

The key year in the transformation of Western thinking on where the world stood in history was 1931. Up to that point it had seemed to many that "Western Civilization had been living and growing continuously" for some twelve or thirteen centuries. To be sure, there had been temporary checks and setbacks. But since the eighth century, "Western Civilization had gone from strength to strength," and it was widely assumed that progress was inevitable. All this changed fundamentally with the worldwide economic depression and the regional political crisis in Asia. Members of a hitherto triumphant society began asking themselves whether "Western life and growth might conceivably be coming to an end in their day."[4]

Toynbee proposed a chronology of Western history for dealing with the West's future. The first period he identified began in 675 A.D. and lasted until 1075 A.D., when the papacy went to war with the secular states, an action which may have been the first breakdown of Western civilization. Toynbee, however, was cautious about making an unqualified judgment, and his subsequent writing suggested that whether or not Western society had broken down was still an open question.[5]

The second period, the era of *Respublica Christiana*, spanned the years from 1075 to 1475. At the beginning, feudalism was prev-

---

3. Toynbee, *The Prospects of Western Civilization*, 13, 14.
4. *Survey of International Affairs*, 1931, p. 1.
5. Arnold J. Toynbee, *A Study of History* (12 vols.; London, 1934–61), IV, 185, 453.

alent. And toward the end, new political relations between the individual and the state appeared and feudalism declined.[6]

The third period, from 1475 to 1875, saw the city-state become the kingdom-state. There was also the development of democracy and industrialism, which prevailed in the fourth period (since 1875). Thus two underlying forces have brought much benefit to individuals but have also led to the deterioration of international politics. The false god of nationalism, having taken democracy and industrialism as its allies, hovers over our future as sovereign nations and as a civilization.

Toynbee's profound anxiety, which contrasts so markedly with Gibbon's optimism, was more than a general feeling. It was based on three factors which were the cornerstones for Toynbee's predictions. The first is a discovery of the predicament the West shares with other civilizations, all of which have declined. The clear symptoms were, and are, militarism and the emergence of the political religion of nationalism. The other factors, which also plagued earlier societies but have been intensified in our day, are war and class. Because of technological progress, they may bring about the end of civilization.

If we consider these factors in discussing the position of the West, a number of issues arise. First, there are "symptoms of things going wrong in the history of other civilizations of which one finds echoes, or partial symptoms, in our own case." One of these is militarism. Assyria destroyed itself by war, despite its achievements in administration and science: "In trying to conquer the world, they bled themselves white and finally provoked their neighbours into annihilating them." Earlier, Toynbee wrote: "Now, in Prussia in our Western world . . . you have another Assyria." Another symptom of decline is the emergence of the political religion of nationalism. The Greeks "put their treasure in a wonderful political institution, the city state." It proved a remarkable instrument for political and cultural growth. But at a subsequent stage in Greek history this instrument became inadequate, yet the Greeks were so much "in love with it, that they could not put it aside." No powerful city-state was willing to sacrifice its sovereignty to a broader form of political organization. Consequently, political unity, which was essential for survival and which was not provided by the city-state, came too late—in the form of the Roman conquest. The parallel in our day is the transglorification of the na-

6. *Ibid.*, 339n4.

tion-state, which has become the principal Western religion. A condition which caused the decline of another civilization is thus a "menace in our own case."[7]

The two factors, then, which take on a unique character in Western society are class and war. The problem of war has been the cause of death for most societies. What is unique about war in Western society is the prospect that "the whole enterprise may come to a stop if we cannot solve the problem of war."[8] Class, likewise, presents an unprecedented challenge because of the need for rapid readjustments in a social environment still geared to nineteenth-century requirements. Our present point in history is defined and determined by our present stage in the life cycle of Western civilization. Our position here is similar to that of other societies at comparable stages in their development. What is unique and distinctive is the accelerated pace of contemporary technological progress, which in turn has transformed war and class into enormities which may bring all civilization, not merely our own, to an end.

Two eloquent illustrations of these underlying tensions were the reactions in twentieth-century Germany and Russia against Western civilization. These reactions were, at the same time, exaggerations of existing tendencies throughout Western society. Scholars in the United States and Europe have, in analyzing the Nazi and Communist movements, emphasized one or the other of two underlying characteristics—a reaction to or an exaggeration of trends in Western civilization. However, few have emphasized that nazism, for example, was both a vast "piratical expedition" against the norms and standards of the embryonic world community and a logical development in the emergence of certain ideas and political principles which had been gaining ground within Western civilization for more than four hundred years. It is the great virtue of Toynbee's evaluation of the two revolts against the West that he appraised them in sociological and political terms, as well as in their moral and legal contexts. Thus he demonstrated that they were a reaction against and an expression of Western civilization.

Nazism, in the first place, was a consummation of modern nationalism. In a profound and tragic sense, it was "the *reductio ad extremum* . . . of a politico-religious movement, the pagan deification and worship of parochial human communities, which had

7. Toynbee, *The Prospects of Western Civilization*, 15, 16.
8. *Ibid.*, 17, 19.

been gradually gaining ground for more than four centuries in the Western World at large." Through exaggeration and caricature, it brought to light the "sinister elements which were latent in some degree in the modern Western institution of parochial sovereignty in every one of its local embodiments." For the more farsighted observers in other Western countries, "the monomania and the fanaticism and the brutality of 'The Third Reich' threw a baleful light upon certain general tendencies of political development which were common to all Western polities in modern times." These included the state's attaining an unrivaled position and the deterioration of the traditional influence of the church.[9]

In the second place, the Nazis, no more than fourteen years after a major military defeat for Germany, launched a recovery program in which an increasing number of Germans could have a stake. Nazism became the chief means of redressing the injustices visited on a great nation by an unfair peace treaty. What made this aspect particularly significant was its relation to modern nationalism: "It is possible, and even probable, that the pagan worship of a parochial community would not have been carried to these extreme lengths . . . if one of the great nations . . . had not been thrown into a mood of peculiar receptivity . . . in consequence of the penalization to which she had been subjected in the Peace Settlement of 1919–20."[10] It was the interaction of the two expressions of modern nationalism and the objective needs of postwar Germany which were principally responsible for the demonic character of the Nazi movement.

In the third place, nazism raised the supreme issue of the age between "the principles of Tribalism and the principles of Christianity." The convulsion in German society was a reflection of the profound struggle going on throughout Western civilization. Troublesome distinctions between hypocrisy and sincerity or myth and fact did not exist in Hitler's policy: "For Herr Hitler the mesh of propaganda was, in all probability, the very substance of reality." Nazism had assumed an "involuntary historical role of exposing the moral perversity of the once Christian society." One of the ways this was done was "its dogma that Mankind was to be classified on a newfangled criterion of physical race in place of the Christian classification by faith and works." The doctrine of racial superiority imposed more rigid qualifications on political and so-

9. *Survey of International Affairs*, 1933, pp. 111, 120–21.
10. *Ibid.*, 112.

cial leadership than religion had ever done, yet it only brought to
the surface a disgraceful social philosophy which had become almost universal in Western society. A second way was "the tacit
repudiation of the God of the Christians, Jews and Muslims" for a
new object of worship. The pure "Nordic race" was fulfilling its
historical destiny in the domination of the German state and ultimately the world. A third way was "the glorification of intolerance and violence and bloodshed which were represented to the
rising generation . . . as splendid manifestations of 'Nordic hero-
ism.'" Racism, atheism, and violence, crucial to the doctrinal apparatus of nazism, symbolized in practice the brazen glorification
of social and political practices sometimes present elsewhere in
modern international politics, although in less blatant form.[11]

The Bolshevik Revolution and its aftermath constitute a second reaction within Western civilization. There are, indeed, fundamental points of similarity between communism and nazism,
as "[a] cult of intolerance and violence and its practical application
in the persecution of dissenters." Since violence and intolerance
are frequently among the by-products of unbridled nationalism,
communism is primarily an exaggeration of a feature of Western
society. But what distinguishes communism from nazism is the
phenomenal success of the former as a crusading political religion.
The shock caused by communism has precedents only if one goes
back to Islam, which challenged Western society until 1683, when
the Turks failed in their attempt to capture Vienna. Islam, as communism, seized upon certain aspects of Christianity, pulled them
out of context, exaggerated them, and built a criticism of contemporary society. But communism is more formidable, for the con-
verts of Islam were confined to areas which had come under Mus-
lim domination. There were never centers of Islamic propaganda
in France or England; but world communism has cells almost everywhere.[12]

It is a legitimate question, therefore, to ask what its sources of
strength are. First, the Marxian creed was "a genuine abstract of
Christianity—but an abstract that was so fragmentary and jejeune
that it had become a ludicrous travesty of its great original." The
fundamental tenet of socialism was: from each according to his
abilities, to each according to his needs. In both practice and teach-

---

11. *Ibid.*, 119; *Survey of International Affairs*, 1936, p. 372; *Survey of International Affairs*, 1933, pp. 121, 122.

12. *Survey of International Affairs*, 1933, p. 123n1; *Survey of International Affairs*, 1931, pp. 4–5.

ing, this was an original Christian doctrine. Second, communism narrowed its application to the material sphere, thus offering a quick and simple remedy to the suffering people throughout the world. Finally, "Communism followed Muhammed in reintroducing the vein of revolutionary violence." In these terms, communism threatens to eclipse Islam as a missionary religion and nazism as the dynamism of an expanding Great Power.[13]

Despite the dynamism of communism, Toynbee did not believe that war between the United States and the Soviet Union was inevitable—in fact, he was outspoken in the view that war was not even likely. It is appropriate to consider, therefore, the nature of his conception of the cold war. As he viewed it, the struggle between East and West is not primarily between rival ideologies, for then the issue would have to be decided through a general war. Toynbee saw the cold war rather as a struggle between two Great Powers, at present the only Great Powers, and it manifested itself in the conflict between their respective foreign policies.

In the 1930s, Toynbee had written confidently about the disappearance of the Communist threat. The victory of the forces of Stalin over the militant world revolutionary group led by Trotsky meant in effect that the Soviet Union represented no threat at all: "From a Machiavellian standpoint, however, the replacement of Trotsky's militant Communist universalism by Stalin's parochial Communist nationalism was to be reckoned as a definite and important gain for the cause of world peace. For a man who has settled down to cultivate his own garden is a man with a stake in the *status quo* who is no longer tempted to disturb his neighbours and indeed no longer concerned with these neighbours at all except in so far as they threaten disturbance on their part." He blithely assumed that the Soviet Union would settle down to pursue a sensible status quo foreign policy. In the 1930s the national interests of the United States, on the other hand, were restricted to the Western Hemisphere and, according to some legislators' foreign policy declarations, to the Far East. Any future conflict between the expanding interests of the United States and the Soviet Union in Europe seemed remote. But even in 1933, there were signs that these public announcements were an imperfect reflection of America's real interests. As Toynbee observed: "Sooner or later, this newly awakened interest of the American people in human af-

13. *Survey of International Affairs*, 1934, p. 355n3.

fairs would overleap its parochial limits and would come to occupy a world-wide field. It was not for nothing that the United
States had been drawn into belligerency in the War of 1914–18 and
had found herself intimately concerned, in the post-war years, in
those international problems which had their focus in the Western
Pacific and in Eastern Asia."[14]

The conditions Toynbee found in 1930 had virtually disappeared in the 1950s, by which time the Soviet and American
spheres of interest had become worldwide. The Soviet Union for a
variety of reasons chose to pursue a foreign policy of imperialism.
Toynbee discussed the challenge: "If man were nothing more than
economic man, there would be no reason why Russia and America
should collide with one another for generations to come. But, unfortunately, man is a political as well as an economic animal."[15]

This statement is a revealing confirmation of the thesis that imperialism is motivated by political rather than economic factors.
It has been widely argued that "one of the considerations that drove
the rulers of Nazi Germany and contemporary Japan into aggressive war was their inability to provide more than a minority of their
young men with jobs." In contrast, both the United States and the
Soviet Union have resources and opportunities which obviate expansion as an urgent need. However, the wellsprings of Soviet and
American foreign policy are fear and the security-power dilemma.
Man is a political animal who "has to contend not only with want
but with fear, and, on the plane of ideas and ideologies, Russia and
America cannot so easily avoid crossing each other's path by staying at home and each cultivating her own ample garden." Natural
political rivalries have been intensified to an explosive point by the
paralyzing fear in both camps that the missionary activities of either might intrude within the garrison state and camp of the other.
As a reaction, the United States has decided on a foreign policy of
containment or counterimperialism.[16]

Students of foreign policy and national power are particularly
concerned, when confronted with a pattern of international politics such as has just been described, to know something about the
comparative strength of the antagonists. There was no question in
Toynbee's mind, when he evaluated the national power of the two
sides, that the United States enjoyed advantages in industrial capacity, national character, and the flexibility of its government and

14. *Ibid.*, 374; *Survey of International Affairs*, 1933, p. 11.
15. Toynbee, *Civilization on Trial*, 143, 143–44.
16. *Ibid.*

diplomacy. The Soviet Union, on the other hand, had advantages which stem from a geographical position ideally suited to defense in depth and to the maximum use of its superiority in total manpower. Militarily as well, the Russians enjoyed an early postwar advantage. It was Toynbee's opinion that America's ideology might undermine its position of superiority:

> The present American ideology lays great stress on the value of freedom, but seems less keenly alive to the need for social justice. This is not at all surprising in an ideology that is a home-grown product; for, in the United States to-day, the minimum standard of living is so extraordinarily high that there is not a crying need to curb the freedom of the able, the strong, and the rich in order to deal out a dole of elementary social justice to the incompetent, the weak, and the poor. But the material well-being of the people of the United States is, of course, something exceptional in the world as it is to-day. The overwhelming majority of the living generation of mankind—beginning with a foreign-born or foreign-descended underworld in the United States itself, and ending with nearly a thousand million Chinese and Indian peasants and coolies—is to-day "underprivileged," and is becoming increasingly conscious of its plight, and increasingly restive at it. . . . Here, for the American, would be his Achilles' heel, and, for the Russian, his opportunity to sow tares in his adversary's field. To look at the situation through Russian eyes, there might seem, in these circumstances, to be quite a promising prospect of at any rate partly redressing, by propaganda, a balance that had been upset by the American discovery of the "know-how" of the atom bomb.

This weakness which Toynbee discovered in the American ideological armor continues to present serious problems in the 1980s especially in poor countries.[17]

Toynbee offered an additional comment, one which was frequently referred to in popular journals in the United States and in England. He asked the rhetorical question: Could it not be that the threat of Russian imperialism and world communism might serve as a stimulus to more spectacular British and American social and economic progress? His allusion to the Soviet Union as a kind of "gadfly" or "catfish" which might prod the Western nations to achieve greater social and economic justice, particularly in pro-

17. Ibid., 144, 145, 145–46.

grams undertaken abroad, is suggestive and undoubtedly true up to a point. It may not be true, however, in the same degree for an emerging garrison state in which the arms buildup reflects the expectation that the antagonist will continue its policy of imperialism. Unfortunately, this more somber picture is closer to the realities of the 1980s, if not those of the 1960s.

Toynbee persistently maintained that the principal cold war issue was the conflict between Soviet and American foreign policies. Is there a contradiction between his emphasis upon the rivalry between ideologies and the paramount attention given Russian imperialism? Did he in fact shift his ground from an original view that the threat to the Western world was Russian imperialism? By emphasizing the relative advantage of the Soviet over the Western ideology, has he given priority to ideologies? This question will be examined more fully later. Here we must observe that Toynbee seems to have consistently interpreted Communist and Western ideologies as instruments of foreign policy rather than as autonomous forces. Although the pathos and peril of the present situation are thus no less serious, Toynbee's frame of reference for interpreting the cold war differs radically from that provided by currently popular psychological versions. Moreover, it is the framework within which the most thoughtful observers have rather consistently analyzed foreign policy for the past three hundred years.

Toynbee was a faithful supporter of ultimate world government. But this philosophy, as expressed since 1945, seldom blinded him to immediate political realities. Because the conditions for establishing world government do not now exist, he proposed an order based on spheres of influence, "a temporary division of the world [which] might be very valuable, because it would give us time." This philosophy has displeased both the more extravagant enthusiasts of world government and the extreme realists. It is important, therefore, to examine his practical solution with some care.[18]

Toynbee favored seeking a political settlement based on spheres of influence to gain time. He recognized that although such a settlement would plainly injure the interests of the smaller nations, the alternative was a war of universal destruction. Toynbee commented on some of the implications of this dilemma by observing: "That would be hard on the countries that happen to be on the bor-

18. Toynbee, *The Prospects of Western Civilization*, 47.

derline, but it would really be much better for everybody if it could be achieved, rather than to have another war with its quite uncertain aftermath."[19]

It is valid to raise the question what particular advantage would result either for East or West if we could gain the time to which Toynbee gave such emphasis. Some political analysts have pointed out that in the future we may anticipate a further increase in relative Soviet strength as it matches if not exceeds American production of nuclear weapons. Might not America's relative position be worse in 1990 or 2000? Toynbee addressed the more fundamental issue which underlies the position of all the nations. He based his recommendation squarely upon it:

> Owing to our great advance in technology, we have been brought sharp up against each other—people with extremely different pasts and traditions and religions and ideologies—without having had time yet to learn how to live together in the same world by grinding off our rough edges against each other.
>
> Russia and the West, Russia and the United States, have not had to live together intimately in the same world until recently. We do not know whether they can or cannot do it, but if it is going to *be* possible for them to do it, they need time to learn how to do it, time to get used to each other. It is very awkward for each of them to get used to the other, and they cannot do it unless they have time and patience. So anything that would enable us to buy time seems worth thinking about.[20]

There is a further question which many intelligent observers of international politics have raised in this connection. If it is assumed that "playing for time" is a prudent political decision now, what guarantees and precedents can one find that political settlement based on spheres of interest is the best means to that end? Toynbee anticipated this question as well: "You may remember that before the First World War, France and Great Britain were great rivals about local frontiers in Africa, and so forth, and Russia and Great Britain went into consultation, worked over the map of the world, and wherever there was friction between them they ironed it out and made a bargain on a fifty-fifty basis: 'You have this, we keep that; and we will forget about that old quarrel of ours.' In 1907 Great Britain and Russia did the same."[21] Other historians have

19. *Ibid.*, 45.
20. *Ibid.*, 46–47.
21. *Ibid.*, 44–45.

pointed out that political settlements such as the one arrived at through negotiations at the Congress of Berlin in 1878 have been effective in mitigating political conflicts and rivalries which threatened to break out in war. In some situations, peace has been preserved for almost a century, and it is undoubtedly this fact which has caused historians to go back to these experiences as precedents.

Political settlements have been negotiated sometimes despite grave obstacles. Often the national interests of nations have not corresponded and their differences have been aggravated by traditional rivalries and dislikes. Usually settlement has been possible only when there was strong pressure from a common enemy about whom each party to an agreement was greatly concerned. In the case of the settlements which Toynbee referred to in Africa and Asia, the common enemy was Germany. In contemporary world politics, where two superpowers stand athwart one another along a band of territory from Stettin to Trieste, one can properly ask whether any other power or force is sufficiently strong to threaten them both in any such way. Toynbee answered:

> But, after all, in the present situation America and Russia have a common enemy, too, of whom I am sure they are likewise afraid, and that is atomic energy. Though, no doubt, it needs great imagination to think of atomic energy as a common enemy whom you must not dare to let loose in the way in which Great Britain and Russia, and Great Britain and France, thought of Germany as the common enemy in the face of whom they must iron out their own former differences, perhaps it is conceivable that American and Russian statesmanship might rise to this.[22]

Toynbee did not provide a blueprint of what might be expected if a political settlement between East and West could be negotiated. Neither did Winston Churchill, Walter Lippmann, or Hans J. Morgenthau. To insist upon a specific outline of boundaries and dividing lines would be to misunderstand profoundly the nature and character of a negotiated settlement. These are points which can be worked out, if indeed they prove capable of settlement at all, only by means of the processes of traditional diplomacy "with all its privacy and gravity." To require the concrete draft of a negotiated settlement before the event is to dispose in advance of the

22. *Ibid.*, 45.

very function that diplomacy is meant to serve. However, Toynbee, as analysts before and following his work, made certain suggestions, as when he observed: "The United States has it in her power to draw the demarcation line between an American and a Russian sphere close around the present fringes of the Soviet Union's political domain. This would give the United States the lion's share of a partitioned globe." He later predicted that the United States would probably obtain in the larger sphere something like "three-quarters of the world's area and four-fifths of its population." This would present the United States with great responsibilities, especially since hundreds of millions of peasants "living at a bare subsistence level in India, China, Indonesia and Japan" would become primarily an American trust.[23] It is a sign of the price of "drifting too long" that at least one of these great areas may no longer cause anxiety and the future of others has periodically been in doubt.

Toynbee also suggested that a political settlement would likely produce no more than two spheres of influence. Neutral countries or areas would inevitably gravitate toward one or the other of the Great Powers. Therefore any buffer zone, if it could be created, would last for only a short time.

One final purpose of a political settlement is the ultimate or long-range one of forming the basis for general world government. The conditions which are necessary for voluntary world government do not exist at the present time. It is one of the gradual and long-run activities of traditional diplomacy to help create those conditions. If the immediate task of diplomacy is to provide for the mitigation and accommodation of political conflicts, its ultimate task is to help establish the foundations of world community. It is on this point, finally, that Toynbee's appeal for political settlement is hinged: "It would give us time, among other things, to try gradually to build these two spheres together and eventually to unite them in a co-operative world government."[24]

The question regarding ultimate world government that Toynbee posed is not whether government will be established. The issue he discussed is rather when and how it will come about. He repeated on numerous occasions that political unity is necessary and possible and will sooner or later be achieved through one of two basic means. He explained: "I believe—and this is, I suppose,

23. Toynbee, *Civilization on Trial*, 145; Toynbee, *The Prospects of Western Civilization*, 50.
24. Toynbee, *The Prospects of Western Civilization*, 46.

my most controversial assertion, but I am simply stating what I do sincerely think—I believe it is a foregone conclusion that the world is in any event going to be unified politically in the near future." Two novel considerations have required that a process which would eventually have taken place for Western civilization naturally, now be accelerated. They are "the degree of our present interdependence and the deadliness of our present weapons." The problem of finding some means of eliminating the specter of war, "which for at least six thousand years has baffled mankind and has many times led to the breakdown of civilizations," requires that this ultimate solution now be considered with a renewed sense of urgency. There is a stronger motive for getting rid of war today shared by more people than has ever been true in the past. That motive is averting universal destruction in a type of conflict which today has been keyed to an unparalleled pitch.[25]

There are two ways in which world government can be achieved—by conquest or by voluntary federation. In structure there might be some similarity between these two, but "the difference between the alternative roads to the same goal makes the whole difference in what happens afterward."[26] World government is inevitable, but whether it will be only another desperate and ill-fated effort to rescue a fading civilization which has already reached a critical stage in its life cycle—as has been true of nearly all universal states in history—or whether it will be a new and creative enterprise depends on the means by which it is achieved.

The precedents in history favoring world government by conquest are innumerable. Larger political units have most often been established in this way. Alexander of Macedon, the Ts'in dynasty in China, and the Roman militarists succeeded in accomplishing by conquest what had been impossible through federation and consent. There has indeed been a steady and consistent diminution in the number of powers in the modern world. In 1860 and 1870, the model state in area and resources was France or Great Britain. Today, the standard size for states that aspire to become "Great Powers" is that of the United States and the Soviet Union. Even those nation-states, however, cannot guarantee the security and well-being of other people. Further, the direction and divergence of their respective foreign policies have not made it any less likely that world domination is a possibility.

25. Toynbee, *Civilization on Trial*, 127; Toynbee, *The Prospects of Western Civilization*, 26.
26. Toynbee, *The Prospects of Western Civilization*, 29.

The conditions for world conquest are present in the political revolution which altered the traditional role of the balance of power. Toynbee observed that the Truman Doctrine might "have given the whole course of international affairs an impulsion away from the new co-operative method of trying to achieve political world unity, and towards the old-fashioned method of fighting out the last round in the struggle of power politics and arriving at the political unification of the world by the main force of a 'knock-out blow.' "[27]

Other factors appear to favor political unification by conquest. As a result of the technological revolution, one state could, for the first time in history, conquer most or all of the world and control it. Furthermore, the new political religion has supplanted universal religion, a traditional force for restraint. One must also consider the psychological factor. Western society has gone to war twice to reject unification on German terms. Toynbee must have been contemplating the rise of a philosophy of neutrality in France, Germany, and to some extent throughout Europe when he wrote: "And I think that after the Second World War, if there were to be a third, by far the greater part of the world, except, I suppose, the United States—and, I suppose, also Russia, though Russia had had a war in her own country twice within living memory, having had the grim experience which neither you in America nor we in England have yet had—the greater part of the world would want peace at any price this time, like France in 1940."[28]

In a sense the political leader who perceived this condition best was Hitler, but the "war-weariness" on which he based his hope of conquest was not yet ripe enough for his project to succeed. Today this mentality has been so intensified that the problem of world conquest has itself been transformed. A world empire would be confronted not with putting down resistance but with assuming unparalleled responsibilities of leadership and reconstruction. To account for the rise in pacifist thinking, Toynbee pointed first to the profoundly antiwar attitude among those who remember the last one. Second, and less obvious, was "a curious feature of nationalism; the tendency of extreme nationalism to lop over into extreme pacifism." Nationalism or its equivalent in other international systems has been the major obstacle to political unity: "And then we see the very people who would not surrender their

27. Toynbee, *Civilization on Trial*, 135.
28. Toynbee, *The Prospects of Western Civilization*, 41.

sovereignty by agreement submit with surprising tameness to having it taken away from them by force by an overwhelmingly superior power. It does not hurt their pride so much to be hit on the head as it does to be asked to surrender their sovereignty by pooling it through a peaceful agreement." Third, class differences have in many countries meant that preservation of privilege was more important than a nation's independence. Some business groups earlier assumed that a sure means of protecting themselves against the laboring class would be to accede to conquest by a foreign power. For this reason, they were willing to make certain concessions to Hitler. They believed that as privileged groups they could save themselves in this way. "The possessing classes throughout the world are still more afraid of communism, and I think this fear would operate very powerfully in a third World War in inducing them to surrender their country's independence."[29]

Therefore the way things have been going in modern international politics, with the gradual decrease in the number of powers and the growth of a defeatist sentiment throughout the world, "it looks, on the face of it, as if the 'knock-out blow' were the obvious line of least resistance, the easiest way for the inevitable unification to come about." Yet if the West chooses to follow this course, it must be aware of the consequences of this form of unity. Accompanying political unity achieved through conquest, a relentless and irrevocable law of karma has inevitably manifested itself. Once having taken up arms to achieve political unity, a conqueror has only rarely been able to give up the means employed for achieving his ends:

> Time is, indeed, working against these unhappy empire-builders from the outset; for sword-blades are foundations that never settle. Exposed or buried, these blood-stained weapons still retain their sinister charge of *karma*; and this means that they cannot really turn into inanimate foundation-stones, but must ever be stirring—like the dragon's-tooth seed that they are—to spring to the surface again in a fresh crop of slaying and dying gladiators. Under its serene mask of effortless supremacy the Oecumenical Peace of a universal state is fighting, all the time, a desperate losing battle against an unexorcised demon of Violence in its own bosom; and we can see this moral struggle being waged in the guise of a conflict of policies.[30]

29. *Ibid.*, 42, 43.
30. *Ibid.*, 43; Toynbee, *A Study of History*, VI, 196–97.

However, the general patterns and the consequences of the rise or fall of universal states has been less happy than this. The universal state has tended to become a mere shell of government and has dissipated its strength by requiring too much of its members in military adventures. It has seldom been a creative force and has had to be patched up and repaired in order even to survive. For nearly all universal states created by the sword, there has come a day of destruction through this same device.

The one practical alternative to the creation of the world government by conquest is world government by agreement. But since the necessary preconditions do not yet exist, any policy to attain that goal must establish ways for creating them. Some writers have suggested that the United Nations may lead in that direction. For Toynbee, however, the United Nations is hampered by the fundamental differences between the Soviet Union and the United States. Although this weakness is a political rather than a constitutional defect, the result is the existence of few bonds of community necessary for effective government. Diplomacy is crucial to the creation of such conditions.[31]

In Toynbee's view, regional federations, such as one among the United States, Western Europe, Canada, Australia, New Zealand, and South Africa, would have the advantage of restoring Europe's status as a first-class power, thus permitting economic assistance on a more mutually profitable basis. In the short run it would provide the surest foundation for security in Western Europe; in the long run it would ensure the recognition of community in a limited area and would increase the possibility of its extension to a broader sphere. The practical problems raised, such as the relinquishment of sovereignty to a Western government, are admittedly difficult but "at least this is a much more practical goal to work for in the immediate future than a world-wide federation would be."[32]

If world government should be created in our times, it would not be a tidy system. Toynbee had no illusions about the sovereign equality of its members. As we have seen, he was convinced it would involve the ascendancy of one or more great powers. Either the United States or the Soviet Union or both would likely be dominant. This would be true whether the government were created by agreement or conquest, for no single power having suc-

31. Toynbee, *A Study of History*, IV, 85; Toynbee, *The Prospects of Western Civilization*, 46–47.
32. Toynbee, *The Prospects of Western Civilization*, 49.

cessfully conquered the world would be able to govern it directly. It would be necessary to have a large measure of local autonomy, and local governments would have to make crucial decisions on the spot. This would introduce inevitably a measure of international cooperation and this could increase the chances of world government by consent. Toynbee summarized his viewpoint: "Whatever great power may provide the nucleus for a world government through its own ascendancy, I think there will also be a genuine element of local autonomy and international co-operation." World government will be a kind of mixed system, and that is all Toynbee chose to say by way of definition. He maintained an eclectic point of view and assumed that the mitigation of conflicts through diplomacy, the extension of economic ties through the Specialized Agencies of the United Nations, and the building of firmer bonds between spiritually and culturally similar peoples would eventually contribute to the creation of world community. From there, it will be a matter of faith.[33]

It was almost inevitable in the nature of Toynbee's philosophy of history that he would suspend judgment on the question of the future of Western civilization. Time and again he called attention to the differences between his method and that of Spengler, particularly in the finality of their conclusions: "I am, as you know, not a determinist, so I certainly think that my work cannot be used for making definite predictions. In so far as Spengler's can, I feel that is a weakness in his work."[34]

Toynbee's reluctance to make definitive prophecies also stemmed from a belief that public judgments may themselves influence the course of history. For that reason, he preferred to proceed with great caution. Then too, he believed, the human drama was a story to follow and observe but the unfolding events were not amenable to accurate predictions. The numbers of past civilizations are so limited as to make predictions little more than rough estimates. Constantly at the center and in control of a large part of his own destiny is the individual. No scientific formula can anticipate the full range of his behavior. Even if in nineteen or twenty civilizations certain recurrent developments have taken place, this offers too limited a basis for confidently supposing that the pattern will be repeated in events of the future. Western civi-

33. *Ibid.*, 48.
34. Arnold J. Toynbee to Kenneth W. Thompson, April 19, 1950, in possession of the recipient.

lization is confronted with unparalleled risks, and the symptoms of its condition are hardly encouraging. Still, for Toynbee, its future remains an open question.

There are, practically speaking, however, three prospects for Western civilization. One is that we suffer a great catastrophe. What makes this so real and so terrifying is our attainments in harnessing the forces of nature and our failure to achieve a comparable mastery over human nature. If the first alternative should be realized, what would be destroyed would be not Western civilization alone but quite possibly the whole human race. The gentle historian wrote: "I can imagine our destroying so much that we should lose all that we have gained during the last six thousand years." Second, we may save our civilization but at a prohibitive price. One example would be survival through the acceptance of complete regimentation. In most utopian schemes and within universal states in general, means are provided for doing away with famine and war. In the process, however, the inhabitants of a "brave new world" would bargain away freedom and human dignity. This gain quite possibly would not be worth the price. The third prospect is to discover a middle way between total destruction and absolute regimentation. This narrow passage represents the one means of rescuing society and assuring it of continually renewed vitality for future tasks and challenges.[35]

We have assumed that Toynbee was principally concerned with the problem of war. Civilizations have broken down and decayed, however, because of class conflicts and social tensions. Unparalleled technological changes, which have taken place within one generation, have made the old cleavages between classes and social groups seem less necessary, and therefore appeals for social reform and social justice have been sounded with greater urgency. It is a perversity of modern technology that although it has been responsible for the creation and increase of a society's wealth, it has also seemed to render intolerable the old differences in status and wealth. All nations and individuals have assumed the right to obtain "equal rations."[36]

Certain facts regarding social classes and their relations with one another are of particular importance in a period of international tension. For one, the middle class has suffered a relative decline in both numbers and influence. It is sometimes assumed that there

35. Toynbee, *The Prospects of Western Civilization*, 104.
36. *Ibid.*, 57.

is a universal and inevitable conflict between capital and labor and that it is in the interests of labor, through its trade unions, eventually to overthrow the free enterprise systems. In this scenario, social transformation would invite and require a fundamental social revolution. Toynbee's theory of international relations hardly contemplated so far-reaching a change: "Recent history has shown that you cannot smash trade unionism without smashing capitalism and cannot smash capitalism without smashing trade unionism." German business groups, for example, assumed that Hitler's destruction of German trade unions would be to their advantage, but business itself was shortly thereafter subjected to enslavement by the same master. The converse was true in the Soviet Union, where the liquidation of the middle classes only foreshadowed the suppression of free trade unionism. The social and economic struggle between labor and capital is primarily for profits and not for the survival of the free enterprise system: "The real nature of trade unionism is the same as the real nature of capitalism; it is an organization freely created to serve their own interests by people who have free play in the economic market." What this signifies, therefore, is the presence of certain well-defined limits within which that struggle goes on: "If either capital or labor pushes the quarrel between them beyond a certain point, they both play into the hands of a third party, the state, which then becomes omnipotent at the expense of labor and capital alike."[37]

One novel aspect of social change in Western civilization is the emergence of an unprecedented frame of mind among the people. Whereas the contending groups in Western economies both seek the maintenance of free enterprise, their attitudes toward work and their scale of values are different: "The capitalist's attitude toward work is what you might call the pre-industrial attitude." The prospect of attaining significant ends inspired the capitalist. The inventiveness of the middle class, the group primarily so stirred, was responsible for the Industrial Revolution. Paradoxically, however, they were never put through the "industrial mill" and never felt the full impact of industrialism and specialization. The laboring groups, in response to the impersonal and monotonous character of work in the new system, developed a defensive and negative attitude. Some members of the middle class, particularly older people in business, have turned to new professions because of fewer opportunities in their own fields. And many have become civil

37. *Ibid.*, 50, 59.

servants and have assumed that traditionally "unenthusiastic" attitude.[38]

Furthermore, as Toynbee observed, "thirty or forty years ago, in all the Western countries, the middle class stood at the height of its power." Today this position has been gradually liquidated through an increase in the number of civil servants, through the merger of the middle class with working elements in Western Europe, and through their outright annihilation in the Soviet Union. This decline has far-reaching significance for the distribution of political power within countries, as well as for the stimulus of Western industrialism. Some writers have asked what all this implies for the future. Toynbee was concerned with a particular historical parallel:

> This Roman civil service had all the virtues of a civil service, but also all the weaknesses. The result was that under the early Roman Empire the world was much better governed, enjoyed much greater justice, and suffered much less brutality and wrong and corruption than during the previous two centuries, but was also a much less lively place, with much less creativeness. . . . That is the sort of situation with which we are, perhaps, going to be confronted in our world today in this chapter of history that is ahead of us. We must, of course, do all that we can to get the best of both worlds. We want to get the order and the justice without having to suffer the loss of enterprise and energy.[39]

The major problem of social transformation in Western civilization is one that Rome was unable to solve: how to reconcile justice with freedom. That problem remains today. Three major experiments in attaining this goal are the North American approach in Canada and the United States, the Western European outlook, and the Russian solution. Each has characteristics peculiar to the problems with which the system has had to deal. In America, it has been possible to achieve security and freedom for a middle class with unusual mobility into and within its own ranks. One primary reason (until the early 1920s) was the steady immigration of one million to two million people a year. Each group of immigrants served to reconstitute the bottom layer of the social pyramid and permitted others to rise in society. American economic and social life was thus dynamic, a characteristic lessened by the

38. *Ibid.*, 61.
39. *Ibid.*, 64, 70.

closing of the frontiers. Immigration continues, as is not the case in Europe, but much of it is illegal. This has contributed to Americans' resisting any threat to the old-fashioned middle-class way of life. The United States has sought to avoid dulling the zest of individuals for new enterprise by turning them into civil servants and industrial workers. New circumstances have made possible a movement toward greater collective action and closer identity with Western Europe. Yet the paramount emphasis has been on the need for protecting the independent and enterprising individual.

The Soviet Union's approach to social transformation has been through the extension of state activities, and the long-standing autocracy of the Eastern Orthodox church has provided the necessary foundations. The absence of an effective middle class has meant that the spur for creative and enterprising action has had to come from elsewhere: "In Russia the industrial revolution has been introduced self-consciously and according to plan, in a country where it never would have arisen if the Russians had not had an industrialized Western World next door to them against which they had to hold their own." The Russians have put both capital and labor under the domination of the state.[40]

The Western Europeans have sought moderation and balance in approaching this problem. Since World War II, there has been insufficient wealth to permit the American solution. It has not been possible to appease the demands of the working class with higher wages. Nor, on the other hand, would it be in the British tradition to extend the powers of government without limitation. So the attempt has been made to achieve some form of mixed system: "In Western Europe, we are trying to effect a cure by merging the working class with the middle class and by mixing the liberal and the socialist ideologies." The real task is to draw the line between the private and socialist spheres in harmony with the changing requirements of the societies involved. This system of trial and error represents the best chance of dealing successfully with social transformation: "Our English provisional solution would not fit other people's conditions in countries where economic and social conditions are rather different. Russia, being a very poor and backward country, probably needs more socialism than we need in England. America and Canada probably need less, because they are in a much more favorable economic position than we are now in Western Europe." Further, Toynbee pointed out that these solu-

40. *Ibid.*, 74.

tions must be worked out in such a way that social justice and individual liberty can be reconciled. A greater number of individuals
must enjoy the privileges of the middle class. But the old sources
of enthusiasm must be maintained. If this cannot be done, then adjusting the post–World War I social forces and demands for social
justice will have too great a cost.[41]

Over the decades, Toynbee discussed the chief political issues
of our time frequently with deep insight. The problems of war and
peace are the most serious of the questions which confront Western minds. But unquestionably for him the supreme issue we face
is neither political nor military but is religious. This assumption
came to the foreground in his theory only in his final years. If one
deals, however, in secular terms, one must draw the conclusion that
in the long historical view the chances for Western survival are no
better than even. One can scarcely point to political or social factors which distinguish that society sufficiently from its predecessors to warrant a hopeful conclusion. Indeed, it would be fair to say
that in the Hellenic world certain political forms and institutions
reached as high a level as had evolved in Western civilization.
Toynbee maintained that the two profound developments in
Western society have been its unparalleled technology and its
original Christian tradition. Western technology has indeed been
exported to all corners of the earth, but the spiritual and moral heritage of Christianity was hardly accepted even within Western society. Its influence, nonetheless, underlies our most important
customs. If we are to bequeath a Western tradition to world history, it must be a tradition in which Christianity is central.

For some students of history, religion has represented a weakening and destructive force in any society. This was the attitude of
some of the well-known Roman emperors, among them Marcus
Aurelius and Julian. It was surely the judgment of Gibbon, who
considered religion responsible for the decline and fall of that civilization: "In the last chapter of Gibbon's history there is one sentence in which he sums up the theme of the whole work. Looking
back he says, 'I have described the triumph of barbarism and religion.'" In the seventeenth and eighteenth centuries the great majority of political and social philosophers held a similar view. An
age of skepticism and toleration found its best object of calumny
in the Wars of Religion, for which Christianity was held accountable. Thus the theory of history so confidently expressed by Gib-

41. *Ibid.*, 76–77.

bon and by Sir James Frazer in *The Golden Bough* became dominant. It was widely believed that throughout the Dark Ages
civilization halted, because of the invasion of Oriental philosophies. Only with the Renaissance was progress possible once
more.[42]

This conception has its roots in bad history and bad ethics, according to Toynbee. Its principal example of the destructive influence of religion is taken from Hellenic civilization. It assumes that
the catastrophe came with the emergence of a more powerful
Christian church in the second century A.D. Toynbee's view, in
contrast to Gibbon's, was that Graeco-Roman society died by its
own hand, for having failed to solve the problem of political unity
among the city-states. That occurred in the fifth century B.C., more
than four hundred years before the appearance of Christianity. It
resulted from a failure to meet a challenge successfully, and thereafter society moved toward its doom. Not "barbarism and religion" but political disunity was the first and most fundamental
cause of the Graeco-Roman decline and fall. Therefore it is doubtful indeed that the ethics of that society were superior to Christian
ones. It would be bad ethics to say that a philosophy responsible
for a society's failure had greater virtues than one which took its
place. On both counts, one is persuaded by Toynbee to reject Gibbon's theory.

Another view is that religion is the chrysalis in which civilizations are born. The Christian church absorbed the internal proletariat of Hellenic civilization and ultimately gave birth to its
successors, the Orthodox Christian and the Western civilizations.
For other civilizations this same pattern was observed. The Islamic church took in the moribund societies of Syrians, Jews, and
Iranians and led to the Islamic civilization. The Hindu religion existed within the ancient Aryan society and nurtured that modern
Hindu civilization which is competing with Islam for mastery in
India. Mahayana Buddhism provided the chrysalis from which Far
Eastern civilization has emerged. All or most great religions have
performed the function of spanning the gulf between dying and
embryonic civilizations: "Christianity is, as it were, the egg, grub,
and chrysalis between butterfly and butterfly. Christianity is a
transitional thing which bridges the gap between one civilization
and another."[43]

42. Toynbee, *Civilization on Trial*, 225–52.
43. *Ibid.*, 231.

There is a significant pattern to the place of religion at various stages in history. Sometimes in the interregnum, there has been no higher religion, as, for example, between Minoan and Hellenic civilization or between Aryan and pre-Aryan civilization in India. If one considers the civilizations alive today as third generation, their predecessors such as the Hellenic and Sinic civilizations as second generation, and defines as first generation those like the Minoan and Aryan which come between primitive societies and the first historic civilizations, then some tentative rules and laws can be established. Toynbee explained: "We find that the relation between higher religions and civilizations seems to differ according to the generation of the civilization with which we are dealing. We seem to find no higher religion at all between primitive societies and civilizations of the first generation, and between civilizations of the first and those of the second generation either none or only rudiments. It is between civilizations of the second and those of the third generation that the intervention of a higher religion seems to be the rule, and here only." This is the first hint of Toynbee's new theme that "the successive rises and falls of civilizations may be subsidiary to the growth of religion." Instead, higher religions are held to be the product of spiritual progress which can be traced from the earliest civilization to our own.[44]

The final view is that disintegration, suffering, and decay in a civilization are stepping-stones to greater spiritual insight and progress. Here, religions are not merely means but ends in themselves. Earlier civilizations and events have allowed for the genesis of churches, instead of churches acting merely as the chrysalis for successive civilizations. In these terms, the higher religions have antecedents in first- and second-generation societies. Christianity is not only the result, therefore, of the transmutation of Hellenic ideas into Western civilization but also the outgrowth of a long, significant pre-Hellenic historical development: "The Christian Church itself arose out of the spiritual travail which was a consequence of the breakdown of the Graeco-Roman civilization. Again, the Christian Church has Jewish and Zoroastrian roots, and those roots sprang from an earlier breakdown, the breakdown of a Syrian civilization which was a sister to the Graeco-Roman. . . . Judaism, likewise, has a Mosaic root which in its turn sprang from the withering of the second crop of the ancient Egyptian Civilization."[45]

44. *Ibid.*, 234.
45. *Ibid.*, 235.

If one accepts this view, then religion and civilization must be considered in fundamentally different terms: "The continuous upward movement of religion may be served and promoted by the cyclic movement of civilizations round the cycle of birth, death, birth." If there is truth to this theory, then Western civilization becomes a "handmaiden" of the one religion which has the greatest chance of surviving when civilizations have come and gone. For this reason, the vain idolatry of parochial institutions stands athwart the progress of religion. The logical culmination of the origin and development of Christianity would be as the prevailing influence in Western society; instead, the two predominant religions are democracy and communism. Both represent leaves taken from the book of Christianity but both are fragments torn out of context and misread: "Democracy . . . has certainly been half emptied of meaning by being divorced from its Christian context and secularized; and we have obviously . . . been living on spiritual capital."[46]

Christianity thus provides the ultimate hope for Western civilization, for without it, there is no other Western tradition on which individuals are agreed. Christianity represents the climax of a particular line of historical development with its origin as far back as the Egyptiac and Syriac civilizations. Tragically, however, "Western Ideas" and institutions have lost their early Christian influence, and forces antagonistic to religion have seemingly gained the ascendancy. The history of Western civilization has provided a battleground between the Christian tradition and an incompatible pagan tradition. The greater part of our present tragedy can be attributed to the preference shown the latter, which expresses itself most dramatically in the political religions of democracy and communism.

Even one who is sympathetic with Toynbee's thesis is obliged to question whether the Christian tradition can accomplish what Toynbee claimed. The sins of omission of the traditional church throughout the Middle Ages were almost as great as were those of commission by its pagan successors. Toynbee gave every impression of being well aware of this problem. He explicitly emphasized that no universal church could assure the establishment of peace or the transformation of the social order—religious institutions are led by imperfect individuals. Although attempts to restore a *Respublica Christiana* broke down by the end of the seventeenth cen-

46. *Ibid.*, 236–37.

tury, the cumulative impact of higher religions was responsible for a rough spiritual progress which, in terms of Toynbee's outlook, is the principal long-range hope: "Thus the historical progress of religion in this world, as represented by the rise of the higher religions and by their culmination in Christianity, may, and almost certainly will, bring with it, incidentally, an immeasurable improvement in the conditions of human social life on Earth; but its direct effect and its deliberate aim and its true test is the opportunity which it brings to individual souls for spiritual progress in this world during the passage from birth to death."[47]

In a religious sense, Toynbee held out hope for the future. He had no illusions about the shortcomings of Christian societies in the past. But Christianity offers us the one enduring tradition of spiritual values in the great struggle with communism. If democracy can be returned to its Christian setting, the hope for survival can be renewed and with it mankind's salvation.

47. *Ibid.*, 251.

PART FIVE

Epilogue

CHAPTER VII

A Critical Evaluation

OST CRITICS would agree that Toynbee's *Study of History* is a work of epic proportions. Several commentators have noted that Toynbee, as a historian who zealously recorded the many contrasting beats of history, himself injected a marked counterbeat into historical writing. Since 1910 few works have exceeded one volume; in literature the short story has been threatening the novel. In contrast, both the length and the temper of *A Study of History* are exceptions to the prevailing ethos. Toynbee consciously struck a blow against the fashionable specialized and "scientific" studies which isolate tiny fragments of experience for the most intensive study. His chief foe, however, was not the discrete use of scientific techniques but rather the idolatry of that method and the ready acceptance of the superficial philosophy of "scientism" with its easy optimism and materialism. His method, in its turn, must be critically assessed, for the boldness of his approach makes it inevitable that certain questions and criticisms should be raised. The first person to anticipate this would have been Toynbee himself, who observed at the time he was launching his major work: "In the world of scholarship, to give and take criticism is all in the day's work and, each in our day, we may criticize our predecessors without becoming guilty of presumption so long as we are able to look forward without rancour to being criticized in our turn by our successors when our day is past."[1]

1. Arnold J. Toynbee, *A Study of History* (12 vols.; London, 1934–61), I, 48.

All historians, including those who construct theories of universal history, have their special competence. Toynbee's was Graeco-Roman history. Its lands and people were so familiar to him as to make them his second "homeland." However, it is exactly his attachment to Hellenic history which causes readers some uneasiness about the pattern of world history he discovered. His conceptual scheme was suspiciously well tailored to the decline and fall of one civilization but it hung rather awkwardly on the twenty-odd others. It is apparent from even a cursory reading that Hellenic civilization had its "Time of Troubles," "Universal State," and "Universal Church" in relentless and seemingly preordained succession. This pattern was more difficult to maintain when Toynbee discussed other civilizations. He was obliged to confess that Egyptiac history comprised one kind of exception (for its universal state was revived after it had run its normal course), Arabic civilization was another exception, and other civilizations were in other ways exceptions too.

When a reader attempts to apply the conceptual scheme derived principally from Hellenic civilization to, for example, Western civilization, Toynbee's problem at once becomes clear. In a table designed to portray the stages in history of the various civilizations, the "Time of Troubles" for Western civilization was charted as having occurred between 1378 and 1797.[2] Elsewhere in the *Study*, Toynbee was more cautious, leaving the impression that although many symptoms of decay may be present, one must wait and see before conceding this decline. If growth and disintegration are as clear-cut as was elsewhere implied, it is curious that the stage in history at which the West finds itself should remain so beclouded for Toynbee.

Furthermore, critics point to flaws in Toynbee's pattern of history which are distinct from the problem of its concrete application to contemporary civilizations. The basic concept in his schema is *civilization*, and yet he never defined by more than a few illustrations precisely what he meant by this term or how it could be distinguished from *society*. As the analysis proceeded he nevertheless talked about these units as if he were using them with all the precision of a zoologist. Yet the species *civilization* appears to be used interchangeably with the generic category society.[3] Most of his definitions are literary rather than scientific, and much of

2. Toynbee, *A Study of History*, VI, 327.
3. Toynbee, *A Study of History*, I, 17–50.

his terminology has that breadth and vagueness which generally characterizes spiritual interpretations of history. For example, in his treatment of the withdrawal and return of creative leaders who inspired growth in civilization, the reader must somehow divine the precise common denominator for the experiences of some thirty individuals. If Toynbee had used Buddha, Caesar, Peter the Great, Kant, and Lenin to point up an interesting parallel, this flaw would not be particularly significant. When he used their experiences to establish scientific formulas and laws, the practice may legitimately be questioned. Indeed, his discussion is curiously marred by the unequal attention given the various personalities and minorities responsible for civilizational growth. In some cases, Toynbee presented shortened life histories of the creative leaders, and the data while interesting often have little to do with the point at issue. At other times, he allowed a paragraph or two to suffice. This difference in treatment can hardly be based upon any systematic principle. Moreover, it is difficult to appreciate the similarity he detected between the quiet habits of Kant, whose thoughts, to be sure, made an impact throughout the world, and the withdrawal and return of Peter the Great, who returned to Russia from Europe with new ideas which he personally put into practice.[4]

This concept is also obscure in Toynbee's discussion of particular creative nations. The notion that England withdrew from the Continent between the sixteenth and eighteenth centuries, only to return as the center of world trade and world power in the nineteenth century, has more meaning as a description of the general foundations of British foreign policy than as an exact statement of historical fact. That is, British policy was based upon England's relative insularity, but this hardly constituted withdrawal. If it is farfetched to assume that a nation even in the sixteenth century could withdraw from relations with others, it is no less extravagant to imagine that other nations in the thick of European power politics would be incapable of making a creative contribution. Any theory which excluded seventeenth- and eighteenth-century France as a creative force would hardly receive support. Yet it would also be erroneous to ignore the fact that the concept of Withdrawal and Return, whether because or in spite of its utter intangibility, illuminates some of the shadowy corners of history which scientific studies have left untouched. However, Toynbee's overly ambitious claims invite critical responses by some honest observers.[5]

4. Toynbee, *A Study of History*, III, 248–377, 278–331.
5. *Ibid.*, 350–63.

Another principle or law which is so indefinite that almost any historical episode can be molded to fit its broad outlines is Challenge and Response. Spiritual and scientific interpretations of history have consistently asked, What is the true mechanism of history? For some, such as Hegel and Marx, it is a particular dialectic or process. Others have found the mechanism in economic conditions or geographical factors. Toynbee's formula is more difficult to verify objectively and more likely to encompass a wider range of events. Between an environment that is too severe and one that is too easy, there is a "golden mean" where civilization can flourish. In general, the basis for this optimum condition is a favorable climate and adequate land and natural resources.

Scientific historians would object that this concept is too simple. New nations and societies have achieved their positions in history because of such rudimentary factors and because the whole context of their historical experience was favorable. The American colonies were blessed with a broad continent with resources of unparalleled variety and richness. This privileged position, however, was only one fragment of the larger historical development in which factors such as outside assistance and unexpected freedom from colonial domination were also involved. There is some question whether Toynbee's formula of challenge and response is sufficiently broad to encompass these various factors and concrete enough to permit their separate consideration. In the eyes of most modern scientific historians, every historic event is a separate entity and therefore so infinitely complex that an observer can evaluate it only in terms of its concreteness. Only by patient research and painstaking scrutiny can such an event be clearly illuminated.[6]

There is a final assumption to which modern historians would probably take exception. Toynbee postulated that civilizations break down and decay because elements within them are inherently self-destructive. Yet the early American civilizations, particularly those of the Incas and Aztecs, were destroyed by external forces. But a spiritual interpretation of history could hardly concede such a point. So A Study of History maintained that these civilizations had already succumbed to the most profound internal malaise before they were invaded and conquered by Spanish adventurers. It is of course likely that societies have been weakened by internal dissension and decay before falling prey to a more

6. Toynbee, A Study of History, IV, 1–584.

powerful foe. It seems naïve to imagine, however, that history does not offer numerous cases of brute force triumphing over weakness and virtue. This has surely been the fate of small nations throughout history. It would be surprising indeed if the same were not true of civilizations such as the early American ones. Toynbee's assumption of transcendent spiritual factors in history makes it difficult if not impossible for him to accept the primacy of force and power as the cause of death for a civilization. His "Time of Troubles" explanation indirectly assumes that the successful conqueror has not himself suffered the same self-inflicted blow and is therefore morally and politically superior. If pursued to its logical conclusion, this principle would mean that in all important respects a conquering invader would surpass his victim. Any list of victorious conquerors shows how fantastic this assumption is. It symbolizes the great weakness in those spiritual versions of history which too complacently identify virtue and power. It reflects the tragic paradox of our times that in Western civilization with the breakdown of common moral standards even the spiritual historian becomes a utopian of power. He finds ways of justifying the proposition that might makes right.

Furthermore, the dilemma which confounds students of human affairs is reflected in the dual problem with which Toynbee grappled. In seeking to establish general principles and laws of history, he chose as his subject great civilizations and found over twenty separate examples. Thus a student of history has the same kind of individual facts with which the physical sciences have traditionally dealt.[7] Civilizations are "affiliated" and "apparented," but this very concept may have served to obscure the empirical unity of history. Particular cultures are interrelated in complex ways, and only in the last volumes of the *Study* did Toynbee demonstrate the degree to which he plumbed the profound and mysterious relations between various societies in history.

Although Toynbee called upon this physical-sciences analogy, he at the same time abandoned a practice central to all scientific pursuits. The criticism leveled most frequently against him has been that his "well-beloved empiricism" is in fact no empiricism at all. He selected his data and imperturbably used them to build a system. But each datum can be used in a variety of ways, and Toynbee may not always have cited those facts which would not support his principal theses. However valid this criticism may be

7. R. G. Collingwood, *The Idea of History* (London, 1946), 159–65.

for Toynbee's empiricism in particular, it is unerringly true with respect to empiricism in general. The cauldron of history is so immense that the individual historian can serve up but a spoonful, and whether this can represent the whole is always doubtful. The limits of Toynbee's history are those of his subject matter. The infinite variety of history is the chief factor which creates the eternal boundaries within which any student must formulate his principles.

There is a further standard by which *A Study of History* can be judged. In sheer erudition and learning, the work is breathtaking and matchless. It is more wide-ranging than Spengler's masterpiece, and its pages literally teem with brilliant passages and flashes of insight. One section includes an extensive account of the history of warfare; another describes the colonization of North America. His accounts of the history of the Jewish people in Eastern Europe and Spain, of the Spartan form of society, and of the Ottoman slave-court illustrate the amplitude of historical experience to which the reader is introduced. Even if one finds that some of Toynbee's main theses are untenable, only the most uninspired of readers would be unable to gain new perspectives on the world. The value of Toynbee's work does not depend on the acceptance of each of its parts as if it were a Euclidean demonstration. It is so rich in historical allusions that the study of its pages has a value independent of full agreement with its assumptions and conclusions.

As a philosopher of history, Toynbee himself held up a warning to all historians and political scientists. He steadfastly maintained the proposition that history in general is unpredictable. The soundest estimates will be confounded by elements of chance and contingency. No one can say in advance how leading participants in the historical drama will act and few have prophesied accurately the more far-reaching events in history. Some think the gradual elimination of this uncertainty will occur when the specialized social sciences delve more carefully into the wellsprings of human behavior. Toynbee affirmed his confidence in the use of some of these techniques, particularly social psychology and statistics. It would be stretching a point, however, to imply that he shared the cheerful and extravagant expectations of some social scientists about the elimination of chance in discoveries that are possible through the use of rigorous social surveys.[8]

In talking about the growth and decay of civilizations, Toynbee

8. Arnold J. Toynbee, Pieter Geyl, and Pitirim A. Sorokin, *The Pattern of the Past* (Boston, 1949), 90–91.

necessarily wrote social history. This is particularly the case in *A Study of History*, for the fundamental criterion by which growth is measured is not geographical expansion but, more unusual, self-determination. It is obvious that a society which turns inward in this way must face up to its social problems. Therefore one finds in the *Study* a large number of rich insights into social ills and social institutions.

Sociologists as a group have laid great stress on case studies, maintaining that a student must first get inside a particular society and appraise it on its own terms. A prominent American social theorist has held that the only clear "case study" in Toynbee's writing is his analysis of Hellenic civilization.[9] Even the staunchest admirer of Toynbee must confess that sometimes the social data hardly provide a clear picture of the uniqueness of a particular community. It is probably fair to say that Toynbee made little or no contribution to the cultural "case study" method as interpreted by modern sociology.

He has, however, provided empirical sociologists with a series of fertile hypotheses which remain to be tested and verified. His theory of challenge and response is of this order. Some of his formulas, however, have already been analyzed more fully, among them his theory of cultural diffusion or radiation wherein a society that has accepted a certain aspect of an alien culture must subsequently acquire all others. Moreover, as early as the turn of the century, modern sociology considered the social phenomenon of imitation, for which Toynbee has constructed his theory of mimesis. One of the social classics anticipated *A Study of History* on this point by nearly half a century: "A society is a group of people who display many resemblances produced either by imitation or by *counter-imitation*. For men often counter-imitate one another, particularly when they have neither the modesty to imitate directly nor the power to invent."[10] There are fewer allusions to the findings of modern sociology in Toynbee's great work than there are to comparable studies in political science and history. Yet it is significant that great social theorists such as Merton have found a community of interest with Toynbee.

The major difference between Toynbee and contemporary sociologists is his individualistic interpretation of social change. Toynbee ascribed to great personalities and leaders what sociolo-

9. Robert K. Merton, "Book Review of a Study of History," *American Journal of Sociology*, XLVII (September, 1941), 213.

10. Toynbee, *A Study of History*, IV, 119–33; Gabriel Tarde, *The Laws of Imitation*, trans. Elsie Clews Parsons (2nd ed.; New York, 1903), xvii.

gists would insist, through more extensive analysis and study, could be attributed to underlying social forces. Research and new theoretical tools may yield the causes of fundamental change in man's social relations and institutions. The neophyte in sociology may be tempted to dissent vigorously from its obsessions with classification, from its sometimes pedantic distinctions between *society* and *community* or between subtypes of sacred and secular societies; he may likewise disagree with Toynbee's extreme individualism.[11] On this point, nonetheless, the paths of the historian and his contemporaries in sociology and anthropology sharply and probably irrevocably diverge.

Students of contemporary religion have been at least as critical of some of Toynbee's views as have scholars in the social sciences. It is most unlikely that philosophers and specialists in comparative religion would accept the strong currents of Christian determinism which emerge in his general conclusion that Christianity is the culmination of religious history.[12] Indeed, by abandoning the neutrality about religions which he maintained throughout earlier accounts, Toynbee invited the unanimous criticism of all relativists in philosophy and religion.

Within religious circles, moreover, particularly among traditionalists, one would expect further differences of opinion on many of the points Toynbee raised. He stated, for example, that religious progress occurred during the breakdown and decay of civilizations. It is historically accurate to say that periods of decay have frequently been marked by profound religious insight. In times of crisis, the idolatrous worship of governments and social institutions has frequently been supplanted by new faiths or old religions. It is far less certain that in all of history, the progress of religion has been an inevitable concomitant of cultural disintegration. One exception is the growth of religious indifference in the past four centuries, during what may prove to be our own "Time of Troubles." Further, it might well be argued that there has been a tendency for religions to identify so closely with historic civilizations that the destruction of one has meant that the other would likewise perish. Toynbee is right if in ideal terms religions prove able to stand apart from their native societies and in times of catastrophe display the courage of interpreting these tragedies as judgments by God. One looks in vain in the New Testament, how-

11. Howard Becker, "Sacred and Secular Societies," *Social Forces*, XXVIII (May, 1950), 361–76.
12. Arnold J. Toynbee, *Civilization on Trial* (New York, 1948), 239.

ever, for a concept of religion mounting to higher dimensions of insight through impending societal breakdowns and destruction. On the stage of human experience, there is always a chance that evil will triumph over the good and an eternal peril that religion itself will be destroyed. From this standpoint, the latter-day revisions of Toynbee's morphology of history may be subject to criticism and possible emendation.

Toynbee also tended to identify religion too completely with a particular ecclesiastical institution. It is not everywhere clear what he meant by his frequent references to the "Church"—sometimes it was the Roman Catholic, elsewhere the Greek Orthodox, and occasionally the Church of England. In general, his hopes for the future were related to the revival of a universal Roman Catholic church under a modern Hildebrand. Thus, the greatest of all questions to be answered in the twentieth century is, "Can Hildebrand arise again in his might to heal the wounds inflicted upon the souls of his flock by the sins of a Rodrigo Borgia and a Sinibaldo Fieschi?" There is a curious naïveté to his statement that although "the Church may actually never yet have expressed Christianity to perfection, there is at least no inherent impediment here to the attainment of a perfect harmony."[13] Elsewhere he seemed acutely aware that all institutions are likely, through domination by hierarchies of leaders, to become closed corporations in which there can be little progress. In general, Toynbee tended to overvalue the virtues of ecclesiasticism and to treat cavalierly the whole tradition of Protestantism. It is one thing to deal realistically with the implications of religious universalism for international affairs. It is something else again to draw further conclusions about the intrinsic merits of religions on that basis. In his emphasis on the primacy of institutional religion, Toynbee surely parted company with Bergson and Augustine.

For the analysis and study of religion, however, Toynbee's contribution is of greatest significance. He identified the particular religions which have been important in various civilizations. He discussed their influence and shortcomings with great insight and unquestioned familiarity. That a secular historian should pay such heed to the religious theme in history has been one of the momentous factors influencing the role of religion in the mid-twentieth century.

More than the majority of historians, Toynbee wrote about political events and trends from the viewpoint of political science. In

13. Toynbee, A Study of History, IV, 647, V, 79n2.

numerous ways, this approach was apparent in estimates of political developments in England and the United States, in analysis of the influence of forms of government upon international politics, and in discussions of political power. But the issues Toynbee spoke of most frequently and on which he propounded formal theories are the nature of political leadership and the nature of the modern state. Each theory carries important implications for democratic theory and practice in the West.

In one view, the leader is merely an expression of prevailing customs or ideas in any society. He is thus an agent for that commonalty and can act only upon its mandate. Toynbee assumed, however, that it is primarily through the energy of the successful creative leader that a society moves forward. Moreover, the bonds of community between him and his followers are so fragile that only through imitation and "social drill" can they respond to his program.[14]

The question one must ask is whether Toynbee's conception leads directly to antidemocratic politics. It is important to observe here that the fundamental assumption upon which a theory of creative leadership is based is not inconsistent with some of the findings of contemporary scholarship in political science and sociology. There is an inherent tendency, we have discovered, for "elitist groups" to ascend to power in both autocratic and democratic governments. The role of the "charismatic" leader is central in this process. The great personality or hero in Toynbee's scheme must first convince the people of his intrinsic worth as a leader before his creative program will be given a try. This would hardly be true for governments which were tyrannies or depotisms, although modern totalitarianism may present a somewhat different case.

On this count, Toynbee's thesis is unqualifiedly democratic, for the great mass of uncreative followers retain the right to accept or reject the leader who is appealing to them. On other grounds, however, there are reasons for some uncertainty. Once a leader who has risen to power has lost his creativity, machinery must be in place to make possible his removal and to assure succession. On this crucial point, Toynbee's references to revolution are inconclusive.[15] Moreover, the system of popular elections, the principal means for disposing of unsatisfactory leaders, is not referred to at any point. If we conceive of Toynbee's theory of political leader-

14. Toynbee, A Study of History, III, 217–48.
15. Toynbee, A Study of History, IV, 133–37.

ship as a detailed account of the political process, then this omission becomes so serious that we may classify his views as antidemocratic. If, on the other hand, we appraise it as a fragment of a broad theory of history, then some qualifications are necessary. In general, spiritual interpretations have tended to accent the importance of struggle, which has often obscured their insight into the indirect channels by which these contests are resolved. If one assumes that the most profound human experiences are a monopoly of the few, it is difficult to build on this foundation a steadfastly democratic philosophy. Yet political leadership, for most moderns, remains little less than an "enigma wrapped in a riddle." It is symbolic of this dilemma that Toynbee should join an intensely individualistic social philosophy with a theory of political leadership which has aristocratic overtones.

Toynbee's view of the state is that of a contemporary English Liberal. In his view, political units in both socialist and free enterprise states have been moving, through trial and error, toward a common set of functions.[16] The major problem in interpreting the role of the state is to bring the discussion to the level of practical experience. If it were possible to find some palliative for the enormity of recurrent wars, then states everywhere could act in many more ways to promote the general welfare. It may be said that Toynbee's conception of political problems is hardly that of a systematic political theorist. To a surprising number of perplexing issues, however, he brings the fresh and creative outlook of a thinker whose intuition has exceeded his ability to formulate general principles and theories.

We have been primarily concerned with Toynbee's theory of international politics. If the scheme he devised for interpreting and evaluating all history moved through successive stages, it is even more true that his concept of international politics was evolutionary. Indeed, his whole outlook on the forces and principles of international affairs was painfully and slowly harmonized with reality.

Toynbee was, in both religion and politics, originally a staunch idealist. His thinking about foreign policy and diplomacy was imprisoned within a crusading nationalism. Sometime during the 1930s, the decade of unparalleled catastrophe, however, he began to employ the tools and principles that four hundred years of mod-

16. Toynbee, *Civilization on Trial*, 147–48.

ern diplomacy have taught. For an absolutist in religious matters, this shift to relativism in politics could not have been easy. He sometimes seized upon new instruments for peace and order as enthusiastically as he had taken to simple formulas.

Thus in the early stages of the experiment with collective security, Toynbee was convinced that this "new dispensation" had taken the place of the old balance of power. The particular problems of collective security with which he was forced to deal concretely were probably what carried him toward political realism. The pathos of these experiences liberated his theory from its earlier utopian fetters. This tendency in his thinking reached its culmination in the counsel he offered for the mitigation of the perilous struggle between East and West since World War II. In time of greatest crisis, no rational student of international politics could afford to ignore the lessons of diplomatic history. Toynbee turned to traditional diplomacy and its well-tested procedures and techniques because he properly identified that struggle as a worldwide political contest.

Moreover, in practice, Toynbee's viewpoint was eclectic. He was able to distinguish between immediate and ultimate objectives. The former can be pursued as practical alternatives; the latter must be conceived as long-range aims which can be achieved only by prudent choices among competing principles. What is striking about Toynbee's theory is that on most fundamental issues he succeeded in maintaining one set of interests without sacrificing the other. Since 1947 he steered the perilous course between a cynical realism and the fatuous assumptions of utopianism. In the 1930s, he was not always able to find this channel but at the height of the cold war when the highest political wisdom is called for, he adjusted his theory to current problems.

Whether the most prudent political insight can carry Western civilization beyond the reach of ultimate destruction is something about which Toynbee was none too sanguine. All he would say was that in the task which confronts Western society and against the catastrophes of internecine warfare, our best hope was in bargaining for time. Toynbee's theory of international politics was transformed because modern society must try to avert its doom. In this common enterprise, the historian of great civilizations and the student of unrelenting struggles for political power offered the same counsel.

INDEX